FAIRE AND GOODLY BUILT

With best wishes

Tim C

The effigies of Thomas Beauchamp and Katherine Mortimer, earl and countess of Warwick, in the chancel of St. Mary's.

FAIRE AND GOODLY BUILT

An incomplete history of St. Mary's Warwick

T I M   C L A R K

BREWIN BOOKS

BREWIN BOOKS
19 Enfield Ind. Estate,
Redditch,
Worcestershire,
B97 6BY
www.brewinbooks.com

First published by Brewin Books 2023

© The collegiate church of St. Mary, Warwick, 2023

The author has asserted his rights in accordance with the Copyright, Designs and Patents Act 1988 to be identified as the author of this work.

All rights reserved. No part of this publication may be reproduced, stored in a retrieval system, or transmitted in any form or by any means, electronic, mechanical, photocopying, recording or otherwise, without the prior permission in writing of the publisher and the copyright owners, or as expressly permitted by law, or under terms agreed with the appropriate reprographics rights organisation. Enquiries concerning reproduction outside the terms stated here should be sent to the publishers at the UK address printed on this page.

The publisher makes no representation, express or implied, with regard to the accuracy of the information contained in this book and cannot accept any legal responsibility for any errors or omissions that may be made.

A CIP catalogue record for this book is available from the British Library.

Front cover image by David Clarke © St. Mary's, Warwick.
Front flap: Warwick the Kingmaker, Beauchamp chapel.
Back flap: Margaret of Antioch, Beauchamp chapel.

ISBN: 978-1-85858-755-4 (Paperback)
ISBN: 978-1-85858-756-1 (Hardback)

Printed and bound in Great Britain
by Bell & Bain Ltd.

CONTENTS

	Key dates in St. Mary's history	7
	Images and acknowledgements	8
	Introduction	15
1.	Foundations	31
2.	Challenges	46
3.	Potential	61
4.	Expurgation	76
5.	Rebuilding	89
6.	Glory	116
7.	Reformation	150
8.	Two Tails	165
9.	Godliness	192
10.	Restoration	218
	Glossary	250
	Further reading	253
	Index	256

The publication of this book has been supported by the generosity of Robert Waley-Cohen and the King Henry VIII Endowed Trust, Warwick.

KEY DATES IN ST. MARY'S HISTORY

1086	St. Mary's recorded in the Domesday Book
1088	Henry de Newburgh created 1st earl of Warwick
1123	Foundation of the college attached to St. Mary's
ca. 1150	Building of the Norman church
1369	Death of both Earl Thomas Beauchamp I and his wife Countess Katherine Mortimer
ca. 1369-94	St. Mary's rebuilt by Earls Thomas Beauchamp I and II
1441	Construction of the Beauchamp chapel begins
ca. 1455	Completion of Earl Richard Beauchamp's tomb
1475	Consecration of the Beauchamp chapel
1544	Dissolution of the college of St. Mary
1561	Ambrose Dudley created earl of Warwick
1588	Death of Robert Dudley, earl of Leicester
1590	Death of Ambrose Dudley, earl of Warwick
1628	Death of Sir Fulke Greville, 1st Lord Brooke
1643	St. Mary's desecrated by Parliamentary forces
1694	Great Fire of Warwick destroyed the nave, transepts, and tower
1704	Completion of the rebuilding of St. Mary's after the fire

IMAGES AND ACKNOWLEDGEMENTS

Frontis	The effigies of Thomas Beauchamp and Katherine Mortimer Andy Marshall / © St. Mary's Warwick	
1	A canon of St. Mary's Getty Research Institute / Internet Archive	17
2	A monk of St. Sepulchre's priory Getty Research Institute / Internet Archive	17
3	A pane in the vestry of St. Mary's, depicting the Last Supper © the author	19
4	A late-medieval vision of hell, from *Les Visions de chevalier Tondal* J. Paul Getty Museum, Los Angeles	22
5	Reliquary box, *ca* 1173-80 Metropolitan Museum of New York	24
6	The Easter sepulchre at St. Mary's © the author	25
7	The collegiate church of the Holy Trinity, Tattershall Lee Beel / Alamy Stock Photo	28
8	Conveyance of Compton Mordak church to St. Mary's Warwickshire County Record Office	35
9	'Warwick church' Royal Collection Trust / © His Majesty King Charles III 2023	36

IMAGES AND ACKNOWLEDGEMENTS

10	The founding charter of St. Mary's, 1123 Warwickshire County Record Office	38
11	St. Mary's crypt © the author	44
12	The memorial brass of Ralph de Hengham Getty Research Institute / Internet Archive	60
13	Guy of Warwick The Morgan Library and Museum, New York	65
14	St. Mary's, Pillerton Hersey © the author	70
15	Earl Thomas Beauchamp I © British Library Board. All rights reserved / Bridgeman Images	73
16	East front, Warwick castle © the author	74
17	Chest to house the Treaty of Calais, 1360 © The National Archives	79
18	House of the vicars-choral From Arthur Leach's *History of Warwick School*	82
19	The church as rebuilt in the fourteenth century © The Warden and Fellows of All Souls College, Oxford	93
20	St. Mary's chapter house © the author	94
21	The chancel David Clarke / © St. Mary's Warwick	98

22	The 'flying ribs' of the chancel © the author	99
23	The effigies of Thomas Beauchamp and Katherine Mortimer © the author	103
24	Thomas Beauchamp and Katherine Mortimer holding hands © the author	105
25	Weepers on the tomb of Thomas Beauchamp and Katherine Mortimer © the author	108
26	The daughters of Thomas Beauchamp and Katherine Mortimer Getty Research Institute / Internet Archive	110
27	The tomb of Thomas Beauchamp II and Margaret Ferrers Getty Research Institute / Internet Archive	113
28	The memorial brass of Thomas Beauchamp II and Margaret Ferrers Alamy	113
29	The arms of Thomas Beauchamp II and Margaret Ferrers David Clarke / © St. Mary's Warwick	114
30	The Beauchamp chapel David Clarke / © St. Mary's Warwick	117
31	The baptism of Earl Richard Beauchamp © British Library Board. All rights reserved / Bridgeman Images	122
32	Saint Alban in the east window of the Beauchamp chapel (detail) © the author	126

IMAGES AND ACKNOWLEDGEMENTS

| 33 | Richard Beauchamp's Garter stall plate
© Look and Learn / Bridgeman Images | 129 |

| 34 | Saint John of Bridlington in the east window of the Beauchamp chapel
© the author | 131 |

| 35 | Richard Beauchamp's tomb
© the author | 133 |

| 36 | Richard II's body being taken from Pontefract
© British Library Board. All rights reserved / Bridgeman Images | 134 |

| 37 | Weeper on the tomb of Philip the Bold of Burgundy
Cleveland Museum of Art, Ohio | 135 |

| 38 | Weeper on the tomb of Earl Richard Beauchamp
Andy Marshall / © St. Mary's Warwick | 135 |

| 39 | Earl Richard Beauchamp's head and open hands
© the author | 137 |

| 40 | Statues in the east window of the Beauchamp chapel
Andy Marshall / © St. Mary's Warwick | 138 |

| 41 | Members of the heavenly orchestra
© the author | 139 |

| 42 | Members of the heavenly choir
© the author | 140 |

| 43 | The Dean's chapel
Classic Image / Alamy Stock Photo | 147 |

| 44 | Anne Beauchamp
© the author | 148 |

45	Richard Beauchamp's seal Reproduced under the terms of the Project Gutenberg Licence	149
46	The sale of indulgences Public domain, via Wikimedia Commons	157
47	Thomas Cromwell © The Frick Collection, New York	160
48	An allegory of the Reformation Bridgeman Images	166
49	Robert Dudley, earl of Leicester © Waddesdon Image Library, Waddesdon Manor	172
50	Memorial to Thomas Oken © the author	178
51	Thomas Cartwright Universal History Archive / UIG / Bridgeman Images	181
52	The tomb of the Noble Impe Andy Marshall / © St. Mary's Warwick	188
53	The tomb of Ambrose Dudley Andy Marshall / © St. Mary's Warwick	188
54	The tomb of Robert Dudley and Lettice Knollys Andy Marshall / © St. Mary's Warwick	189
55	Historiated initial of the founding charter of the Lord Leycester hospital Lord Leycester hospital	190
56	The ragged staff in the form of a mouchette © the author	190

IMAGES AND ACKNOWLEDGEMENTS

57	The memorial to Fulke Greville © the author	195
58	The tomb of Sir Francis Vere Angelo Hornak / Alamy Stock Photo	195
59	Samuel Clarke Art Collection 2 / Alamy Stock Photo	198
60	The ledger stone of Cecily Puckering David Clarke / © St. Mary's Warwick	205
61	The tomb of Thomas Beauchamp and Katherine Mortimer Look and Learn / Bridgeman Images	208
62	The memorial to Thomas Puckering © the author	210
63	Robert Greville, 2nd Lord Brooke Carnegie Museum of Art, Pittsburgh	214
64	The depiction of the day of judgment in the Beauchamp chapel David Clarke / © St. Mary's Warwick	223
65	The depiction of the day of judgment on the wall of the Sistine chapel MB_Photo / Alamy Stock Photo	223
66	A late seventeenth-century fire engine © Museum of London / Bridgeman Images	227
67	The tomb of Thomas Fisher Getty Research Institute / Internet Archive	229
68	One of Sir Christopher Wren's designs for the new St. Mary's © The Warden and Fellows of All Souls College, Oxford	234

69	Francis Smith Yogi Black / Alamy Stock Photo	235
70	All Saints', Northampton © the author	238
71	The portal to the Beauchamp chapel © the author	240
72	The nave David Clarke / © St. Mary's Warwick	243
73	The tower (detail) David Clarke / © St. Mary's Warwick	245
74	Shields on the north face of the tower David Clarke / © St. Mary's Warwick	246
75	One of Sir Christopher Wren's designs for the new tower © The Warden and Fellows of All Souls College, Oxford	247
76	Blind tracery © the author	251

INTRODUCTION

I

RICHARD BEAUCHAMP, thirteenth earl of Warwick, who died in 1439, directed that a chapel of Our Lady be 'well, faire, and goodly built' at the collegiate church of St. Mary. It certainly was, for his executors created what has justly been called one of the finest mortuary chapels in Europe, where the earl is, in the words of the sixteenth-century traveller John Leland, 'entombed most princely'. Earl Richard's effigy is one of the greatest pieces of English late medieval sculpture, the depiction of the heavenly choir and orchestra in the windows of his chapel is incomparable, and around the east window is arguably the best grouping of late medieval statues inside an English church.

But Richard's executors were not the first to undertake work of quality, drama, and imagination at St. Mary's, and neither would they be the last. Over six centuries, the builders of St. Mary's created one of the most magnificent parish churches in England, of such grandeur that visitors often assume that it is a cathedral. This book tells how such a splendid church came about, and considers the many exceptional and surprising features of St. Mary's besides the peerless Beauchamp chapel, including the size of the crypt; the design of the chancel roof; the tomb of Earl Thomas Beauchamp and his wife Countess Katherine; and 'sin's trophy' in the chapter house. We will see why, almost exactly one hundred and fifty years after Earl Richard's death, the Beauchamp chapel became the resting place of Ambrose Dudley, earl of Warwick, and his more famous brother Robert, earl of Leicester, the favourite of Elizabeth I. Then, in 1694, the disastrous Great Fire of Warwick partly destroyed the church, the rebuilding of which has given us the distinctive and controversial nave and tower that are familiar today.

The history of St. Mary's was intertwined with the earls of Warwick for over three centuries, its fortunes ebbing and flowing with their attitudes and ambitions. We will, therefore, be looking at the many facets of the earls' achievements, or lack of them: from the unlucky and the incompetent to the determined, the honourable, the valiant, and their rise to becoming some of the most powerful, and richest, men in England. After the Reformation, the influence of the castle on St. Mary's shifted from financial to spiritual, a change that we will also follow.

We will gain an insight into the lives of those connected with St. Mary's or living in its parish, both before and after the Reformation, and meet some characters without whom its history would be less colourful. An earl of Warwick was likened to a dog returning to its own vomit – by the pope, no less. A canon of St. Mary's found himself in the Tower of London, another was excommunicated at least three times, and a third absconded with church funds, which led to a brush with none other than Thomas Cromwell. We will see how one well-known man of Warwick struggled to come to terms with the implications of the Reformation. Then there was the thirteen-year-old boy baptised at St. Mary's who wrote down all his sins – not that it did him much good; the MP who smashed up the church; a vicar who dragged a preacher out of the pulpit; and another who threatened to pistol whip his own assistant priest, as well as, allegedly, inciting his brother to put the mayor of Warwick in fear of his life.

This book is an 'incomplete history' in that it only covers the period up to and including the rebuilding of St. Mary's after the 1694 fire, the most recent major construction work. As a result, important topics fall outside its scope, such as the role of St. Mary's in the community in the eighteenth and nineteenth centuries through its administration of the Poor Laws, and the changing faces of the church during the Georgian and Victorian eras. Perhaps these omissions will be made good in the future.

II

St. Mary's was founded as a collegiate church in 1123, meaning that it had attached to it a college of priests known as canons, one of whom would be appointed dean, or head of the college. It was a secular foundation, from the Latin *saecularis*, meaning 'worldly', in contrast with one that was 'regular' (from *regula*, 'rule', 'regulation'), such as at a monastery or priory. The key difference is that, unlike monks, canons did not live together as a community, and so they were not supported by the communal funds of a regular house. Rather, they

INTRODUCTION

1 and 2. Illustrations of (left) a canon of St. Mary's and (right) a monk at St. Sepulchre's priory both taken from Sir William Dugdale's invaluable Antiquities of Warwickshire, *first published in 1656.*

received their own income known as a 'prebend', which they were responsible for collecting.

Canons were, however, required to observe the eight 'canonical hours' every day – times of prayer and contemplation known collectively as 'the offices' – in much the same way as monks were. Characterised by prayer and chanting, in Latin, and with particular focus on texts from the Book of Psalms, some of the names of the offices are familiar to us, such as matins (before dawn), and vespers (late afternoon, before supper). The detail of the liturgy of the hours varied across England, but by the fifteenth century (and probably much earlier) St. Mary's was following the most common one, known as the Use of Sarum (Salisbury).

With no requirement to reside at a secular college, St. Mary's canons could observe their offices elsewhere, or in private; even if a canon were in Warwick, some of his acts of worship might have been performed at home before a portable altar, or perhaps at one of the altars in St. Mary's that was out of public view, such as those in the vestry and the sacristy.

Absent canons were represented by their vicars (from the Latin *vicarius*, a deputy), who were paid by the canons out of their prebends. Vicars were responsible for day-to-day clerical duties in the parish, and therefore were the public face of St. Mary's. They heard confessions; baptised infants by plunging them, naked, into the font; married couples in a brief ceremony conducted at the church door; encouraged the giving of alms; tended to the sick; and prayed for the dying, invoking the help of saints to intercede for their soul. The prominence of vicars in the community is evidenced by gifts such as that of a property in Saltisford in about 1240, expressly given for the benefit of St. Mary's and the vicars' common fund. As we shall see, vicars at St. Mary's were poorly paid, and did not receive the support from the canons that they should have done.

The focal point of worship before the Reformation was the mass. Also known as the Eucharist (from the Greek *eukharistia*, thanksgiving), it has its origins in the Last Supper, when Christ blessed bread and offered it to his disciples, telling them to 'take, eat; this is my body'. Then he gave them wine as his 'blood of the new testament, which is shed for many for the remission of sins' (Matthew 26: 26-28). When the officiating priest consecrated the bread and wine at mass, it was believed that the body and blood of Christ actually became present, a miracle known as transubstantiation. He then raised them aloft, so the congregation could witness Christ's presence.

High mass, the most elaborate form, was celebrated in every church at least every Sunday and on holy days, of which there were at least forty a year, and probably daily in a collegiate church like St. Mary's. It was normally held at eight or nine o'clock, before breakfast, and always at the high altar. The Lady mass, in honour of the Virgin, took place mid-morning in a Lady chapel or at an altar dedicated to her. It was always celebrated on Saturdays but, like high mass, may have been celebrated daily in larger churches. By the late Middle Ages, both high and Lady mass at St. Mary's would have involved choral singing, accompanied by an organ.

Parishioners were required to attend mass at least once a week, usually opting for the Sunday morning high mass, not least because fasting was required beforehand. For wealthier members of the congregation, it was an opportunity to be seen and to reinforce one's status. Attendance was not compulsory, in the

INTRODUCTION

3. A detail from a pane in the east window of the vestry of St. Mary's, depicting the Last Supper. Its provenance is unknown, but it probably dates from the mid- to late-sixteenth century. Christ is being offered unusual fare; it looks like a rat. It is placed immediately behind Judas, who is fleeing the table with his thirty pieces of silver while Christ points towards him. By the time the pane was made, 'rat' had come to mean someone deceitful, and this might explain why a rat is shown between Christ and Judas.

sense that many had good reason not to go, but absence without excuse was frowned upon and persistent offenders risked social denunciation and even public penance, imposed by the church authorities. The nature of this penance varied, but it could range from a requirement to offer a candle at high mass (in effect, a fine), to being beaten round the church.

People were summoned to services by the ringing of the bells, and entered at the west end of the church through a south door, crossing themselves with holy water as they came in. Opposite the entrance was usually an image of a benign Saint Christopher, the patron saint of travellers, bearing the infant Christ on his shoulders. St. Mary's would have been vivid with colour: painting, statues, cloths, and, especially on saints' days, pennons and banners. Flowers were displayed in summer. The Virgin, and numerous saints, would have been represented throughout the church, some as statues within niches that would also have been painted. On the walls were scenes from the bible and, perhaps, roundels illustrating the four Evangelists. There might be shown such didactic images as the seven deadly sins, the seven acts of mercy, the expulsion from the Garden of Eden, or the consequences of breaking the Sabbath. Borders and aisle arches could have been adorned with secular images such as foliage or pastoral scenes, or even jocular illustrations such as a saint tweaking the Devil's nose. Overall, there were a range of messages conveyed, from comfort to fear, to guide and cajole the faithful into living a virtuous life in this world and to prepare for the next.

Many churches had a depiction of the day of judgment painted on the east wall of the nave, so as to be in full sight of the congregation when it faced the high altar. In doing so, the worshippers were looking towards the direction of earthly paradise, and the direction from which Christ would return to judge the world. Christ would be shown separating the dead to his right or left. Those on his right had been chosen to enter the Kingdom of God, those on his left condemned to the eternal fire tended by the Devil (Matthew 25:31-34, 41). The Virgin and John the Baptist were shown alongside Christ, interceding on behalf of the worthy.

Some artists went to town in their illustration of hell in doom paintings, with grotesque devils, fire-breathing monsters, and flames torturing the damned. Even bishops or cardinals might be shown heading towards hell, as a reminder that no one was exempt from His judgment. It might also be an opportunity to caricature unpopular locals: Holy Trinity church in Coventry has a good example, featuring women accused of watering down the ale that they sold. It was designed to shock, to emphasise relevance to everyday life, and to be a potent reminder of the fate that would befall the unrepentant sinner.

There were probably no pews in St. Mary's until, at the earliest, the rebuilding of the nave, which was completed in 1394. Before then, the congregation knelt, standing for the reading of the gospel. People divided themselves into social groups – the nearer the front, the higher the status. Important benefactors to St. Mary's such as Walter Power, and powerful laymen like Thomas and John Huggeford, all of whom we shall meet later, may well have had seats in the chancel.

INTRODUCTION

There might also have been separation of men and women, for all except those of the highest status, until the practice died out by the fifteenth century. Often women stood, or sat, on the north side, the men on the south, which is the basis of the tradition of the bride's and groom's sides at weddings. The explanation may be that the north side, to the left of the nave as one faces the high altar, mirrors the side of the cross on which the Virgin Mary stood. However, such a division was not a hard and fast rule, and we do not know if it was practised at St. Mary's.

High mass started with the priest and his assistants walking in procession from the chancel around the nave, in a clockwise direction, sprinkling the congregation with holy water as they went. They then returned to the chancel, which was divided from the nave by a gated stone screen called a pulpitum. The service continued out of sight and in Latin, though the priest was supposed to explain to the congregation, in English, what was happening. Spiritual enrichment came from the drama of the occasion, rather than active participation. Sermons were rare, though from 1281 priests were instructed to preach four times a year on subjects such as the Ten Commandments or the seven deadly sins. Otherwise, the priest would read from a book of homilies, often about caring for the poor. Prayers were said for matters concerning the community, such as for the sick, the recently deceased, or for a good harvest, and public announcements were made. At St. Mary's, such addresses to the congregation were probably made from a gallery along the top of the pulpitum.

Some may have attended mass for the sake of appearance, but people were generally devout and respectful. Gossiping or wandering around during the service was frowned upon. There were those who questioned the validity of transubstantiation and other aspects of daily worship, but there is no history of organised resistance to them in Warwick before the Reformation. For the vast majority, the fear of one's soul being condemned to eternal damnation was real, and witnessing the mass reminded them that Christ died so that their sins could be forgiven. Forgiveness and eternal peace were at the heart of Christian belief, and most people wanted to maximise their chances of attaining them.

Forgiveness required acknowledgement of one's sins, penance, and atonement. The dead could not acknowledge sin, hence the need for a last confession, but penance could be made, and atonement obtained, by the soul in purgatory. The doctrine of purgatory is not in the Bible, but it emerged as a practical solution to the problem of how anyone other than saints or martyrs could get to heaven: through purification of the soul by the fires of purgatory. This was reinforced by the influential scholar Thomas Aquinas (died 1274), who argued that if the soul were purged of its sins, perfection was achieved, and the gates of paradise opened to it. Quite how this purification happened attracted the attention of subsequent writers and thinkers, notably the Italian poet Dante Alighieri (died 1321) in his *Divine Comedy*. Purgatory came to be seen as a place of torment and incomprehensible pain as the soul's sins were eradicated. It was cleansed by means appropriate to the crime: the proud had to carry hefty boulders on their shoulders, liars were to be strung up by their tongues, and what happened to fornicators is best left to the imagination.

Not surprisingly, it became a priority to reduce one's time in purgatory, and make the experience less traumatic. Money was left to pay for priests to say masses

4. A late-medieval vision of hell, from Les Visions de chevalier Tondal, *Franco-Flemish, 1475. It is the story of Tondal, a knight who is taken to hell by an angel, and then on to paradise. Hell is a fiery pit in the mouth of a monster; devils prop the jaws open; and tormented souls writhe in agony within.*

The book was commissioned by Margaret of York, duchess of Burgundy, (died 1503), a cousin of Richard Neville, sixteenth earl of Warwick.

for the soul, the more the better; tombs bore inscriptions that implored worshippers to pray for the soul of the deceased; alms were bequeathed to the poor. A vigil was held in church on the evening of All Hallows Eve, 31 October, bells were rung for souls in purgatory, and two days of feasting followed. It was a big thing.

More comfort was to be had from saints who could intercede with God on your behalf, and help protect you from misfortune. Each saint had their own special area of influence, fuelling the display of their images in church. But even better was to worship before a relic, an object associated either with the life of Christ (such as the Cross on which He was crucified), or with that of a saint, perhaps a part of their body or some of their clothing. Churches, abbeys, and priories competed for the pilgrims' penny: their offerings, their buying of candles and souvenir badges. It became an important source of revenue. There was even a day for special veneration, Relic Sunday, the third after Midsummer's Day, a festival that smacks of commercialism.

St. Mary's fully exploited this opportunity. By 1455 it had accumulated an astonishing thirty-nine relics, including such perennial crowd pleasers as a piece of the true cross on which Jesus was crucified, a thorn from the burning bush where Moses received the message from God to lead the Israelites out of Egypt into Canaan, and the Virgin Mary's hair. These were, it must be said, pretty common: it was said that the abbey at Bury St. Edmunds alone had so many pieces of the true cross that the monks could have reassembled it.

Relics of the popular saints of the Middle Ages were also well represented at St. Mary's, including some oil of Saint Katherine; clothing and hair of Mary Magdalene; and the hairshirt of Thomas Becket, who quickly became the most revered English saint after his martyrdom in 1170. St. Mary's also had what purported to be a phial of the Virgin's breast milk, though its actual contents were probably chalk dissolved in water. This may have been a blatant attempt to tap into the market dominated by Her shrine at Walsingham, Norfolk, though there was plenty of competition. In 1543 the Frenchman and leading reformer Jean Calvin, whose arguments were to be a major influence on the Church of England, memorably remarked that 'there is not perhaps a town, a convent, or nunnery where [her breast milk] is not shown in large or small quantities. Indeed, had the Virgin been a wet-nurse or a dairy [cow], she could not have produced more than is shown as hers in various parts'.

5. *An English reliquary box for the keeping of a relic of the archbishop of Canterbury, Thomas Becket, made shortly after his martyrdom in 1170. Such boxes would often have been kept beneath an altar slab, and brought out for display on appropriate occasions.*

III

Easter was the most devout time of the year. This was usually the only time that the laity took communion (or 'the sacrament'), when they were offered the blood and body of Christ. This could not be done before the recipient had confessed his sins, and Shrove Tuesday comes from 'to shrive', meaning to hear confession. The priest normally sat within the sanctuary of the parish altar (which was in the nave, in front of the pulpitum) as penitents knelt before him at the rail, acknowledging their sins.

After mass on Palm Sunday, the start of Easter week, the priest distributed 'palms' – branches of yew, box, or willow – to the congregation, which then processed to a cross in the north-east of the churchyard, accompanied by the choir singing anthems. There was a gospel reading, after which everyone circled the church, singing hymns, and returned to the nave through the west door. The service then continued at the parish altar.

Later in Easter week ceremonies were focussed on the sepulchre, a representation of Christ's tomb in the garden of Gethsemane. Usually these were temporary wooden structures, placed on the north side of the high altar, but some larger churches had permanent ones made of stone, as does St. Mary's. Typically, during Holy Week the sepulchre would be covered with a pall and surrounded by candles, with a white cloth placed at the back of it. On Good Friday the Crucifix was blessed before the congregation approached it, barefooted and on hands and knees, and kissed its base: a ceremony known as

6. *The Easter sepulchre, built into the north wall of the chancel of St. Mary's.*

'creeping to the Cross'. It was then paraded around the church and placed in the sepulchre along with the Host and linen sheets to represent the grave clothes. A vigil was kept by the sepulchre until Easter Sunday, when the Host and the Crucifix were removed, and the cross paraded again, this time in celebration of the risen Christ.

Events in celebration of Easter combined worship with social interaction, and church liturgy could be particularly convivial on other occasions, such as saints' feast days, or walking the boundaries of the parish to seek blessing for an abundant harvest. Rogationtide was three days of celebration that marked Christ overcoming the Devil. Processions were made around the parish, and perhaps beyond, in which the Devil was represented as a dragon, and Christ as a lion. There was plenty of drinking and eating, though not meat. More soberly, at Candlemas, 2 February, parishioners took candles around the church to honour the Purification of the Virgin Mary and the presentation of the newborn Jesus at the Temple: the basis of the 'churching' of women after childbirth. Candles representing the Virgin and the priest Simeon were taken to the high altar. Parishioners took away candles after the ceremony, believing that to do so would protect themselves and their home against thunderstorms.

6 December, the feast of St. Nicholas, heralded a period of much jollity: the reign of the 'boy bishop'. As its name suggests, the tradition had originated in cathedrals, but it was adopted by some larger churches, including St. Mary's, where it seems to have been embraced enthusiastically. On that day, the choristers chose a boy from among their number to act as a bishop, and his colleagues took the parts of canons. The chosen boy was dressed in child-size bishop's vestments, kept at St. Mary's for the occasion. He would have looked the part. One cope (a ceremonial cloak) was of white satin decorated with gold-coloured trefoils, while there were two of blue silk, with golden roses. There was even a mitre, also made of white silk, with the letters T and M embroidered on it, presumably for Earl Thomas Beauchamp II and his wife Countess Margaret, a sure sign of comital approval, and possibly donation.

The boy bishop sat in the dean's stall in the chancel, accompanied by boy canons, and took his role in the observance of the offices. He also attended at mass; he could not, of course, elevate the Host, but he may well have given a blessing and delivered a light-hearted sermon after the service. He then toured the parish, in full regalia and accompanied by his fellow choristers, offering blessings and seeking donations for the church. The boys might also have performed plays, as in 1464 St. Mary's had a book called the *Kings of Cologne*, a version of the story of the Magi, which was a common subject for dramas. The boy bishop's term of office ended on 28 December, with a grand, indigestion-inducing feast to celebrate Holy Innocents Day.

This is the backcloth against which the history of St. Mary's unfolds: one of devotion and certainty of belief, but also of entertainment and a sense of community based on the church. But it would all be challenged in the sixteenth century. Within a generation, transubstantiation, prayers for the soul, purgatory, images, relics, Palm Sunday processions, creeping to the Cross, walking the boundaries, Candlemas, boy bishops, and much more were swept aside by the 'reformed' Church of England. It was a social as well as a religious revolution. The continuing and bitter divisions of the sixteenth and seventeenth centuries were played out at St. Mary's as they were throughout the country, but Warwick was influenced by some particularly vociferous reformers, some of whom clashed with more conservative vicars. Underlying tensions erupted into civil war, the execution of the king, and a short-lived republic. The scales then steadied towards something approaching equilibrium, with a greater acceptance of diverse opinions, and we shall see that St. Mary's offers an unusual insight into the practical consequences of this shift.

IV

Some housekeeping is required before we go any further. I have tried to keep the use of technical terms to a minimum, but unfortunately some are unavoidable and there is a glossary towards the end of the book.

I have modernised the spelling in quotations from older sources, but not the vocabulary or grammar. Biblical references are all taken from the King James Version. Several street names in Warwick have changed their names since the seventeenth century, and I have used the current ones to make them easier to relate to. Amounts of money are shown in the currency of the time, when one pound was divided into twenty shillings (shown as 20s), in which were twelve pennies (12d). The mark, a common unit of currency in the Middle Ages, was worth 13s 4d, or 66.6p. With apologies to the purists, I write (for example) 6d rather than sixpence, to avoid any confusion with 6p.

I have made no attempt to equate monetary sums to present day values, which I find at best unhelpful and at worst misleading. Better, I think, to compare them either to contemporary incomes, such as a week's pay, or to something we can visualise. The guides at St. Mary's will rightly tell visitors that the Beauchamp chapel cost about two thousand five hundred pounds, and are often asked what that would be worth now. The online National Archives currency calculator gives a figure of over one and a half million pounds, but I would defy any quantity surveyor to build it for that today. More usefully, the entire collegiate church of the Holy Trinity in Tattershall, Lincolnshire, of similar size to St. Mary's and finished to a high standard, cost about twelve hundred pounds: just under half that of the Beauchamp chapel, which was built about the same time. Or, to put it in ways that would have made it unimaginable to most of St. Mary's parishioners, the cost of the Beauchamp chapel was well over three hundred times what a fully-employed labourer would earn in a year, and it would have bought about six thousand oxen. But it was also about the same that Richard, duke of York (died 1460) spent on a single item of jewellery, and it pales in comparison with the four thousand two hundred pounds (at least) paid by Henry IV in 1406 for farewell celebrations when his twelve-year-old daughter Philippa left England to marry the king of Denmark.

7. *The collegiate church of Holy Trinity, Tattershall, Lincolnshire, was built by Rafe, Lord Cromwell, one of Earl Richard Beauchamp's executors. It is roughly contemporary with the Beauchamp chapel, which cost at least twice as much.*

INTRODUCTION

The 'further reading' section towards the end of this book lists those sources that I have found particularly useful, but I should single out some of them. Charles Fonge's *The cartulary of St. Mary's collegiate church, Warwick* is a transcription of documents relating to the church from the foundation of the college until the early fifteenth century, and includes a most useful introduction. It is a product of his PhD thesis at the University of York, which includes more detailed argument. His material is a major source for the earlier chapters of this book, and I have shamelessly relied upon his summaries of each document in the cartulary rather than reading them in the original. My excuse is quite simply that medieval church Latin is way beyond my abilities.

I also acknowledge a large debt to Michael Farr's *The Great Fire of Warwick, 1694*, which reproduces documents of the Committee and Court of Record established to administer the rebuilding of the town. Mr. Farr was the county archivist at the Warwickshire County Record Office from 1967 to 1989, and his scholarship in producing this book was invaluable to me.

No work on the history of St. Mary's could fail to draw upon the writings of Philip Chatwin, who succeeded his father as the church's architect. He oversaw the restoration of the Beauchamp chapel between 1922 and 1928, and designed the stunning window for the chapel of the Royal Warwickshire regiment in the north transept of St. Mary's, unveiled in 1952. His numerous articles, written over a period of some thirty years, are meticulous, enlightening, and thought-provoking. Fittingly, his ashes are interred in the Beauchamp chapel, the first burial in it for over three hundred years.

I should add my appreciation of three other works. *The Newburgh earldom of Warwick and its charters, 1088-1253*, edited by David Crouch and with an introduction by Richard Dace, is the go-to account of the Newburgh earls and their countesses. Nicholas Orme's *Going to church in medieval England* is a comprehensive study of the experience of pre-Reformation worship. My discussion of the wider context of St. Mary's history during the years from Henry VIII to Elizabeth I draws heavily on Peter Marshall's *Heretics and believers*. I make no apologies for this, as it is the most comprehensive yet readable account of the numerous twists and turns of religious changes during this period that I have come across.

Last, but by no means least, I want to thank everybody who has supported me in this project, and some require special mention. Robert Waley-Cohen and the King Henry VIII Endowed Trust, Warwick, have provided generous financial backing. The staff of the Warwickshire County Record Office have, as always, been most helpful. Karen Newton, Simon Pickard, Judith and Keith Russell, and Mo Sutherland have all been kind enough to read drafts as the text has evolved; this book is much the better for their comments and advice. The knowledge and dedication of my fellow guides at St. Mary's has been a great influence on me. But most of all I thank my wife, Amanda, for her unflinching enthusiasm, encouragement, patience, and love.

– 1 –

FOUNDATIONS

I

THE EARLIEST documentary evidence of St. Mary's is the Domesday Book, a survey of land ownership and resources undertaken for William the Conqueror. Dating from 1086, it records that St. Mary's owned enough land to support one plough (about one hundred acres) and three cottars (peasants who held about five acres each), plus four acres of meadow. It also had a female serf, most likely British, the widow or daughter of a serf, and a dairymaid or weaver. Serfs were common, accounting for over ten percent of the population of Warwickshire, and often held by churches or monasteries. Technically serfs were not slaves (though the words share a common derivation): serfs could not be bought or sold, but they were tied to their lord's land. It is a distinction that was of little or no practical effect, and nowadays historians tend to treat serfdom as a form of slavery. However, the days of serfdom in England would soon end, as landlords began to find it more profitable to rent land to freemen.

St. Mary's also had a hide of land – reckoned to be enough land to support a family, about thirty acres – in Myton, on the south side of the River Avon, that previously had belonged to Edwin, earl of the Mercians. It was given to the church by a wealthy Saxon *thegn* (broadly, a nobleman below the rank of earl), Turchil of Arden, who may have been the sheriff of Warwickshire, and, therefore, responsible for keeping the king's peace in the county. Turchil held extensive lands in Warwickshire from the Crown, and he was one of the few Anglo-Saxons to keep his position after William the Conqueror's replacement of officials by fellow Normans. He is St. Mary's earliest recorded benefactor.

It is possible that St. Mary's was founded at the time that Turchil made his gift, shortly after Edwin's death in 1071, but there is good, if circumstantial, evidence that points to St. Mary's being some one hundred years older than this. The first half of the tenth century saw a large increase in the number of churches, and this period coincides with Warwick's growth after its founding as a *burh*, (hence 'borough'), or planned community, in 914. That was when Aethelflaed, Lady of the Mercians and daughter of Alfred the Great, established a defensive position at Warwick to help protect her realm, under threat from the Vikings' base at Leicester. Warwick's street pattern is typical of Saxon development, and churches were often situated on the edge of towns. It is quite possible that St. Mary's was, when it was built, at the northern boundary of the settlement. In short, one might expect a church where St. Mary's now stands, and its dedication to the Virgin may reflect an intensity in devotion to her towards the end of the tenth century.

St. Mary's is the only church in Warwick mentioned in the Domesday Book, but there may have been others. It is probable that St. Laurence's (West Street) and St. Michael's (Saltisford), were both Saxon, on the basis that they, like St. Mary's, would have been at boundaries of the *burh*. St. Helen's, on the site of, and later incorporated within, the priory of St. Sepulchre's, may also pre-date the Norman Conquest. St. Nicholas's was said by John Rous, the fifteenth-century priest of Warwick and author, to have had a nunnery that was destroyed by the Vikings in 1016, but it is questionable whether the Danes reached Warwick at all in that campaign, and, indeed, if St. Nicholas's even existed then. In any event, its supposed nunnery is probably a myth.

One church that certainly had been established by 1086 was All Saints', probably the first church in Warwick. Rous's claim that it was founded by Dubricius (died *ca.* 550), as the first bishop of Warwick, can be readily dismissed, but it may date from the seventh century. It was probably a collegiate minster church, responsible for a wide area known as a *parochia*. The fact that there are churches at Leamington Priors, Leek Wootton and Sherbourne dedicated to All Saints suggests that they could have been within the *parochia*; we do not know if St. Mary's was.

Warwick was developing into a substantial town. The castle was rebuilt and expanded in 1068 to remind the locals that the Normans were now in charge, and the castle's increasing importance stimulated local trade and enterprise.

The Domesday Book tells us that Warwick had 244 dwellings, which implies a population of between one thousand and one thousand five hundred, large by the standards of the time. Warwick was the dominant town in the region, bigger than Coventry, ten times the size of Stratford-upon-Avon, while Birmingham barely existed. There was also a significant settlement of up to five hundred people in the suburb of Cotes (hence 'Coten End') centred on Smith Street and St. Nicholas Church Street. It was probably a horticultural community, supplying the castle.

St. Mary's may have flourished in this economic vibrancy, but All Saints' did not. Churches within *parochiae* were becoming independent of their minster, part of a national trend towards establishing the smaller parishes that are still familiar today. If All Saints' had been a mother church, it had ceased to be so by 1123. And, fatefully, All Saints' had been encircled by the castle, making it unsuitable for public worship, and perhaps became nothing more than the earl's private chapel. St. Mary's was now the most important church in Warwick, and no trace of All Saints' has survived.

II

William the Conqueror died in 1087, and under the terms of his will his eldest son, Robert Curthose, received his lands in Normandy, while the English crown was bequeathed to his second son, William Rufus. This led Curthose to raise an armed rebellion, which Rufus defeated. The Norman nobleman Henry de Beaumont, otherwise de Neubourg and hence Newburgh, was a trusted ally of Rufus, and his fidelity was swiftly rewarded with the earldom of Warwick in 1088. The accompanying land, known as an 'honour', was assembled from estates held by the king, including the castle and the rest of his holdings in Warwick; by local landowners like Turchil; and, with his agreement, by Henry's own brother Robert, count of Meulan. The honour was spread over a wide area beyond Warwickshire, with lands in Gloucestershire, Rutland, Wiltshire, and elsewhere.

Rufus was killed in 1100 while hunting in the New Forest, resulting in another contested succession for the throne. The winner was William the Conqueror's youngest son, who became King Henry I, and Earl Henry had again backed the winning side. About seven years later he was granted the honour of Gower in South Wales, which extended way beyond the peninsula of that name. It included the island of Sweins ey in the mouth of the river Tawe, where Earl Henry built a castle of wood to house a garrison that would help protect his new acquisitions against the Welsh princes. Just as Aethelflaed's military construction had stimulated the growth of Warwick, so Henry's did for Swansea.

Earl Henry actively reinforced his newly acquired rights, quickly extracting payments from land holders in recognition of his lordship. He also, as would have been expected of him, made large donations to religious houses in both England and Normandy, but the clearest demonstration of piety was to establish a new religious house. This he duly did, and it was a foundation of some distinction: a college in Warwick of the order of the Canons of the Holy Sepulchre, the first of its kind in England. It is known more succinctly as St. Sepulchre's priory, its curious name deriving from the fact that *sanctus* is Latin for both 'holy' and 'saint'. According to John Rous, it was established at the request of pilgrims to the Holy Land, though it may be more to do with the fact that Earl Henry's brother-in-law was a prominent participant in the First Crusade, with its capture of Jerusalem in 1099 giving rise to the founding of the order. As we shall see, St. Sepulchre's was a thorn in St. Mary's side for centuries.

All Saints' had retained its collegiate status despite its decline, while St. Mary's probably had only one priest. However, in about 1115 Earl Henry began the process of creating a college at St. Mary's by granting it the church of Compton Mordak (Verney), to provide a prebend for a canon. The prebend was worth fifteen marks a year, which would be the most valuable to be attached to St. Mary's.

Earl Henry created a second canon of St. Mary's, William, described as his chaplain. The prebend William received had previously been held by a priest named Herlewin, who presumably had been a canon of All Saints', and comprised a tithe from both the toll of Warwick and from one of the castle mills; land in Brailes in the south of Warwickshire; the land that Herlewin had occupied (the document does not say where this was); and a dwelling in Coten End.

St. Mary's was increasing its importance relative to All Saints'. However, we cannot be sure if Earl Henry intended its new college to be separate from, or in succession to, that at All Saints'; he died in 1119 before doing anything that might have given us more evidence. He had retired a year or so beforehand

8. *The conveyance of the church at Compton Mordak to St. Mary's at the direction of Earl Henry in about 1115. This document seems to be either a copy of the original or confirmation of a transfer that had not previously been recorded in writing, and is thought to date from the time of Earl William (died 1184).*

to one of the religious houses that he had endowed, the monastery of St. Peter of Préaux about ten miles north-east of Rouen, where he is buried. Henry may have initiated the foundations of the colleges at St. Sepulchre's and St. Mary's, but his spiritual home was still in Normandy.

III

Earl Henry was succeeded by his son Roger, who continued the process of founding a college at St. Mary's. One of his first acts was to move the school from All Saints' to St. Mary's, a clear statement of intent as to St. Mary's new status. This threat to All Saints' led to its prebendaries appealing to the Crown for confirmation of their rights and privileges, including possession of the school, which they claimed to have held since the time of Edward the Confessor (reigned 1042 to 1066). The king upheld their case, but it was a Pyrrhic victory. Roger promptly translated the college from All Saints' to St. Mary's, and amalgamated the two.

9. This image of 'Warwick church' (i.e. St. Mary's) has been cut out from a book, the identity of which is unknown, but which probably dates from the nineteenth century. The apsidal chancel suggests that it is intended to depict the Saxon church, but other features are anachronistic to that era. The image has no basis of accuracy at all, but it shows the interest there was in the history of St. Mary's.

The collegiate church of St. Mary and All Saints was created by two charters issued by the earl, and a third by which the bishop of Worcester, in whose diocese Warwick fell, confirmed his consent. The reference to 'All Saints' in the college's title appeared in a document some thirty years later, but seems to have been dropped soon afterwards.

The first two charters clearly go together, seemingly executed at the same time as they were witnessed by the same people. The first of them is undated, which was not particularly unusual, but the second is dated 1123. That date is not entirely free from doubt, as the second charter refers to Simon, bishop of Worcester, who was not consecrated until 1125. Perhaps it was prepared to replace an earlier one that had been lost. Despite these uncertainties, it is generally accepted that St. Mary's college was founded in 1123.

The first charter is a short document. After reciting that Earl Roger is implementing the wishes of his father, it grants the right for the Warwick canons to have a dean and chapter at St. Mary's, and to hold their possessions 'as the canons in the cathedrals of London, Lincoln, Sarum (Salisbury), and York': all secular foundations. St. Mary's may not have been a cathedral, but it was given the constitution of one.

Despite their earlier objections, the prebendaries of All Saints' readily agreed to move to St. Mary's as long as they retained their position, stipends, and rights. This is documented in the second charter, which also sets out the details of St. Mary's endowment, much of which was transferred from All Saints'. It included six of the seven other Warwick churches, those of Saints Nicholas, Laurence, Michael, Helen, Peter, and John.[1] Earl Roger later added the seventh Warwick church, St. James's, above West Gate. St. Mary's also received the church of the neighbouring parish of Budbrooke, and, inconveniently, that of Greetham in Rutland, where the manor formed part of the Warwick honour.

St. Mary's was to be the mother church for all nine of these churches, and so had responsibility for their functioning. They were not, at this stage, fully under St. Mary's control, as they retained their own rectors, and received income on their own account, paying a proportion of it to St. Mary's. St. Mary's held the advowsons though, except in the case of St. James's, where it was retained by the earl.

---

1   St. Peter's was at the crossroads of Castle Lane and High Street, but was moved to above East Gate in the fifteenth century. St. John's was in the Market Square.

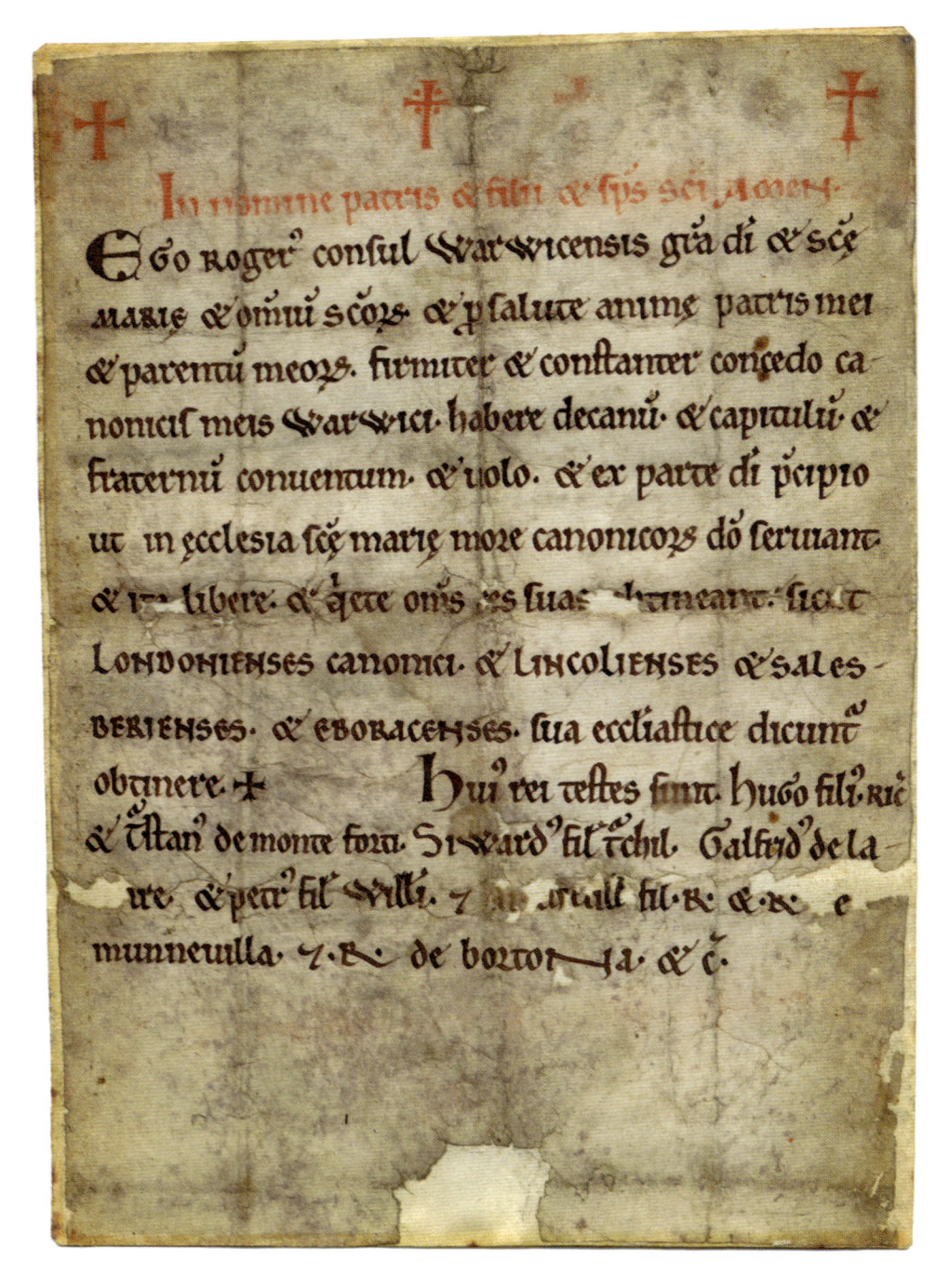

10. The 1123 charter, establishing the college at St. Mary's. It is the oldest document at the Warwickshire County Record Office.

St. Mary's also obtained sixty-five houses; land in at least sixteen local villages including Barford, Charlecote, Sherbourne, Snitterfield, and Wellesbourne; and various rights in other villages, including in Claverdon, where it received the earl's share of its tithes and the right of pannage (the foraging of pigs in woodland), which the peasantry would be charged for. Earl Roger added land at Brailes to the endowment by 1128. It looks like a sound basis, but, as we shall see, appearances can be deceptive.

IV

St. Mary's was well established as a secular college by the time Earl Roger died in 1153. It seems to have had a usual complement of six canons, though there were sometimes more, with the right to appoint them vested in the earl. But why was a secular college created at St. Mary's at all? It was very much against the trend.

Pope Gregory VII (died 1085) had discouraged secular colleges, partly because they were open to too much influence from their patrons, and partly because they could become power blocs threatening the authority of cathedrals. Monasteries, on the other hand, were promoted as centres of greater spirituality that were isolated from the vices of the world, and less susceptible to external interference.

As a result, patrons wishing to demonstrate their piety were now favouring regular communities. Sentiment was so strong that some secular colleges became monastic, such as that at Daventry, which was refounded within a Cluniac priory in about 1108. By 1123 there were only fifty or so secular colleges in England, excluding cathedrals and academic colleges, and only one other in the Worcester diocese.

Four years elapsed before Roger continued the process started by his father, though admittedly some of this may have been taken up by negotiations with the canons at All Saints'. However, the bishop of Worcester, Theulf, died in 1123 and his replacement was not appointed until 1125. This may have given Roger a window of opportunity so that the new bishop, Simon, was presented with a *fait accompli* when he confirmed his consent to the college. Perhaps Roger did not want the bishop interfering in what the earl considered a necessity.

On the face of it, the reason why the college at St. Mary's was a secular foundation seems obvious: to move the one at All Saints' to somewhere more suitable. Certainly that was the reason given in the bishop of Worcester's charter of confirmation. It may also be that Earl Roger took the line of least resistance with the litigious All Saints' canons, by simply translating them to St. Mary's.

There are other possibilities though. One was to curry favour with the king. Whereas his father had assiduously courted royal favour, Roger lost it, and more, almost straight away. He soon became associated with intrigues against the king in which his brother and cousins were prime movers. Fearing that the de Beaumont family was becoming too powerful, Henry I fined Roger heavily and stripped him of part of the Warwick honour. Some of it was given to the king's treasurer, Geoffrey de Clinton, who promptly built Kenilworth castle on his new estate, with financial help from the king. It was deliberately intended to create a formidable presence in Roger's backyard.

Earl Roger may have tried to recover his standing by founding the college as a demonstration of piety, devotion, and loyalty to the king. This suggestion comes from wording in the second of St. Mary's foundation charters, which, notably, includes a list of persons for whose souls its priests were to pray. They include not just Roger's father and grandfather, but also the royal family. This could be a smokescreen for a wider intent, but the wording of the charter implies that praying for souls was a motive behind the establishment of the college.

If this is right, the college at St. Mary's resembles a chantry foundation. Possibly this had become the *de facto* function of All Saints' by 1123, albeit limited to Newburgh souls. But what makes this suggestion particularly interesting is that we are two hundred years ahead of the popularity of chantries, and the first college founded explicitly as a chantry was at Marwell (Hampshire), established by the bishop of Winchester between 1129 and 1171, and so post-dating St. Mary's.

But there were other good reasons to establish a secular college, those same reasons why they were disliked by Gregory VII: to enable its patrons, the earls of Warwick, to influence it and to benefit from it. A secular college, coupled with St. Mary's role as a mother church focussed on Warwick and its surrounding villages, gave the earl a structure through which he could protect and extend his authority and influence locally, and built on the connection between the earldom and the church that had been established at All Saints'. To suggest, as one historian has done, that it would have enabled him to use priests to further his own interests in relation to parishioners may be going too far, but there was certainly an opportunity for the earl to use the clergy as his eyes, ears, and mouth.

But perhaps the most important advantage that a secular college offered was the prospect of patronage. Clerks could hold positions in the earl's household and have their pay supplemented by prebends. This is exactly what happened when Earl Henry appointed William, his chaplain, to be a canon of St. Mary's, and numerous other examples were to follow. By making someone a canon, with the income that went with it, the earls could fulfil an obligation or favour that they felt that they owed, or encourage a relationship that might prove useful. Moreover, patronage engendered a sense of mutual obligation: if the earl showed favour, he could expect favour or loyalty in return. It has even been said that prebends could be treated as commodities, to be bought and sold through the currency of patronage.

Whether or not patronage was the principal reason for the founding of St. Mary's college, it was certainly a valuable asset that could, occasionally, be granted to others, in return for some economic or political advantage. As early as 1143, Earl Roger had agreed to confer the right of preferment to St. Mary's on his brother Rotrou, bishop of Évreux (just over thirty miles south of Rouen), but for some reason he reneged, and instead gave it to the archdeacon of Coventry. Presumably Roger considered this to be more expedient, but in doing so he incurred the displeasure of Pope Lucius II who, after Rotrou's complaint, censured Roger, memorably invoking Proverbs 26:11 against him – 'as a dog returneth to his vomit, so a fool returneth to his folly'.

A later earl, Waleran, also conferred the right to prefer canons to St. Mary's on a third party, in his case Hubert Walter, who was granted it personally for life in or after 1194. Walter was arguably the most powerful man in England besides the king: he was archbishop of Canterbury, justiciar (chief minister and, in effect, regent during the king's frequent absences abroad) and, later, chancellor. The earl was undoubtedly seeking to demonstrate loyalty to, and to curry favour with, both Church and Crown. It was another way of exploiting St. Mary's for personal benefit.

It was a short step from the earls having the right to appoint canons to a claim to be entitled to nominate the dean of the college. Despite the pope's somewhat vivid rebuke, Earl Roger supported the archdeacon of Coventry in the ejection from office of the then dean, Richard. This struck at the college's independence, and Richard duly appealed to the pope. The decision, in 1146, was that no secular person was to interfere with the election of the dean, which was entirely a matter for the college itself, subject only to papal and episcopal authority. Roger's meddling had been against the terms of the charter that he himself had granted, but he also came up against wider policy considerations.

Dean Richard seems to have been reinstated, but the 1146 decision did not change the earl's behaviour. In response, in 1155/56 the canons of St. Mary's wrote to their counterparts at Sarum, who (not surprisingly) confirmed that the adoption of their constitution meant that the dean was to be elected by the chapter, and not be appointed by a third party. St. Mary's then seems to have petitioned Rome on the issue, for in November 1157 Adrian IV confirmed the papal ruling that had been given eleven years beforehand.

Nonetheless, the ability to choose the dean was a matter of considerable interest to the earls. It may be that they simply saw the church as part of their possessions, and therefore considered that they had a right to require it to behave as they wished. Rotrou's objection to his brother's disposal to the archdeacon of Coventry of the right of presentation at St. Mary's could have been more to do with the fact that it was going out of the family, rather than any particular wish of his to have it. Be that as it may, the personal link between the earls and St. Mary's through patronage was forged for some three hundred and fifty years.

V

The college of St. Mary may, therefore, have been founded out of expediency, as an act of fidelity to the Crown, from Earl Roger's desire to offer paid positions to men that he wished to reward, or as a means of exercising control locally. They are not mutually exclusive, of course. But whatever the reason, the elevation of St. Mary's to collegiate status was followed by the building of a new church. Most histories of Warwick date this from 1123, to coincide with the first two founding charters, but there is no documentary evidence to support this, and its architecture points to a rather later date.

The first part of the new church to be built would have been the crypt, which can still be seen. The design of the crypt's vault is very distinctive, and is found in England only at St. Mary's and in two other nearby churches – the chancel at St. Nicholas's Beaudesert, and the crypt at St. John's Berkswell. Both are within the Warwick honour. The building of all three seems to be connected, and similarities between the crypts at Berkswell and St. Mary's suggest that the former was influenced by the latter, to the extent that they may be by the same masons. Berkswell's crypt was probably built between 1160 and 1180, and Beaudesert's chancel can be dated to much the same time, so this suggests that work on the new St. Mary's began in around 1150. This is reinforced by architectural features within the crypt such as scalloped capitals and chamfered ribs, both implying a mid-twelfth century construction.

Dating it is not the only mystery afforded by the crypt, as there is a more fundamental question: why did St. Mary's have a crypt at all? They are uncommon, and Berkswell's is the only other one in Warwickshire. We can confidently rule out two reasons why crypts have been built elsewhere. One was sloping ground, the crypt providing a level platform for the chancel above; St. Mary's is built on an incline, but it would not have been necessary to dig as deep as the crypt to counter it. Another was to protect the chancel from flooding, but the crypt at St. Mary's is remarkably dry. Therefore, the indications are that the purpose of the crypt was to provide usable space, rather than structural utility.

Twelfth-century crypts are often associated with the display of relics, the popularity of which was increasing just at the time that St. Mary's was being rebuilt. There is no evidence that this is what St. Mary's crypt was for, one way or the other. However, there is an alternative, or additional, reason why the crypt might have been built: as a mausoleum for Earl Roger, housing his tomb, along with, typically, a relic, and an altar. The crypt is certainly grand enough, both in terms of its size and in the use of contrasting courses of grey and red sandstone, suggesting that it was an area of prestige.

We do not know where Roger was buried, but it was probably in Warwick. If so, St. Mary's is the most likely possibility, as he had a poor relationship with St. Sepulchre's. And if work on the crypt started in, say, 1150, Earl Roger would have been about fifty, and considering his final resting place. If he wanted to be buried at a new St. Mary's to provide a lasting memorial to his faith, now was the time to start building.

A clue might be found in the similarities between the crypts at Berkswell and St. Mary's. The manor of Berkswell was held from the earls of Warwick by the de Mondevilles, and they built the church there. Berkswell's crypt is unusual in that it seems to have been altered during its construction to accommodate a newly acquired relic. It is in two distinct parts, a conventional

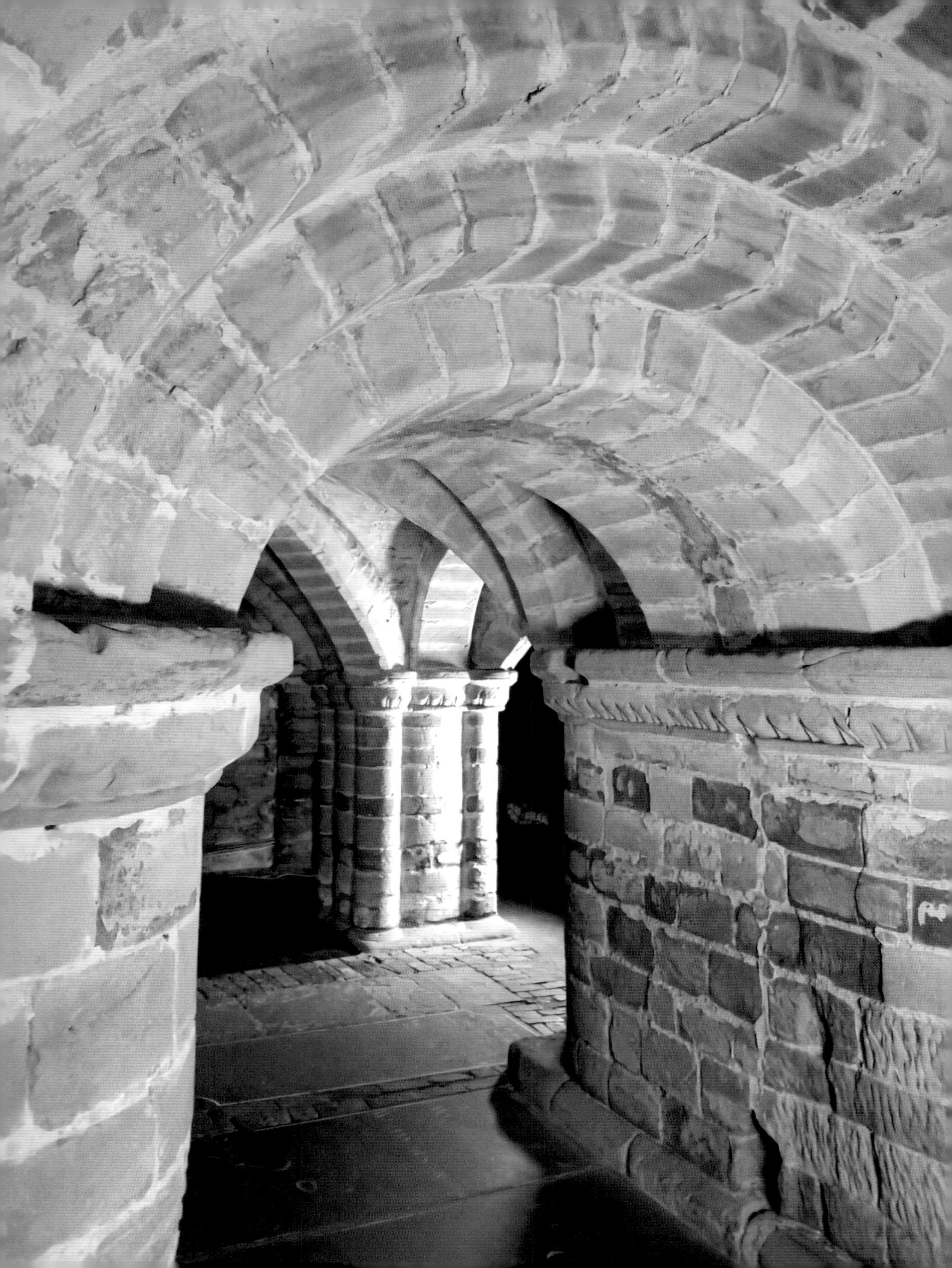

eastern section beneath the chancel, and an octagonal chamber to its west, beneath part of the nave. It may be that this chamber was used as a viewing area by the public, affording sight of a relic placed in the eastern part, along with, perhaps, a de Mondeville tomb. The crypt at St. Mary's also extends beyond the footprint of the chancel, predominantly to the north. Indeed, it is exceptionally large, extending northwards beneath the present-day vestry and chapter house. Does this suggest a separation of space in the crypt between public and private, with devotees using the northern section, and were the de Mondevilles imitating their lord's church of St. Mary's in the architectural design of their crypt, and in its function? These are intriguing possibilities.

Left: 11. The crypt at St. Mary's, looking from the north. The scalloped capitals and the chamfered ribs of the vaulting can be seen clearly, as can the contrasting bands of stone though there has been some unsympathetic restoration. The large piers and extensive vaulting suggest that a north tower was intended, though there is no evidence of it having been built.

The text of the first founding charter of the College of St. Mary

In the name of the Father and of the Son and of the Holy Spirit Amen. I, Roger, earl of Warwick, by the Grace of God, St. Mary, and All Saints and for the health of the soul of my father and of my ancestors, firmly and steadfastly grant to my canons of Warwick to have a Dean and Chapter and brotherly meeting, and I will, and on God's behalf grant, that they may serve God in the Church of St. Mary after the manner of canons, and may hold all of their possessions as freely and as quietly as the canons of London and Lincoln and Sarum and York are said to hold their possessions in ecclesiastical fashion. Of which thing these are witnesses Hugh, son of Richard & Thurstan de Montfort, Siward son of Turchil, Geoffrey de la Mare, & Peter son of William & Anschetill son of R. & Ranulf de Mundeville & Robert de Borton etc

Translation reproduced from P. Chatwin, 'The charter of Roger, earl of Warwick, founding the Collegiate Church of St. Mary, Warwick, 1123' *Birmingham Archaeological Society Transactions* LVII (1934), pp.65-66.

– 2 –

CHALLENGES

THE ONE hundred and fifty years that followed the foundation of the college saw St. Mary's struggle, surviving as best it could. It had little financial support from Earl Roger's successors, and there were few townspeople willing or able to make grants to it. One reason was the continuing preference for regular houses over secular, another was that Warwick was stagnating. Moreover, St. Mary's became embroiled in disputes over its income, and over the rights of the bishop of Worcester to supervise the activities of the chapter. But before looking at the detail, we should set the scene and discuss the context of St. Mary's difficulties: an earldom beset with incompetence, misfortune, and debt, and the connected topic of the under-performance of Warwick's economy.

I

As we have seen, Earl Roger's earldom did not get off to a good start, with the loss of Kenilworth, and his tribulations continued throughout his life. In around 1140 Roger was unable to prevent the earl of Hereford from seizing some of his lands in Gloucestershire. He was to suffer one final ignominy. By 1153 the legitimacy of King Stephen's claim to the throne, after the death of his uncle Henry I in 1135, remained unresolved, and the cause of the late king's daughter, Matilda, had passed to her son, the future Henry II. Earl Roger had placed Warwick castle and its garrison at Stephen's disposal, but while the earl was at Court his wife, Countess Gundreda, opened the castle gates to Henry's forces. It was said that the shock and humiliation killed Earl

Roger as soon as he heard the news, and his failure to control his own castle – and his wife – quickly became the cause of much derision. Roger did not enjoy the best of epitaphs, with one contemporary writer calling him 'feeble … rejoicing more in pleasure than in resolution of mind'.

Earl Roger's successor was his son William, who seems to have played no part at all on the national stage. That may have been a blessing if his attempt at negotiating his own marriage is anything to go by. A prospective bride's main attractions, beyond her ability to bear children, were her dowry – land settled on the married couple by her father ostensibly to provide for her during the marriage, but in which his son-in-law had a half share; her prospects of inheritance; and the opportunities her family brought for advancement.

Earl William's marriage to Matilda de Percy had all the makings of a good match for an impoverished earl. She was co-heir, with her elder sister, of the rich, well-connected, and recently deceased, William de Percy. Earl William made a substantial payment to de Percy's estate for the privilege of marrying Matilda, funded partly by selling land, and partly by mortgaging the honour of Gower to Bruno, a London moneylender.

Earl William had saddled himself with a large debt to finance a marriage that quickly proved disappointing. With Matilda's sister doing much better than she did out of the distribution of their father's estates, William's expectations of a windfall soon dissipated, and he had to raise more money by selling some of his lands. Even so, the debt to Bruno could not be serviced, and it was purchased by King Henry II, who foreclosed on William's death in 1184. Gower was lost to the earldom.

William's heir, his brother Waleran, made more of an effort to revive the earldom. We have already mentioned that he used St. Mary's to foster relationships with the archbishop of Canterbury and the Crown, and we shall be coming back to this. Waleran was followed, in 1204, by his young son Henry, who was about twelve years old when his father died. Henry grew up to be one of the more competent Newburgh earls, but he had little opportunity to stabilise the earldom's finances, and he owed over eight hundred marks shortly before his early death in 1229.

Henry's son, Thomas, set about consolidating the progress made by his father by spending money he could not afford on litigating against his stepmother over her entitlement. Despite the good fortune of inheriting substantial holdings in Oxfordshire from his uncle, he was still in debt when he died, childless, in 1242. John Rous thought that Thomas was buried in Warwick, but this cannot be substantiated, and, if he was, it might have been at St. Sepulchre's rather than St. Mary's.

The earldom drifted for the next twenty-five years. It passed from Earl Thomas to his sister Margaret and, by royal favour, to her husband John de Plessis. On John's death in 1263, William Mauduit, the grandson of Earl Waleran, inherited the earldom. He played his part in draining the coffers by seeing Warwick castle captured by the rebel de Montfort forces, its defences destroyed, and himself and the countess imprisoned at Kenilworth. The ransom was a mere 1,900 marks. It was quite an achievement in only five years.

Such ineptitude and debt was exacerbated by a perpetual problem with widows. A marriage settlement required the groom to provide his wife with a 'dower' – property that, should he die first, would belong to her for the rest of her life, and then revert to his heir. It was customarily one third of the husband's lands. In other words, the heir could expect his income to be reduced by about a third during his mother's widowhood, even if she remarried. There was also a considerable indirect cost, in that he was unable to manage a significant proportion of his estates, and had to forgo the trappings and opportunities of lordship, such as patronage. Less land, less income, and less patronage did nothing to enhance the standing of an indebted earldom.

The Newburgh earls had a particular knack of marrying women who brought little worth with them, but who enjoyed generous dowers, long and wealthy widowhoods, and litigation (see table, page 49). The statistics are startling. All six dowagers outlived their husbands by at least twenty years, one of them by an impressive fifty-six. Two of them were alive for the twenty-three years between 1242 and 1265. Countess Matilda survived the entire earldom of her brother-in-law, Earl Waleran, bar two months. The Warwick honour was free from dower in only twelve years between the death of Earl Henry I in 1119 and that of Countess Ela in 1298. The manor of Claverdon was in dower for over half this period. Every dowager was involved in disputes over her entitlement. One earl, the hapless William, sold land that had been promised to his widow, bequeathing to his successor a lawsuit from both her and the purchaser, the bishop of Winchester, who had to be compensated. It was a catalogue of disasters.

The devastation caused to the earldom's finances by poor management and long-lived dowagers was so great that it has been said that Earl Thomas controlled little more than his holdings in Warwick, and Earl William Mauduit only one third of the whole honour. There were serious implications for both Warwick as a town and for St. Mary's.

The Newburgh era earls and their dowagers

Earls	*Dowagers*	*Length of dower*
Henry I 1088-1119	Margaret	*ca.* 38 years
Roger 1119-1153	Gundreda	*ca.* 22 years
William 1153-1184	Matilda	*ca.* 20 years
Waleran 1184-1204	Alice	*ca.* 22 years
Henry II 1204-1229	Philippa	36 years
Thomas 1229-1242	Ela	56 years
Countess Margaret II 1242-1253		
John de Plessis 1247-1263		
William Mauduit 1263-1268		

II

St. Mary's finances suffered directly from uninterested, distracted, unimaginative, and impecunious Newburgh earls, who did virtually nothing for the church after Earl Roger's death, but there was a double hit: the earls conspicuously failed to invest in the town of Warwick, which in turn restricted the support that St. Mary's might otherwise have had from a growing entrepreneurial class.

Warwick was the largest settlement in the county in 1086, but it was soon overtaken. By the early 1200s it was well behind Coventry, while Stratford-upon-Avon was growing fast, its population quadrupling between 1160 and 1250 to equal Warwick's. With most urban economies expanding, Warwick got left behind.

There are two principal, inter-connected, reasons for this. First, the basis of Warwick's economic strength, the castle, became a drag on the town's growth as traders became complacent. With a ready outlet for their goods, there was little or no incentive for innovation, and seemingly no desire to rock the boat. Towns like Coventry and Worcester had seen the emergence of merchants and artisans pressing for initiatives to encourage and regulate commerce from 1150 onwards, securing financial and administrative concessions from their lord in a partial rebalance of power and responsibility.

These were the early signs of the emergence of town corporations, and most towns had gained some form of self-governance by 1400. However in Warwick an official of the earl's household, John Huggeford, was both constable (custodian) of the castle, and steward of the town, responsible for collecting tolls, as late as 1478. It shows how closely the administration of Warwick remained tied to the earldom, and how politically backward the town was.

Secondly, the earls did not invest in Warwick to stimulate trade to any meaningful extent. Some of their contemporaries had seen that establishing markets grew the local economy, generating wealth and increasing returns for landowners. A lord might forego traditional sources of income, such as tolls to enter a town, to encourage traders and buyers from farther afield. The cost of his concession was outweighed by the lord's increased profits from a larger and more successful market; it was free trade, medieval style. Hence Coventry's burgesses (those who owned property in the borough) were granted freedom from tolls by about 1150, and those in Stratford from about 1200.

Some lords went further, creating something akin to modern enterprise zones, encouraging building through development in infrastructure and low rents and taxes. Stratford is a prime example, a speculative venture by the local lord, the bishop of Worcester, who in about 1200 rebuilt the town bridge to improve access from the south, and laid out streets to serve building plots offered on low rents. It was a stunning success, and Stratford soon competed effectively with Warwick for the trade to be had from the villages between them.

In the opposite direction, Coventry was receiving new investment, most notably from the Cistercian abbey at Coombe. The order was renowned for its sheep farming, and in Coventry it ventured into a form of vertical integration, developing the area within what is now Much Park Street, Earl Street, and Upper Park Street for downstream industries such as fulling and dyeing. The monks created a ready supply of processors of their fleece, and benefitted from their rents. It was a sound and prosperous strategy, paving the way for Coventry's heyday as a centre for wool.

Fairs were another means by which good profits could be generated for the host town, attracting travelling salesmen offering specialist and luxury goods not normally available locally. Stratford had had a fair since 1214, Coventry since 1218 with a second in 1227. There were few similar initiatives in Warwick, even though the benefits were to be seen literally up – and down – the road. Far from giving concessions to enterprising townsmen, Earl William granted the market tolls of Warwick to Alan, his master cook and chamberlain, in part payment of the retainer payable to him as a squire. It suggests that William, at least, was unconcerned with the greater good of the prosperity of the town, but perhaps the financial disaster of his marriage to Matilda de Percy left him little option. Admittedly a new bridge across the Avon probably dates from about 1200, the same time as Stratford's, but it was not until 1261 that Earl John de Plessis granted a charter for an annual fair in Warwick, to be held for eight days starting on 31 July.

The fact that de Plessis found it necessary to institute a fair implies that Warwick's economy needed boosting. De Plessis gave freedom from toll to those who attended, presumably to encourage its establishment on the circuit, but the concession was only for six years, and after that the customary rates would apply. Traders from outside the town still had to pay to erect their stalls. It was better than nothing, but it fell well short of the terms on offer in competing towns.

III

Warwick was, therefore, insular and stagnant from lack of investment, the stimuli evident in towns like Coventry and Stratford absent. Consequently, St. Mary's had to fend as best it could; its endowment was not enhanced significantly in this period, and even those who might be expected to have the closest connection with St. Mary's spurned it.

There is no evidence that any of the Newburgh earls, or their countesses, left bequests to St. Mary's. Countess Margaret II was a benefactor of St. Michael's leper hospital in Warwick (another of Earl Roger's foundations), but not of St. Mary's. Countess Ela, the widow of Earl Thomas, gave land in Claverdon to St. Sepulchre's in return for prayers for the souls of her late husband, herself, and her family. However, the main beneficiaries of Ela's piety were the abbeys of Lacock in Wiltshire, which had been founded by her mother; Godstow, in Oxford; and Osney, also in Oxford and where she is buried. Indeed, other than Earl Roger, the only record of any grant to St. Mary's by the Newburgh earls or their countesses is one by Earl William who, despite his financial difficulties, gave five now-unidentifiable properties in or near Warwick.

The local gentry did not support St. Mary's either. For example, Hugh FitzRichard of Hatton, a major tenant of the earl, preferred to endow a nunnery at Wroxall (about six miles north of Warwick) and to give land to St. Sepulchre's. Successive descendants of his continued to support Wroxall. As we have seen, the foundation of St. Mary's as a secular college was against popular sentiment, and, as the bequests to St. Sepulchre's and other regular houses show, that did not change quickly. There may also have been a feeling that St. Mary's was 'the earl's church', and therefore not considered by those who wished to demonstrate their piety. This may have influenced a wealthy corn merchant in Warwick, Richard the Kentishman (died 1203), who does not seem to have been a benefactor of St. Mary's.

Some grants were made to St. Mary's by townspeople, with gifts of rental income being more common than outright donations of property.

For example, Philip of Itchington let a property in Saltisford, for which the tenant was to pay 12d a year to the church. Many rents were allocated for particular purposes, such as that made by one Gilbert in about 1250, who gave to St. Mary's the annual rent of 18d from land he owned in Warwick, to be used to provide candles at the altar of Saints Katherine and Margaret: the earliest reference we have to the dedication of an altar in the church. Some forty years later Roger Young gave rents from several properties, to be divided equally between the resident canons and vicars on the anniversary of his father's death, and with a mass to be said for the persons he named. And John de St. Amand, a canon of St. Mary's, donated rental income of 12d to the church's common fund, for the benefit of his soul and that of Archbishop Hubert Walter of Canterbury, in whose service he had been.

This link between the payment of rent and spiritual provision could also be seen when St. Mary's was the landlord. In 1230 Walter, a tanner, leased a property in Saltisford from St. Mary's in return for an annual rent of 12d which was to be used to pay for a torch. In this way, Walter could relate his payment to part of the church liturgy, candles and torches being particularly revered as representing the light of God, symbolic of faith and holiness.

One lease granted by St. Mary's, that cannot be dated more accurately than the middle of the thirteenth century, is particularly disturbing. The tenant of a property owned by the church was expressly prohibited from assigning it to a person of Jewish faith, and the tenement was probably in Jury Street, 'the street of the Jews', or Smith Street. St. Mary's would not have inserted this restriction into the lease in isolation from prevailing opinion. There was an ineffective attempt to expel Jews from Warwickshire in 1234, and, for no obvious reason, the bishops of Worcester seem to have been particularly intolerant. Despite this, and thankfully, Warwick's Jewish community was not subjected to the appalling violence and atrocities that took place elsewhere.

IV

As well as not receiving any significant new endowments, St. Mary's faced difficulties in managing what it had. Its holdings were fragmented; it did not have a complete manor, and Earl Roger had divided local benefits between different institutions, probably to prevent any of them from becoming too powerful in any locality and so threatening his authority. Thus, he gave the tithes of Wellesbourne to St. Mary's, but the church and its advowson, a useful source of patronage, to Kenilworth abbey. St. Mary's was a significant landowner in Brailes, but again the church and advowson was with Kenilworth. St. Mary's had the tithes of Claverdon, but St. Michael's in Warwick held land there, and the Cistercian nuns of the nearby Pinley priory were entitled to a portion of the income of the manor.

There were two important consequences of this fragmentation. First, St. Mary's had little control over its sources of revenue, which was under pressure. Inflation was particularly high after 1180, and landowners took action to preserve the real value of their income, such as reducing costs by converting arable farming to livestock, which was less labour-intensive. St. Mary's was powerless to follow suit. The secular structure of the college did not lend itself to managing whole manors anyway; regular houses were in a much better position to do this, as they could take collective initiatives to boost their finances. St. Mary's could not have generated income in the way that St. Sepulchre's did when, in 1249, it leased some ninety acres at Stivichall, Coventry, for thirty years. In effect the priory took over the management of the estate on the owner's behalf, who received a third of the harvest in return. And St. Mary's was certainly in no position to undertake projects such as the Cistercians at Coombe did.

The other difficulty with holding split local property interests was the considerable scope for argument over rights and money. For example, there was a long-running dispute between a canon of St. Mary's and the abbot of Bordesley abbey (Worcestershire) over the entitlement to the tithes of Bidford-on-Avon. The manor of Bidford had been granted to the abbey by Matilda, daughter of King Henry I, on or shortly after its foundation by Earl Roger's cousin Waleran, but Earl Roger had given a share of the tithes as part of a prebend of St. Mary's. The abbot challenged this right, but Matilda's son, King Henry II, twice commanded him to restore the tithes to the canon. Nonetheless the dispute rumbled on for another twenty years or so before it was settled on the basis that the abbot retained the tithes after all, in return for an annual payment to the dispossessed canon of fifteen shillings. It was still being paid in 1544.

Sometimes disagreements arose between prebendaries, as in about 1200 when the dean and chapter gave judgment on a dispute between two of St.

Mary's canons over tithes at Walton and Warwick. This seems to have been a particularly fractious time. In 1203 the college had the temerity to question the right of the earl to the advowson of St. Laurence in Warwick (with good reason), and again in relation to St. James's four years later (less so).

V

Like all parish churches, St. Mary's was dependent upon tithes and offerings from its parishioners. These critical income streams could, and did, lead to tensions, most notably a protracted turf war between St. Mary's and its ecclesiastical neighbour, St. Sepulchre's priory, barely half a mile away.

The church of St. Helen had been annexed to St. Mary's by Earl Roger's founding charters, but it quickly became St. Sepulchre's priory church and seems to have been subsumed into it as early as 1127/28. The benefit of the revenue that would have accrued to St. Helen's was thus lost to St. Mary's, and the priory was supposed to pay an annual pension of 2s 6d to St. Mary's by way of compensation. That obligation was honoured only haphazardly.

The priory also encroached on St. Mary's receipt of burial payments. Churches could not charge a fee for burial, which was a sacrament, but they could expect to receive offerings from the deceased's estate, family, and attendees at the funeral. By 1146 an agreement had been reached whereby the priory cemetery was to be used only for its own brethren, but two years later the pope had to instruct the archbishop of Canterbury and the bishop of Worcester to warn the priors to adhere to the agreement. Petitioning the pontificate to issue the necessary decree would have been expensive, but the college clearly thought it worthwhile. It did not have the desired effect. Within two years, the pope mandated the archbishop and the bishop to enforce the agreement against St. Sepulchre's. Then, in late 1157 or early 1158, the archbishop and an archdeacon of Worcester (the see being vacant at the time) ruled that the prior was not only still in breach, but was also guilty of poaching parishioners. The prior was ordered to desist on pain of excommunication.

The squabble was, to say the least, unseemly and unbrotherly, but it was not over yet. Within three years St. Mary's again appealed to the pope, at more expense, and, with the see of Worcester still vacant, Gilbert, bishop of Hereford, was mandated to settle the dispute, with no right of appeal.

Having heard evidence from both priests and laymen, he found the priory guilty of both unlawfully refusing to pay the pension due to St. Mary's in lieu of income from St. Helen's, and of appropriating St. Mary's parochial rights, which probably meant that St. Sepulchre's was still admitting St. Mary's parishioners for worship. In other words, nothing had changed.

Despite such a strong finding in favour of St. Mary's, a compromise was necessary. St. Mary's, apparently on the initiative of Gilbert to try and get rid of the case once and for all, agreed to pay the prior personally for the rest of his life a share of parochial revenues, in return for an annual payment from him of ten shillings.

If Gilbert thought that this was the end of the matter, he was wrong. Shortly after this judgment comes another of his, this time in the case of the wife of one Gilbert le Nurric. It seems that either she had been buried at St. Sepulchre's, or that she intended to be, with land being given to the priory by way of burial offering. This was, of course, contrary to the arrangements made between the priory and St. Mary's, and it shows how the priory was prepared to disregard them openly, as was Nurric, despite the recent injunction against the poaching of parishioners. Nurric must have known that the priory cemetery was supposed to be for its brethren only, yet he was prepared to give away land for the privilege of a burial there. The desire to be buried at a regular house took precedence over legal niceties. The prior was ordered to hand over to St. Mary's the land that had been given by Nurric, and to make a public declaration of the nature of the dispute and of the papal judgment.

The Nurric decision was made no later than March 1163, but by August of that year St. Mary's complained that the prior was still refusing to comply with the papal instruction. The pope again appointed Gilbert, by now bishop of London, who must have been sick and tired of the whole thing. He was told to re-iterate his decision, and to ensure that it was honoured. Even the king, Henry II, instructed Gilbert that St. Sepulchre's must comply with the ruling, twice. The priory finally seems to have accepted the position, though it had taken decisions of at least three popes, a king, an archbishop, two bishops, and an archdeacon to bring it to heel.

VI

With no requirement for St. Mary's canons to be resident in Warwick, absenteeism was frequent, and holding other appointments was the norm. This pluralism was permitted for those priests, like canons, who did not 'have cure' of souls; that was a responsibility delegated by the canons to their vicars. The low value of St. Mary's prebends made pluralism inevitable, and at times the consequences became serious. When Bishop Cantilupe of Worcester visited the church in about 1263 the entire college was absent, with services conducted by six hired chaplains. That in itself was not a major problem; the issue was that the chaplains were not being paid, either by the canons themselves (as they should have been), or by St. Mary's. Being a chaplain was not a great job anyway, badly paid, low status, no job security, but those at St. Mary's were living in poverty, solely dependent on the offerings of parishioners.

Bishop Cantilupe ordered the canons to pay their chaplains, which they ignored, and they were summoned to Worcester to explain themselves. They ignored that instruction as well, and were excommunicated for their pains. Even so, in 1270 the bishop, by now the diligent but prickly Godfrey Giffard, had cause to warn one of the canons, John de Plesset, about his behaviour, and he was excommunicated, again, in 1274.

Most churches were subject to visitations, a sort of parochial Ofsted that, in theory, took place every three years, and enabled the bishop to be satisfied that standards were being maintained. This is what had brought Bishop Cantilupe to Warwick in 1263. Representatives of the laity were asked about the priests' attendance, dress, moral conduct, and performance of duties, and enquiry was made as to the physical condition of the church, the availability of books, and the moral standards of the parish. Both Cantilupe and Giffard were assiduous about visitations, and they took the opportunity to deliver sermons to clergy and laity alike. But there was more to visitations than being subject to scrutiny: parishes had to pay for them, along with the not-inconsiderable expense of feeding and housing the bishop and his entourage of up to thirty men during their stay.

In 1282 the dean of St. Mary's, Robert de Plesset, initiated a claim against Bishop Giffard, alleging that he had no jurisdiction over the administration and behaviour of the chapter. It was not a spurious argument. At the time that the college was founded, diocesan powers were ill-defined, and the bare reference to St. Mary's enjoying the same rights as four secular cathedrals left a lot of room for uncertainty. When the dean of St. Mary's wrote to his counterpart at Sarum between 1155 and 1165 asking for clarification, he was told (not surprisingly) that the prebendaries had considerable independence, being answerable to the college, not to the bishop, and were not required to pay any money to the diocese. This appears to have gone unchallenged until 1246.

Robert de Plesset had been one of those excommunicated in 1263, and was very probably a relative of the errant John, and may even have been the son of John de Plessis, earl of Warwick. As one might expect, Robert's claim of independence provoked a lively response from the bishopric; Giffard rejected the contention, provocatively referred to Robert as the 'so-called dean' and the canons as 'his accomplices', and applied to the archbishop of Canterbury for a ruling. The following year, 1283, Giffard made a point about who he thought was really in charge, by absolving a priest who had been excommunicated by Robert. Giffard then excommunicated Robert again, this time for irregularities in administering Earl John de Plessis's will, of which he was an executor. The archbishop upheld Giffard's appeal, fined St. Mary's twenty marks in costs, and confirmed Robert's excommunication, along with that of the rest of the chapter.

A third (at least) excommunication for Robert, for disobeying the bishop's rulings, came in 1286, and finally Giffard urged the earl, now William Beauchamp, to appoint someone more suitable to the deanery. Robert was duly dismissed. In theory the dean was appointed by the canons, not the earl, a principle that had been upheld by the pope in 1146, but if that was being observed before this incident, it certainly was not afterwards.

Giffard was not to be trifled with. On one occasion, he ordered men who had assaulted members of the clergy in Little Comberton (Worcestershire) to be paraded barefoot and publicly beaten, not only in the nearest town of Pershore, but also in the marketplaces of Worcester, Gloucester, Bristol, and Warwick, *pour décourager les autres*. Including Warwick in the itinerary had the advantage of reminding the chapter of Giffard's authority. Nonetheless, the dispute between St. Mary's and the bishop over jurisdiction did not end with Robert de Plesset's sacking. In 1308 the bishop-elect called the then dean, a decidedly belligerent character, 'a roaring lion' – it was not a compliment. The church was still accusing the diocese of unlawful interference as late as

1343. There were some later minor skirmishes, but ultimately St. Mary's had to back down.

VII

Like Warwick's economy, St. Mary's was treading water during the lordship of the Newburghs, who did not consider it an appropriate beneficiary of their pious donations. They were ready to use the advantages of the secular college to further their patronage, and they took control over the appointment of the dean, but beyond that St. Mary's was left to fend the best it could.

Secular foundations like St. Mary's could not command the same degree of allegiance as regular houses. Moreover, in about 1263 a Dominican friary (the Black Friars) was founded in Warwick, situated just beyond West Gate and giving its name to Friars Street. This would have compounded St. Mary's difficulties, with the friars' ethos of mendicancy (they were forbidden from owning property), preaching, and simplicity putting churches at even more risk of being seen as bloated, complacent, and increasingly divorced from humbleness.

Perhaps this is what provoked the canons into taking a harder line with the bishop of Worcester over his jurisdiction; the visitation that seems to have sparked off the dispute was at about the same time as the establishment of the friary. Given the problems that the college had faced with St. Sepulchre's, it might well have feared the consequences of the new arrival, and felt that it was in a better position than the diocesan archdeacon to decide how to face the challenges that it posed. It would, though, be naïve to rule out the canons' basic desire for non-interference, and to avoid having to pay the bishopric for the privilege of suffering its visitations and other dues.

But the college was not simply a querulous bunch of largely absent prebendaries, taking the fruits of their preferment without performing any of their responsibilities. They could support St. Mary's and press its case without being there day in, day out. For example, Walter, a canon preferred by Earl Roger, was also archdeacon of Oxford, and his authority helped to broker the deal between St. Mary's and St. Sepulchre's over burial rights. Another canon, the arch-pluralist Ralph de Hengham, the prebendary of Compton Mordak by 1295, was a close friend of Bishop Giffard, so a factor behind his appointment may have been an attempt to defuse the situation between him and the college. He was also a canon at Hereford, Lichfield, and St. Paul's cathedrals; for a time he was archdeacon of Worcester; he was a prebendary at four other collegiate churches; and he held other positions in no fewer than ten different counties.

Hengham was more than a pluralist cleric; he was also a top lawyer. He became a judge in 1271, and three years later he was made Chief Justice of the King's Bench, which heard criminal cases. However, he fell from grace in 1290, was dismissed on what was probably a technicality, and imprisoned. He paid an astounding ten thousand marks in return for his release and a pardon; the amount reflected his ability to pay rather than the crime. He was reinstated as a judge in 1300, and was Chief Justice of the Common Bench, or civil court, from 1301 to 1309.

Despite Hengham resuming his legal career at such a high level while at St. Mary's, he is recorded as being involved in the church's affairs some half a dozen times, and he could well have attended other meetings of the chapter to impart the benefit of his wisdom and experience.

By the end of the 1200s St. Mary's was in less than rude health: financially insecure, its chaplains unpaid, its canons embroiled in arguments over their independence. Thankfully, the church was about to be swept on a course that would, eventually, transform it.

12. The memorial brass from the tomb of Ralph de Hengham in St. Paul's cathedral, and destroyed in the Great Fire of London. De Hengham was a canon at St. Mary's from at least 1295 until his death in 1311.

– 3 –

POTENTIAL

THE NEWBURGHS may have failed to enhance the standing of the earldom, but the same can hardly be said of their successors, the Beauchamps. Within fifty years of the death of Earl John de Plessis, a Beauchamp earl of Warwick was a prominent, even infamous, national figure, and the next three generations produced, in succession, a feared military commander; a rebel against the king; and one of the wealthiest men in England. And, in pursuing their advancement, the Beauchamps demonstrated another way of getting on in life: propaganda. Their self-promotion included a spurious embellishment of their ancestry, the use of motifs so distinctive that they are still familiar today, and the building of powerful reminders of the family's importance: Warwick castle, and a new St. Mary's, taken to its zenith in the second half of the fifteenth century with the building of the incomparable Beauchamp chapel.

I

The first Beauchamp earl of Warwick was William, who became earl in 1268 following the death of his uncle, Earl William Mauduit. He was descended from Walter de Beauchamp, who died in 1130 or 1131, and had been a royal dispenser (steward) and both sheriff of Worcestershire and keeper of its forests.

Walter made what turned out to be a fortuitous marriage, to the daughter of one Urse d'Abetot, who had arrived in England with William the Conqueror. The Domesday survey records that Urse held Worcester castle and land in seven counties, though mainly in Worcestershire, for where he had been appointed sheriff for life. Urse died in 1108, leaving a son, Robert, but some two years later Robert was expelled from England for killing a royal official. Walter hit the jackpot, receiving the lands that his brother-in-law had forfeited. They included Robert's inheritance from Urse, and about half of the estate of Urse's brother, also Robert.

The next three generations of Beauchamps, all Williams, need not trouble us, so we come to the earl himself, another William. His position was also elevated by a combination of marriage and luck. His wife, Matilda FitzGeoffrey, had two married brothers, so William could have had little expectation of a profitable alliance. Yet both brothers died young and childless, and Matilda became heir to a quarter of her father's substantial estate. William benefitted further from the marriage of his father to Isabel, the sister of William Mauduit, who had become earl of Warwick following the two childless marriages of Earl Thomas and of Countess Margaret II. With Mauduit also dying without issue, the earldom passed to his nephew, William Beauchamp. Serendipity indeed.

St. Mary's was sorely mistaken if it hoped that the new regime would bring a swift transformation of its prospects. Apart from anything else, William's inheritance was burdened with debt. There was a Beauchamp dower until 1280, and he also had Countess Ela's to contend with. She finally gave up the dower manors of Claverdon and Tanworth in 1289, in return for appropriate compensation, but she kept the advowson of the church of the latter, showing the desirability of having a right of presentation to clerical livings. William remained impecunious almost until his death, despite King Edward I underwriting, or using his influence to have written off, over seven hundred pounds of his debt, as a reward for his loyalty. In 1295, three years before he died, William owed four hundred pounds to Italian bankers, though there was some improvement when his wife's inheritance finally fell in.

No new endowments for St. Mary's were forthcoming, but Earl William did not totally ignore it. We have already met one of William's appointees to St. Mary's, the influential lawyer and cleric, Ralph de Hengham, who was a useful person to have on board. But more difficult to understand are the discussions that took place in 1285, some ten years before Hengham's appointment, between Earl William and Godfrey Giffard, bishop of Worcester, over the creation of six additional canons at St. Mary's, to be endowed by the bishop. Presumably the bishop would have had the right of their presentation. Perhaps this was an attempt at reconciliation between the Beauchamps and the diocese, who had had a long history of conflict over their respective interests in Worcester going back to the time of Urse d'Abetot. William himself was engaged in a power struggle with Giffard over territory that included the family seat of Elmley castle, near Evesham. Even so, William must have had doubts about increasing and embedding the influence of the diocese over St. Mary's, seemingly to the extent of giving the bishop control of the chapter.

This proposal was being discussed at a time when the dispute between St. Mary's and the diocese over jurisdiction, spearheaded by the dean, Robert de Plesset, was still bubbling. As recently as 1282, three years earlier, de Plesset had objected to the chapter's presentation of one Peter de Leycester to Budbrooke. No doubt the fact that de Leycester was a diocesan official did not endear himself to de Plesset, but he was in a minority of one in resisting de Leycester's appointment, so perhaps his colleagues were prepared to be more conciliatory towards the bishop. One can only imagine de Plesset's reaction when, the following year, de Leycester was appointed the bishop's proctor, or representative, in a case between Giffard, de Plesset, and another canon of St. Mary's.

As it was, nothing came of the proposals to increase the size of the college. However, the incident implies that the earl viewed it first and foremost to provide an outlet for patronage, that it was subservient to his purposes, and something to be offered up as a sacrificial pawn in a wider political strategy.

Notwithstanding William's engagement with the college, the Beauchamp roots stayed very firmly embedded in Worcestershire. The family's principal residence remained at Elmley castle, Worcestershire was its power base, and Worcestershire its spiritual home. When William died, at Elmley in 1298, he was buried at the Franciscan priory in Worcester. But he took one step during his life that would, indirectly and in time, benefit St. Mary's immeasurably. By naming his son Guy, he emphasised the connection between the Beauchamps and the ancient lineage of the earldom of Warwick.

II

Guy of Warwick is one of the greatest English medieval ballads, written possibly in celebration of the marriage of the future Earl Henry II in 1204, or, perhaps, to boost the image of Earl Thomas Newburgh (1229-42). It is the eponymous story of the son of the steward to Rohund, earl of Warwick, who falls in love with the earl's daughter, Felice. Their difference in rank demands that she refuses Guy until he has proved himself worthy of her, so he travels to Rouen to compete in tournaments. He is so successful that he is offered the hand of the daughter of the German Emperor, but he refuses it and returns to Felice. Unfortunately for Guy, Felice is not as impressed as he would have hoped, and he is sent away to do better. Indeed, the heiress to the earldom of Warwick clearly had high standards, as Guy needed to be the best knight in the world. He goes back to the Continent, and in Constantinople (Istanbul) his gallantry results in a proposed marriage to a sultan's daughter, which he naturally declines. He returns to Warwick via Northumberland, where he had taken the opportunity to slay a dragon that was terrorising the local population, despite him falling from his horse and sustaining three broken ribs.

This time Felice is won over, marries Guy, and immediately falls pregnant with a son, Reinbrun. But within two weeks after the wedding Guy has a crisis of conscience and, fearing that his devotion to Felice has meant him neglecting God, he sets out on a pilgrimage to the Holy Land. Felice tried to persuade Guy to build churches and abbeys instead, where prayers could be said for him 'forever, night and day, without end', but to no avail. Guy's journey back from Jerusalem features his killing of a diabolical giant, Amorant, in the cause of a certain Earl Jonas, who was trying to free Christian prisoners held by the king of Alexandria. When Guy reaches England he joins King Athelstan, who is being threatened by Danish forces near Winchester. Guy kills a second giant, the Danish champion Colbrand, and both the city and the realm are saved by his valour.

Guy travels to Warwick incognito, and, presenting himself at the castle gate as a penitent, receives alms from his unsuspecting wife. Unrecognized, Guy becomes a hermit. He receives a visitation from an angel telling him of his impending death, and he sends to Felice a ring that she had given him. Guy duly dies, as does Felice two weeks later, and they are buried together, with Guy's soul bypassing purgatory and being taken straight to heaven by his fellow dragon-slayer, Saint Michael the Archangel.

Guy's exploits do not attract much sympathy from a modern audience, and it is easy to be sarcastic about them, but to medieval ears it was an irresistible

13. An illustration from the beautiful English sixteenth-century manuscript *Descents of the earls of Warwick and Essex*, a fine example of how descent from Guy of Warwick was valued more than three centuries after the legend was written. The *Descents* is, as the name implies, a family tree of the houses of Warwick and Essex, and Guy and Felice are shown as the founders of both houses. Guy has his foot resting on the slain giant Cobrand, while behind him is the base of the family tree, deliberately echoing a ragged staff, from which the family sprouts. Felice's hand is on the head of her son, Reinbrun, and she has a bear at her feet. The ragged staff represents the earldom of Warwick, while the bear was a badge of the Beauchamps. Between Guy and Felice is a shield with the arms of Newburgh (appropriated to represent Guy), impaling a fictive variation of the Beauchamp arms (representing Rohund, Felice's father).

concoction of self-aggrandisement, valour, courage, prowess, perseverance, loyalty to a lady, service to kings, and an exceptional piety that embraced a denial of worldly trappings. Guy progresses from a steward's son to a true successor of glorious warriors. The giant Amorant may have fought with the sword of Hercules bathed in a river of hell, but Guy had a shirt of mail from Charlemagne, a helmet from Alexander the Great, and the sword of Hector. In short, Guy was just the sort of hero that an earl would wish to be the true descendant of, and to honour his son with his name.

This is not the place for an account of the evolution of the legend of *Guy of Warwick* over many years, though two changes made in the fifteenth century are worth noting as they show how Guy's connection with Warwick, and hence the Beauchamps, was embellished. First, Guy's place of birth, originally said to be Wallingford in Oxfordshire, was moved to Warwick. Secondly, the early versions tell of him living as a hermit in a forest, but this later became a cave at Guy's Cliffe, just outside the town. It was the site of a medieval hermitage, when it was called Gybcliffe, and it assumed its present name only when it became associated with Guy. This association became so powerful that King Henry V, no less, intended to build a chantry at Guy's Cliffe in honour of the hero.

Guy of Warwick was tremendously successful in promoting the earldom of Warwick throughout England and beyond. The library of Canterbury cathedral had a copy in 1279. The Smithfield *Decretals*, an illustrated copy of a collection of documents prepared for Pope Gregory IX (died 1241) and made in the south of France at the turn of the fourteenth century, portrays Guy with a lion lying prostrate before him. The *Langtoft Chronicle*, which dates from about 1300, has an image of King Athelstan, the defender of England, paying homage to Guy, who is dressed as a hermit in a hair shirt, barefoot, holding a pilgrim's staff, and raising his left hand in benediction. Robert Mannyng's *Handlyng Synne*, written in 1303, is a devotional text enlivened with moral tales that included the story of Guy. A misericord at Wells cathedral, dating from 1330-40, shows Guy receiving alms from Felice, while one at Gloucester carved a little later depicts Guy slaying Colbrand. Guy appears on the lid of a drinking bowl made in the first half of the fourteenth century, mounted on his horse, fighting a dragon, and carrying a shield on which the Beauchamp arms can clearly be seen. The lid is stamped from a die, implying that it was one of a number made for general sale.

An international industry and mystique were building around Guy, fuelled and exploited by the Beauchamps. *Le Rommant de Guy de Warwik et de Herolt d'Ardenne*, probably dating from the early fourteenth century, may be an attempt to present the tale to a courtly audience, and therefore increase the Beauchamps' prestige among their peers and superiors. In 1305 Earl Guy (who had succeeded his father, Earl William, in 1298) gave a copy of *Guy of Warwick* to Bordesley abbey, where the heroic Guy's relics supposedly were. Earl Guy's son, Earl Thomas Beauchamp I, named his eldest son Guy and another son Reinbrun (both pre-deceased him), and even left to his heir 'the coat of mail sometime belonging to that famous Guy of Warwick'. A copy of *Le Rommant de Guy* was given by Earl Richard's daughter, Margaret, to Margaret d'Anjou in 1445 on the occasion of her marriage to King Henry VI as a reminder of the Beauchamps' rightful place in the hierarchy of the English nobility.

All this helped to project the image of a family and an earldom with a glorious and honourable heritage, with the line between fiction and fact becoming increasingly blurred. An aura was developing around the Beauchamp earls of Warwick, boosting their reputation and status. The time would come when that would pay dividends for St. Mary's.

III

If the Newburgh earls can be criticised for failing to make an impact on the national stage, the same can hardly be said of Earl Guy Beauchamp. Subjecting King Edward II's favourite, Piers Gaveston, to a trial (of sorts) at Warwick castle in 1312, and then beheading him on Blacklow Hill, three miles away, was not the act of a shrinking violet. Earl Guy was one of the leaders of a group of conspirators against the king, though they would plead, with some justification, that by disposing of Gaveston they were protecting the monarchy from his malign influence. Indeed, with Edward II severely weakened following the disaster of Bannockburn, Guy had been pardoned within eighteen months.

It was Guy who began the move of the family's principal residence to Warwick. By 1298 Elmley castle was falling into disrepair, and was declared worthless in 1315. But Guy founded a chantry of eight chaplains and four clerks at Elmley chapel in 1308, despite the ruinous state of the castle, and St.

Mary's continued to be neglected. Guy was buried, not in Warwick, where he died, but at Bordesley abbey. The draw of a monastic house that the family had long supported was stronger than that of the local secular church – and, of course, it was held to be the resting place of the earl's legendary namesake.

These were difficult times. Years of mismanagement had had a serious impact on St. Mary's finances. Some of its assets had gone for good. Greetham in Rutland had passed to St. Sepulchre's by 1235, and possibly much earlier. Other possessions had been lost either through neglect, legal squabbles, or deliberate disposal by canons who failed to distinguish between their prebend and their other assets. And then the earldom suffered a minority for fifteen years after Earl Guy's death in 1315, its lands controlled in succession by Hugh Despenser, Roger Mortimer, and the Crown, all of whom pursued short-term profit for their own benefit. Warwick castle itself was neglected and becoming dilapidated.

There were more devastating concerns. Crops failed nationally in each of the years 1314, 1315, and 1316, the last being the worst harvest on record, and between 1319 and 1321 there was widespread disease among cattle and sheep, as well as further crop shortages. The result was a tripling of grain prices and wholesale famine, exacerbated by drought conditions in 1325-26. Thousands starved. Tithe income dwindled, and this may explain why Robert de Leicester, who became dean of St. Mary's in 1314, became involved in a legal claim over the tithes of Snitterfield with its rector.

Beyond disputes as to entitlement, one suspects that many of those who funded prebends through payment of tithes would have wondered if absentee and pluralistic canons were worthy recipients of a share of their produce, even before these hardships, and even though failure to pay tithes could result in excommunication. And parishioners could not afford to make offerings at their customary level, even if they felt the need to support the church in their quest for spiritual succour.

Some attempt had been made to preserve St. Mary's income. In 1305 the pope ordered the prior of Studley (Warwickshire) to oversee and enforce the efforts of the canons to get back what they, or their predecessors, had unlawfully disposed of. There was to be no appeal against such actions, even if a purchaser could produce letters of confirmation of their entitlement. Not surprisingly, St. Mary's prebendaries were also warned as to their future conduct.

In 1262 Robert of Longbridge (just outside Warwick, to the southwest) surrendered land to a canon at St. Mary's which he had obtained from a previous holder of the prebend, but recovering lost lands could be easier said than done. In 1310 Richard Greynye of Coten End, and his wife Christina, sued the dean of St. Mary's, Richard Tankard, in the royal courts. They claimed that Tankard had unlawfully attempted to retake possession of their meadow. The Greynyes abandoned their suit, presumably settling out of court, but it shows that the process of restoring prebendal assets was not straightforward. A few years later, in 1328, one of Tankard's successors took legal action to recover eighty acres of land, two acres of meadow, and four buildings at Coten End, that had formed part of a prebend but was now claimed by four different parties. And in 1333 St. Mary's recovered a property in Warwick in the face of opposition from the diocese of Coventry and Lichfield.

There are no recorded grants of new land to St. Mary's at this time, though this was not just because the town was impoverished. The Statute of Mortmain of 1279 had made it illegal to give property to the Church without a licence from the king, on the basis that once it had been given the land stayed with the religious institutions, who were thus becoming too dominant, while at the same time depriving the Crown of income. It was not a total bar, and it was not easy to enforce, at least for small gifts, but it was a deterrent.

Some rents were given to St. Mary's, though much fewer than there had been. Particularly generous was a donation by Roger Younge of Warwick, who in about 1289 gave rents totalling 10s 6d a year, to be distributed among the resident canons and vicars in return for an annual mass for his soul and others he named. The fact that Roger excluded absentee canons from benefitting is a telling reflection of his attitude towards the college.

St. Mary's income from parishioners' offerings all but dried up. In theory the parishioners were responsible for the upkeep of the nave, but St. Mary's finances had deteriorated to such an extent that it could not afford its basic functions of divine service and charity, let alone repairs. Earl Guy's son, Earl Thomas I, had to intervene, and in 1334 he obtained a licence under the Statute of Mortmain to grant to St. Mary's the church of Pillerton Hersey, in the south of Warwickshire, specifically to pay for the repair of the tower, which was in danger of collapse. It was another seven years before Pillerton Hersey was appropriated to St. Mary's, but it brought a useful income

14. St. Mary's church, Pillerton Hersey, appropriated to St. Mary's Warwick in 1341. The tower is probably late thirteenth century, and altered and heightened in the fifteenth, the latter while under St. Mary's stewardship.

twelve marks a year, less half a mark to be paid to the diocese. It was the first endowment to St. Mary's by an earl for over one hundred and fifty years, bar Earl William Beauchamp's hardly generous gift in 1296 of a rent of 6d per year, payable for a house in Jury Street.

It was Earl Thomas I who would take the first steps in rebuilding St. Mary's, creating the magnificent chancel we see today, by strengthening its endowment and overhauling its management. Before we look at this, we should say something about his life, and what influenced his plans for St. Mary's.

IV

Earl Thomas I, eleventh earl of Warwick, was about eighteen months old when his father, Earl Guy, died, and he was sent to live with his guardian,

Roger Mortimer of Wigmore (Herefordshire). Ironically, Mortimer himself had had a guardian, none other than Piers Gaveston, murdered by Earl Guy.

Thomas soon became betrothed to Mortimer's daughter Katherine, in order to settle a violent dispute between the Beauchamps and the Mortimers over a large area of land known as Elfael. It lay between the Wye and the Severn, and comprised much of modern-day Powys. At least, Elfael was the reason given in the pope's consent to the marriage, required because the couple were related in the third (uncle/aunt and niece/nephew) and fourth (first cousins) degrees of consanguinity. Settlement of conflict to avoid bloodshed was one of the recognised grounds for papal dispensation, though which of the Beauchamps was prepared to fight for Elfael on behalf of the infant Thomas is far from clear. Besides, in 1318 Mortimer received a payment of 1,600 marks out of the Warwick estate in consideration of the marriage, so perhaps Elfael was not the real reason for the betrothal after all.

With Thomas still only five years old, if that, and Katherine probably a few months younger, the wedding could not yet take place, and it was called off when Mortimer was imprisoned in 1322. The match was restored after Mortimer's release, his power strengthened through his close, and sexual, relationship with Edward II's wife, Queen Isabella. Thomas and Katherine probably married at Hereford in May 1328 in the presence of the new king, Edward III.

Thomas's prospects were not dented by his father-in-law having first committed adultery with the king's mother, and then being executed for the murder of the king's father. On the contrary; Thomas was granted his earldom before he reached the age of majority, and quickly became one of Edward III's most valued and trusted leaders. He fought for Edward against the Scots, showing such skill that he was given command of the army of the north while still in his early twenties. In 1343 he topped the leader board in the king's tournament held at Smithfield. The following year the abbot of Abingdon described him as a 'magnificent and powerful man and most energetic warrior'.

Thomas frequently served in the French campaigns. At Crécy (1346) he commanded the prince of Wales's division, which saw the heaviest fighting, and he was at the ensuing siege of Calais. His bravery and tactics at Poitiers (1356) were decisive, and it was said that he was so committed to the fight that 'his hand was galled with the exercise of his sword and poll axe'. Thomas was at Calais again in 1369, and according to a fourteenth-century chronicle written by monks at York, the duke of Burgundy and his army retreated from outside the town under cover of darkness to avoid confrontation with 'that devil Warwick'. Another account of the same incident has the enemy fleeing even before Thomas had landed, news of his imminent arrival being enough to send them packing. He was now in his mid-fifties, but his reputation as Edward III's most feared commander was undiminished.

This summary of Thomas's military career barely does justice to his reputation and success, but it shows his importance in national affairs. This, and the fact that the earl remained fiercely loyal to Edward III throughout his life, brought ample reward. Thomas was paid one hundred pounds in 1340 for services rendered in France the previous year, and £610 in 1341 when he stood hostage for a loan taken out by Edward III. Florentine bankers defaulted on a promise to discharge the debt, and Thomas was imprisoned until the king could negotiate his release. The incident embarrassed the king, and strengthened his bond with Thomas. In 1344 Thomas was made sheriff of both Warwickshire and Leicestershire for life; three years later he was granted the rather precise sum of £1,366 11s 6d 'for good service in war beyond the seas', and shortly afterwards he was awarded an annual pension of one thousand marks. In 1354, possibly thanks to some dubious interference by the king in legal proceedings, he even regained the lordship of Gower, though Richard II reversed this in 1397.

War brought other opportunities for financial gain, most notably through the capture of foreign dignitaries. The archbishop of Sens was seized at Poitiers for the crime of being in the wrong place at the wrong time, and Earl Thomas is famously said to have received eight thousand pounds for his ransom. More accurately, that was the amount paid for the archbishop's release, and not all of it came to Thomas: the king normally demanded one third, and if the archbishop had been captured by one of Thomas's men, he would have had been rewarded as well. However, Thomas did receive three thousand pounds as his share in the ransom of the bishop of Le Mans.

All told, it has been estimated that by the 1360s Thomas's annual income was about £3,200: not super-rich, but very comfortable, and about three times that of his grandfather's. But Thomas received more than money for his service to the king: he gained considerable prestige. Edward III founded the Order of the Garter in the wake of the glory of Crécy, an exclusive

15. *Thomas Beauchamp I in the robes of a knight of the Order of the Garter. The image is taken from the* Bruges Garter Book *(ca. 1430).*

group of twenty-five knights who had proved their worth through military success, loyalty, and moral purity, with membership in the personal gift of the sovereign. All of the founder members had fought for the king in France, at least eighteen of them, and possibly as many as twenty-three, at Crécy. An invitation to join was public recognition that you were the elite of the elite. Each member was given a numbered stall in the collegiate chapel of St. George at Windsor castle. The first stall was allocated to the king himself; the second to his son Edward, prince of Wales (the 'Black Prince'); the third to the earl of Lancaster; and the fourth to Thomas, earl of Warwick. The tenth was that of Thomas's brother, John. The Beauchamps had well and truly made it.

Thomas started to transform Warwick castle into something more palatial. Exactly what work he was responsible for, and what was done by his son, also Thomas, is a matter of conjecture, but between them they created the iconic and photogenic east front. Its distinctive barbican and curtain wall are flanked by two towers: Caesar's, overlooking the river, its French-style double tier of battlements suggesting a commemoration of the success at Poitiers; and Guy's, on the town side, facing towards Guy's Cliffe.

16. The east front of Warwick castle, built to impress by Thomas Beauchamp I and his son, Thomas II. Caesar's tower is to the left, Guy's to the right.

The former was probably built by Thomas I shortly after Poitiers, the latter almost certainly by Thomas II. Dating the rest of works is more problematic, but a detailed study has concluded that most of the east front at least was done by Thomas I.

Thomas also set about rebuilding St. Mary's, but first he had to put the college's finances, management and constitution on a sounder footing. How he did that is the subject of the next chapter.

– 4 –

EXPURGATION

I

ROOT-AND-BRANCH REFORM of the college's administration and finances had become essential. For one thing, the dispute with the diocese over jurisdiction rumbled on, involving St. Mary's in considerable expense as its canons sought to defend what they saw as their legitimate interests. In 1311 the chapter petitioned the pope, yet again claiming that the archdeacon of Worcester had interfered with the exercise of their legitimate rights, usurped their functions, and wrongfully suspended and excommunicated them. It sounds all too familiar. The pope appointed no fewer than three clerical dignitaries, the abbots of Alcester and Pershore and the prior of Great Malvern, to adjudicate. Twelve years later, St. Mary's accused the archdeacon, along with four others, of acting prejudicially towards the prebendaries and causing them material loss. No doubt money was at the heart of the matter, and perhaps falling income in the wake of the recent famines was causing the canons to be more protective of their alleged rights.

Meanwhile, St. Mary's fabric continued to deteriorate, and the grant of Pillerton Hersey to the church in 1341 was only a stop-gap measure while a more radical solution could be implemented. In the spring of 1364 Earl Thomas I was in Avignon, negotiating the terms of a crusade to the Holy Land with Pope Urban V. Such was Thomas's reputation that the pope appointed him co-commander of the entire forces, which were assembling in Venice. But infidels were not the only item on the agenda at Avignon: so was St. Mary's. Thomas obtained papal consent to change St. Mary's constitution, and to take other measures to secure its future. As a result, on 24 December 1367 William Whittlesey, bishop of Worcester, issued a comprehensive set of statutes governing St. Mary's. They record that they were made at the request of Thomas, and he surely had a considerable say in the detail, given that he had a personal interest in the future conduct of the chapter and its financial stability.

The dean and canons of St. Mary's were said to have petitioned for the statutes, which may seem unlikely, given the attitudes of their predecessors towards the diocese. The explanation is simple: Thomas had packed the college with his supporters, with the entire chapter having been appointed in the preceding six years.

We know little about the dean of the time, Nicholas de Southam, except that he became the priest at Budbrooke in 1349, and was a guardian of St. Michael's leper hospital. His appointment to the deanery in 1361 probably signifies that it was made by Thomas with his reforms in mind. Five other canons were all known Beauchamp loyalists: Albanus del Fen, William Morton, Robert Mile, Richard Pirton, and John Blake. As a sign of their closeness to Thomas, all except Mile were appointed executors of his will. The college had come to resemble an administrative department of the castle.

Albanus del Fen was appointed in 1363 but little more is known about him. William Morton was the parson of Elmley castle, became Countess Katherine's treasurer, and would later be Thomas II's attorney. He was appointed to the prebendary of St. James's in August 1367. Robert Mile served the Beauchamps from at least 1351 until his death in 1405, and is named as Earl Thomas's steward in 1364. He became a canon at St. Mary's in 1361, and held a number of other offices in Thomas's gift. Richard Pirton, presumably from the manor of that name in Worcestershire held by Thomas, had been a Beauchamp affiliate since at least 1344. He was Chamberlain of the Exchequer – an official of the Crown's treasury and a position in the hereditary gift of the earls of Warwick – from 1353 to 1363, and was installed to the prebend of Compton Mordak in 1364. He frequently acted as Thomas's representative in his absence, being described as his attorney-general, and performed the same role for Thomas II.

Pirton is probably the only canon of St. Mary's to have been imprisoned in the Tower of London, when in 1365 he was accused of framing a clerk for embezzlement. He may or may not have been guilty, and the charges were brought while Earl Thomas was abroad, but he had to stay there until he had repaid the loss. His career survived, and it has been said that when he died in 1387 Thomas was 'deprived of an experienced administrator who was an important figure in London…'.[2] He had, meanwhile, become archdeacon of Colchester and a canon of St. Paul's cathedral, where he was buried alongside Thomas's brother, Sir John Beauchamp.

Pirton had been presented to his prebend by John de Buckingham, acting as Earl Thomas's deputy during his absence. Buckingham was very much Thomas's man. He was born in about 1320, and was a predecessor of Pirton's at Compton Mordak, to which he had been appointed by 1344 and held for almost twenty years. In 1346 he became rector of Sutton Coldfield, a church within the Warwick honour. Like Robert Mile, Buckingham was also Chamberlain of the Exchequer, from 1347 to 1350, and went on to serve the Crown in several other capacities, including as Controller of the Wardrobe, in effect the chief accountant for the royal household, and as a judge of the Court of Exchequer. Between 1360 and 1363 he was Keeper of the Privy Seal, one of the three great offices of state (along with Chancellor and Treasurer). The regard that Edward III clearly had for Buckingham culminated in the king appointing him an executor of his will.

Buckingham's *curriculum vitae* of ecclesiastical appointments strengthened alongside his royal service. He was a founding canon of Edward III's prestigious college of St. Stephen, Westminster in 1348, and later became a canon at Lincoln and York cathedrals and dean of Lichfield. He then, most unusually, was appointed to a second prebend at St. Stephen's. However, he resigned all his ecclesiastical and governmental appointments in 1362, including his prebend at St. Mary's, when he became bishop of Lincoln.

Buckingham, a man of humble origins and without the advantage of the university education that was normally required for a bishopric, is an excellent example of medieval social mobility based on patronage, personal quality, and ambition. Earl Thomas clearly had the ability to spot potential, which he was prepared to nurture and use to further his own ends. But it went beyond that. Such was Thomas's regard and affection for him that he bequeathed to him a gold cross that had belonged to Edward III and which contained 'part of the very cross of Christ'. The respect was mutual; Buckingham's arms were a single gold crosslet on a red background, an obvious echo of his first patron's.

---

2   Anthony Goodman, *The loyal conspiracy* (London, 1971), p.145.

17. A chest made to house the Treaty of Calais, 1360, concluded while John de Buckingham was Keeper of the Privy Seal. Buckingham was still a canon of St. Mary's at the time, and remained so until 1362. His arms are those on the far left, clearly referencing those of his patron, Earl Thomas Beauchamp.

Buckingham was instrumental in reshaping the membership of the college at St. Mary's to make it sympathetic to Earl Thomas's agenda, and continued to be so even after he became bishop of Lincoln. Besides appointing Pirton to the college in 1364, John Blake of Lincoln became a canon in 1366. He quickly rose in the service of the Beauchamps, becoming not only an executor of Earl Thomas's will, but also Thomas II's treasurer.

II

By 1367, the canons were all loyal, trustworthy, able, and understood exactly what their earl expected of them, starting with their approval of the new statutes. They begin by describing the background to their making. They recite, correctly, that previous earls had allowed their devotion to St. Mary's to cool, and their virtue to be silenced. They then accuse past canons of mismanagement and of the deliberate disposal of prebendal property: also true. The consequence of this, they say, was damning: the chapter itself had undermined the original purpose of the foundation, and it was responsible for the deterioration of the church. It was a very sharp episcopal rap on the knuckles for St. Mary's.

As a result, the statutes continued, it was necessary for the earl to ask the bishop of Worcester to take control of the college, with the dean required to swear obedience to him. Arguments over diocesan jurisdiction had been resolved at a stroke, with the college not so much having its independence wings clipped as amputated. The liberties conferred on the prebendaries by the adoption of the terms of the constitution of the college at Sarum, almost two hundred and fifty years beforehand, were swept away.

Structural reform was also necessary to address the problems occasioned by each canon being responsible for his own prebend. First, as we have seen, there was the temptation for incumbents to treat prebends as their own property. Secondly, canons received stipends according to the value of their prebend, and so were not remunerated equally. As the statutes explain, this was not so much a question of fairness, though no doubt it implied a hierarchy and could give rise to resentment; rather, it was the implications it had for absenteeism. The wealthier prebendaries had no need to attend, while the poorer ones could not afford to – it was not worth their while when they could supplement their income elsewhere. A good example is given by Peter de Leycester, whom we have already met in connection with his disputed appointment to Budbrooke, and who later became a canon. He complained to the bishop that the stipend from his prebend was less than five shillings a year – what a labourer might earn in little more than two weeks. It was due, at least in part, to the loss of prebendary assets through the negligence of Leycester's predecessors. As a result of circumstances such as these, the statutes declare, funds had been misappropriated, and divine services had suffered.

To address these shortcomings, the new constitution provided that, henceforth, all income from prebends was to be paid into a common fund. This followed the precedent of St. Stephen's chapel at Westminster, and, of course, John de Buckingham had first-hand experience of how it worked, which might well explain its adoption at St. Mary's. Moreover, stipends were linked to attendance. Those who were present for five days out of seven, taken as an average over a year, would receive an annual payment of twenty marks, otherwise it was less than a sixth of that, at a mere two pounds. Even that was eight times the value of Leycester's prebend. The pay of vicars was also put on a proper footing, as they were now to receive ten marks a year.

The dean was required to be at the college permanently, and would have a stipend of forty marks a year. He was no longer 'first among equals', but that had become a fiction anyway. Moreover, he would be appointed by the earl rather than by his peers within the chapter – a codification of what had long become the norm.

This new regime was to be administered by a treasurer, appointed by the dean and canons, and who had to be resident. It is a sign of how precarious St. Mary's finances were that it was the only one of sixty-six colleges founded (or refounded) in the fourteenth century to have one. From now on the treasurer, not the individual canons, would be responsible for the prebends, and he was charged with keeping proper accounts and with managing the church's property. The parish chest, which may well be that on display in the nave, had three keys, held by the dean, the treasurer, and a resident canon, and all three had to be present for it to be open. He was assisted by a layman, whose job it was to collect the income due to St. Mary's, and to check the condition of its churches. The treasurer was required to present the accounts to the dean and chapter every year, with a full record of proceedings kept by a public notary. It was a seismic change.

III

The canons lived close to the church, either in Church Street, Northgate Street, or Canon Row, which was on the south side of Tink-a-Tank. The five houses granted to St. Mary's by Earl William de Newburgh (1153-84) may have been for housing prebendaries, and his successor, Waleran, granted a prebend to Nicholas Brito which included a house that had been held by two of his predecessors. It was a stone building, and therefore prestigious, but again it is not known exactly where it was, or if it was to be his residence. In 1415 the treasurer had a large house opposite the west end of the church, probably on the south-west corner of Northgate Street. The dean's house is thought to have been either on the site of the Beauchamp chapel, or, perhaps more likely, on the edge of the churchyard. Either way, it was moved to the Butts when the Beauchamp chapel was built. The archery field from which the Butts gets its name may have been within the precincts of the church, as this was not uncommon.

The six vicars – later increased to ten – lived rent-free in a house built about 1340 to the south-east of the church, but it too was relocated to the Butts, between 1455 and 1464, under the terms of Earl Richard's will. They had separate rooms, with a shared hall and other communal areas. The costs of repairing the building were met by the church, unless the damage was due to the vicars' neglect. The vicars' house later became the grammar school, and was demolished in 1880 following its relocation to Myton Road.

Rules of behaviour for both canons and vicars were imposed by the bishop of Worcester in 1441. The former were to:

> ...wear habits that are not too short, ridiculous, or conspicuous but which at least reach the middle of the shin; their hair should not be worn too short or be of uneven length or too long so as to look effeminate, but they should cut their tonsures to cover only the upper part of the ears...

18. The house of the vicars-choral in the Butts, as illustrated in Arthur Leach's History of Warwick School *(1906).*

They were also fined for failing to attend mass without permission, the money being deducted from their stipend and paid into the vicars' fund.

Vicars faced tighter regulations than the canons, perhaps reflecting the importance of maintaining their standing in the local community. Quarrelling among themselves rendered them liable to a fine of 6d, or 3s 4d if they drew blood. They could not be in town alone, were prohibited from entering taverns, and faced a sunset curfew. Not surprisingly, women were banned from their residence.

Each vicar had a chorister, who was provided with accommodation, probably in the vicars' house, and who received a subsistence allowance of two pounds a year. The choristers were taught both singing and grammar in the school, though they had to leave when their voices broke. They were required to stand during mealtimes, and any of them who failed to attend mass were flogged.

The school was under the authority of the dean, with separate masters for grammar and singing. 'Grammar' encompassed classical literature, argument, philosophy, and rhetoric, while the song school taught singing, reading and writing. A dispute between the two masters arose during the deanship of Robert de Leicester (1314-39) over which of them should teach the music pupils a form of grammar known as Donatism. There were allegations of 'undue encroachment', which would have impinged not only upon the pride of the masters, but, as importantly, their income. The dean resolved the matter in favour of the grammar master, and took the opportunity to set out regulations for other aspects of the masters' duties. The master of grammar was required to attend church services on all feast days, when not teaching, and to process with his scholars for mass in the Lady chapel every Saturday during school terms, carrying two wax candles of three pounds in weight, to be left burning throughout the mass. The song master had to attend mass daily in the Lady chapel, along with two scholars who were to sing all the music in the latter part of the service, during and after the communion.

Being the song master could be prestigious and financially rewarding. In 1409 William Wytteneye's appointment was confirmed for as long as he was reasonably able to perform it; he was to have a pension of three pounds a year for life in appreciation of his role as organist; and he was granted an exceptionally long lease for eighty years of a house in Church Street for himself, his wife, and his mother, on favourable terms.

IV

Besides reforming the administration of St. Mary's, it was necessary for Earl Thomas to put its balance sheet on a firmer basis. The 1367 statutes recite that he had agreed to make good past losses of assets, and to add to the church's endowment, but more was required.

One measure was a review of the churches that had been given to St. Mary's by Earl Roger. It concluded that both St. Helen's, absorbed within St. Sepulchre's priory, and St. Mary's at Greetham, were irretrievably lost. Budbrooke remained in the fold, and its status was unchanged. All the appropriated churches in Warwick, except for St. Nicholas's, were declared redundant. St. Michael's (Saltisford) had only three parishioners, all poor peasants who were in no position to be generous with their offerings. The church was close to ruin, there was no parsonage, and its cemetery was small, with few buried in it. It was simply unviable. St. James's (West Gate) also had a small congregation, and the living had been vacant for many years. It did not have a cemetery, and therefore no income from burials, and neither did St. Peter's (High Street) nor St. John's (Market Square). St. Laurence's in West Street did, but that was not enough to save it.

Under the new order, the townspeople had to pray, and to be buried, at either St. Mary's or at St. Nicholas's. Whatever would have gone to the other Warwick churches by way of offerings and fees – not that it would have been very much – now came to St. Mary's. On the debit side, St. Mary's was to provide two vicars for St. Nicholas's, one serving that part of its parish that lay north of the river, the other that to the south. To maintain a connection with the past, each of the five redundant churches was to retain its name in a prebend, and altars were to be put in St. Mary's to their dedicated saints, with their images provided. It was an unusual arrangement, the only other known example in England being Beverley minster. Nonetheless, it was sufficiently important in 1441 for the canons to be reminded of it by bishop of Worcester.

The subsumption of these churches was not entirely smooth, and there seems to have been some resistance from the incumbents. St. Laurence's remained in use for at least another forty years, and the building was still standing in 1632, but there is no record of it after that. St. Peter's survived until 1400, but it was probably demolished around 1425. It was replaced by a chapel above East Gate which survives, albeit much altered in the eighteenth century. St. John's was housing the grammar school by 1410, and continued to do so until at least 1544; it was demolished sometime between 1694 and 1711. St. Michael's became the chapel of the adjacent leper hospital, and was almost totally rebuilt in the fifteenth century. Despite being reported as ruinous almost five hundred years ago, it is still standing. St. James's was gifted to the guild of St. George in 1383 (a topic we will come back to), and replaced by a new chapel that survives, albeit much altered, as part of the Lord Leycester hospital.

But the closure of the redundant churches was not enough to secure St. Mary's finances. Just eighteen years later, in 1385, Earl Thomas II obtained a mortmain licence to authorise an enlargement of St. Mary's endowment, on the ground that the church remained so poor that it could not perform divine services – one of the reasons that had been given for the grant of Pillerton Hersey forty years earlier. Indeed, the situation had become a lot worse, as the Black Death of 1348 to 1350, with subsequent reinfections in 1361, 1369 (probably claiming the lives of Earl Thomas I and Countess Katherine) and 1375, had reduced the population of England by at least a third, perhaps as much as a half.

Fewer people meant less income for St. Mary's, and to address its financial deficit it was granted five more churches. Earl Thomas II gave two in Warwickshire, Haselor (where St. Mary's also received the manor, the first it had), and Wolfhampcote, plus Whittlesford in Cambridgeshire. His brother William, Lord [A]Bergavenny, gave Spelsbury in Oxfordshire and Chaddesley Corbett in Worcestershire. These were rich pickings, particularly Chaddesley Corbett and Whittlesford, valued at forty-five and forty marks a year respectively, and Wolfhampcote at twenty-five marks. By comparison, the wealthiest of the five redundant Warwick churches had been St. Laurence's at a mere nine marks, and all of them combined were worth barely twenty. These later acquisitions, plus Pillerton Hersey, increased St. Mary's endowment by 157 marks, though local vicars and other costs had to be paid for out of this.

The handover of these churches was marked by due ceremony. A canon from St. Mary's would present himself at the church door and read, in English, the papal authority for the appropriation. He formally took possession of the church by receiving its books, chalices, and donations from the parishioners at the high altar. Then the bell was rung to announce that the process was complete.

The handover also confirmed the rights and payments to which the vicars of the appropriated churches would be entitled. For example, at Spelsbury the vicar was to receive the hall of the rectory with a room above, a bakehouse, brewhouse, and other outbuildings, a dovecote, two crofts, and a kitchen. He did not receive a stipend, but was granted in lieu the church's meadows, several tithes, and the offerings of his parishioners. However, out of this income he had to pay for a deacon to assist him in his ministrations, for the parish's dues to the diocese, and for the repair of the chancel. The local vicar was, therefore, assuming costs that would otherwise have fallen on St. Mary's.

This arrangement did not work, and in 1447 St. Mary's agreed to pay to the parishioners of Spelsbury – not the vicar – forty shillings a year, of which 26s 8d was to be used to employ a deacon who could sing and read, appointed by the parishioners themselves. The balance was to be used for repairing the church's ornaments, or be given in alms to the poor, chosen by the vicar and twelve of the parishioners. The payment could be withheld if the deaconship was left vacant for more than two months, or if the parishioners said or did anything contrary to St. Mary's. It is a useful insight as to how the laity within a relatively small parish could become involved in the administration of their church, and how St. Mary's, over a day's journey away, delegated responsibility.

The boost to St. Mary's income from the churches given by Earl Thomas II and Lord Bergavenny, welcome though it was, barely covered the cost of paying its clergy, and in 1399 another mortmain licence was obtained, this time to allow St. Mary's to be granted property worth one hundred marks a year. It shows how great the shortfall was, and the benefit of the licence was felt almost straight away. Two years later Walter Power granted to St. Mary's the nearby manor of Heathcote, valued at twelve marks. He was to receive in return two obits a year, on the anniversaries of his death and that of his wife, but there was a distinctly proprietorial (but not unusual) air to the transaction. If the church failed to provide the obits, it was to pay to Power's heirs the sum of forty shillings, and, in the absence of payment, distraint could be levied on the manor to satisfy the debt.

Power was a significant benefactor to St. Mary's, for as well as Heathcote he gave it a silver bowl with a communion cup, together weighing a hefty thirty-nine ounces (just over a kilo) and worth five pounds. His generosity did not finish there, for he also donated a gold pyx valued at £8 6s 8d, and on his death he bequeathed a canopy for the high altar, topped by three crowns and a silver and gold ball, worth another five pounds. These gifts truly enriched the liturgical ceremonies at St. Mary's.

In the same year that St. Mary's received Heathcote, Robert Walden paid the king twenty-two pounds for a licence to give rent and land in and around Warwick worth just over nine marks, to provide a chaplain for a chantry at the altar of Saint Anne at St. Mary's. Mass was to be said once a day for himself, his family, the king, Margaret, dowager countess of Warwick, and Earl Richard and his wife. As this gift was earmarked for a specific purpose, the common fund would not have benefitted, but it is indicative of a new wave of willingness to support St. Mary's.

A third donor was Guy Spyne. He was in receipt of an annual pension from the earls of Warwick of ten pounds, which he gave to St. Mary's in 1404 – even though at the time he was being pursued for a debt of forty pounds.

Power, Walden, and Spyne were all closely connected to Earl Thomas II. Power, from Avon Dassett, had been a faithful Beauchamp retainer since 1381. He was a guardian of the future Earl Richard during his minority, and later became his shield-bearer. In 1392 Earl Thomas granted him a pension charged on the manors of Budbrooke, Haseley and Grove Park, to add to the five pounds per annum that he already enjoyed from the earl's manor of Chedworth in Gloucestershire. Walden, the only one of the three from Warwick, had been one of the earl's councillors, and was MP for Warwick four times between 1377 and 1397. His estates were forfeited to the Crown in 1397 when Thomas II was imprisoned by King Richard II on charges of high treason, and then exiled to the Isle of Man: an indication of how close to the earl Walden was seen to be. Presumably the estates were restored, along with the earl's, by Henry IV after he deposed Richard II in 1399.

Spyne, of Coughton, near Alcester, had also been an MP, representing Warwickshire in five parliaments. Like Walden, Spyne had had his property forfeited in 1397 along with Earl Thomas II's, but when the duke of Surrey was given Warwick castle and other estates in Warwickshire, Spyne switched his allegiance, and was appointed receiver-general for the duke's Warwickshire interests. Despite his disloyalty, Spyne somehow retained his pension from Earl Thomas. Perhaps its assignment to St. Mary's was either guilt money or a blatant attempt to curry favour, but either way Spyne felt it expedient to use it to benefit his lord's church.

* * *

Earls Thomas I and II had, between them, given St. Mary's a constitution that was much more appropriate to its needs, and one that imposed on the canons the discipline of a residential dean and, unusually, a treasurer. It discouraged absenteeism by giving a significantly better stipend to those who attended at Warwick. It demanded that vicars be properly remunerated. St. Mary's endowment had been increased significantly, and its position as a premier church strengthened. And, having set the scene, it is time to tell of the rebuilding of St. Mary's.

– 5 –

REBUILDING

I

DESPITE THE repairs that had been done after the appropriation of Pillerton Hersey in 1341, St. Mary's was still being described as collapsed and ruined, which must have been a considerable embarrassment to Earl Thomas Beauchamp. It hardly fitted the image of the patronal church of the scourge of the French, a Knight of the Garter, and a direct descendant of the giant- and dragon-slaying Guy. Warwick castle was being rebuilt, deferentially more modest than Edward III's at Windsor, which was being transformed at the same time. St. Mary's, in contrast, would have seemed almost disrespectful when set against the king's great collegiate foundations, St. Stephen's Westminster and St. George's Windsor.

Beyond the need to address this blot on Earl Thomas's image, the fact that his son William, Lord Bergavenny, endowed St. Mary's with two churches, Spelsbury and Chaddersley Corbett, shows its importance to the family. And there was another, crucial, factor to consider: Thomas's wish to be laid to rest at St. Mary's.

It was a surprising choice, and not just because Earl Thomas was shunning Bordesley abbey, the burial place of his father and, reputedly, of Guy of Warwick. Choosing a parish church to be buried in was itself novel for a man of his rank. Admittedly, the fourteenth century saw a shift away from burial in monastic houses towards secular churches, particularly those with chantries, but this was a trend of the gentry, not the nobility. Indeed, of the twenty-two English founder Knights of the Garter, only four were not buried in a regular house. Three of them chose secular cathedrals, and Thomas was the only one who opted for a parish church. He did not neglect Bordesley completely, as his will directed that masses be said for his soul, and alms distributed, there as well as at St. Mary's, but clearly there was such a strong attraction to being buried at St. Mary's that the earl was prepared to defy convention.

In one sense Earl Thomas was deliberately turning his back on the past, investing heavily in Warwick as a demonstration of his own identity and maturing status. But at the same time he was connecting with his heritage, not that of Worcestershire but of the earldom of Warwick going back, of course, to the heroic Guy and beyond. It was a palpable switch of allegiance, culminating in a desire to have a resting place in the town of his comital forebears in a church founded by one of them and, in effect, refounded by himself. And with St. Mary's in dire need of restoration and revitalisation, there was a golden opportunity to create a suitably impressive memorial to himself.

Received wisdom has it that Earl Thomas paid for the new St. Mary's out of the spoils of Poitiers, and especially the ransom received for the archbishop of Sens. That is an exaggeration. Poitiers was certainly lucrative for Thomas, but it was only one of many sources of his wealth. Furthermore, Poitiers was at least twelve years before work started on St. Mary's, and Thomas had, in the meantime, undertaken extensive works at the castle: if any structure deserves to be associated with Poitiers, it is the castle's Caesar's tower. And the cost of rebuilding St. Mary's would have been nothing like the ransoms that Thomas received; about one thousand five hundred pounds would have covered it.

Neither did Earl Thomas meet the entire cost of the new church himself. Rather, he resorted to medieval crowdfunding. His visit to Avignon in 1364, when he obtained the pope's consent to issue new statutes for St. Mary's, also resulted in a financial deal. Visit St. Mary's on a feast day, contribute to the church, and as a reward your soul will spend one year and forty days less in purgatory. Contribute on a feast day of the Virgin Mary – and there were at least six of them a year – and the credit became a more tempting three years and one hundred and twenty days.

The idea of getting time remission for one's sins in return for performing specific acts of devotion, known as indulgences, had been introduced by Pope Urban II in 1095 to encourage participants in the First Crusade. Indulgences later became mainstream, with an entry-level benefit for remaining present throughout mass. One person who needed no persuading about the efficacy of this was Gerald of Wales (died *ca.* 1223), who attended 395 masses in forty different churches, thereby reducing his stay in purgatory by an impressive ninety-two years. Indulgences came to be used to finance church building, as in the case of the nave at Beverley minster in 1308.

Indulgences were getting a bad press by the time St. Mary's was being rebuilt. Central to the problem was the pardoner, whose job it was to raise money by visiting churches and extracting cash from their parishioners, offering a reduction of time spent in purgatory in return. Pardoners' tactics were, to say the least, morally dubious, and they were becoming increasingly resented. Reflecting popular sentiment, Chaucer's *Canterbury Tales*, which date from the same time as the rebuilding of St. Mary's, has a pardoner tell a tale using words from 1 Timothy 6:10 as its theme: 'Greed is the root of evil'. Even Pope Urban V, who authorised the scheme for St. Mary's, criticised pardoners who took over the daily service, diverted offerings from the parish, and who so outstayed their welcome that there was no time for mass. Presumably that explains why indulgences for giving to St. Mary's required personal attendance.

II

There are no surviving contemporary documents that tell us about the construction of the new St. Mary's, so an excursion into the dark art of looking at surrounding evidence is required. The first question is when the rebuilding started. One theory is that work on the extension of the crypt and on the nave began in the 1350s, was halted, and recommenced after the promulgation of the new statutes at the end of 1367. This is not the place for a lengthy rehearsal of the pros and cons; suffice to say that there are difficulties with this. A more logical sequence is that followed in the preceding chapter: address the most urgent work by using the income from Pillerton Hersey, sort out the constitution to prevent history repeating itself, increase the endowment for financial stability, and build. This puts construction as starting not before 1368.

Who built the new church has also provoked debate. John Harvey, a renowned architectural historian who specialised in this period, thought that it might be the work of Robert Skyllington. One of the leading masons of the fourteenth century, Skyllington was active in the area at the time, being responsible for John of Gaunt's Great Hall at Kenilworth castle (1389-93) and perhaps the tower of St. Michael's Coventry, the 'old cathedral' (1373-95). Harvey saw similarities in the tracery design, an acknowledged distinguishing feature of medieval builders. An opposing view is that St. Mary's was built by masons from Gloucester. The reasoning is somewhat esoteric, but, like Harvey's, is based on a comparison of architectural details. This argument is reinforced by circumstantial evidence that work on the east end of Gloucester cathedral finished at about the same time that it would have started at Warwick. However, if this were so, one might expect to see more similarities in style than there are. There is insufficient evidence to reach any firm conclusion, but Skyllington must be a prime candidate, and it is quite possible that he oversaw a team from Gloucester, and incorporated some of their designs.

In any event, Earl Thomas's will, dated 6 September 1369, directs his executors to 'new build the quire [chancel] of the collegiate church of Warwick'. He died on 13 November, and his funeral must have been spectacular, as he left five hundred pounds to cover the cost. If work on the chancel had not started beforehand – the wording of the will does not exclude this possibility – then it did soon afterwards. His son, Thomas II, implemented his father's wishes, and the chancel was probably finished by 1392.

Thomas II went beyond replacing the chancel, as a new nave, transepts, vestry, and chapter house were completed by 1394. Only two parts of the Norman church were retained. One was the crypt, which was extended westwards to be coextensive with the new chancel. Why it was is a good question. One possibility, obviously, was to enlarge the space, and another was to maintain windows on the east elevation, and, significantly, those in the south wall of the Norman section were altered at the same time. The need to preserve light suggests that the crypt was being used regularly, though not necessarily for its original purpose. It seems that the only entrance was now from a staircase that led from the vestry, which implies that access was limited to the clergy. Intriguingly, part of the crypt became known as the 'priests' kitchen', and there is evidence it contained a fireplace, but it is not known when such use started.

St. Mary's also kept its Norman tower, recently repaired. The tower was crowned with crenellations and pinnacles, but lacked grace and appeared

19. The rebuilt church. There are two drawings that illustrate St. Mary's before the 1694 fire; this one was prepared by Sir Christopher Wren's office, and is thought to have been drawn by Nicholas Hawksmoor, who worked for Wren at the time. The other drawing is similar, though it shows six clerestory windows in the south wall of the nave, not five, and the detailing of the tower differs.

rather squat alongside the new nave. There was a sundial on the south-east corner, a common feature, that enabled the peal of eight bells to be rung at the correct time for a daily office or mass. A prominent buttress to the south-west shows that structural integrity was a problem, and did nothing to improve the tower's looks. There were porches on both the north and south sides, dating from the fourteenth century, the latter with a room above used as a study and library by the historian John Rous and then as (probably) the song school. Architecturally, it was a bit of a mess.

The rest of the church was new. To the north of the chancel lies the vestry, originally incorporating what is now the outer vestry: the stone screen that now divides them probably dates from the sixteenth century. Somewhat unusually, a chapter house was provided; they were not routinely built at collegiate churches, and the fact that St. Mary's has one reflects a desire to demonstrate status. It is likely that it replaced a Norman structure on the same site. It is the sole surviving chapter house at an English parish church, though Howden minster in Yorkshire has the ruins of one, and the St. Katherine

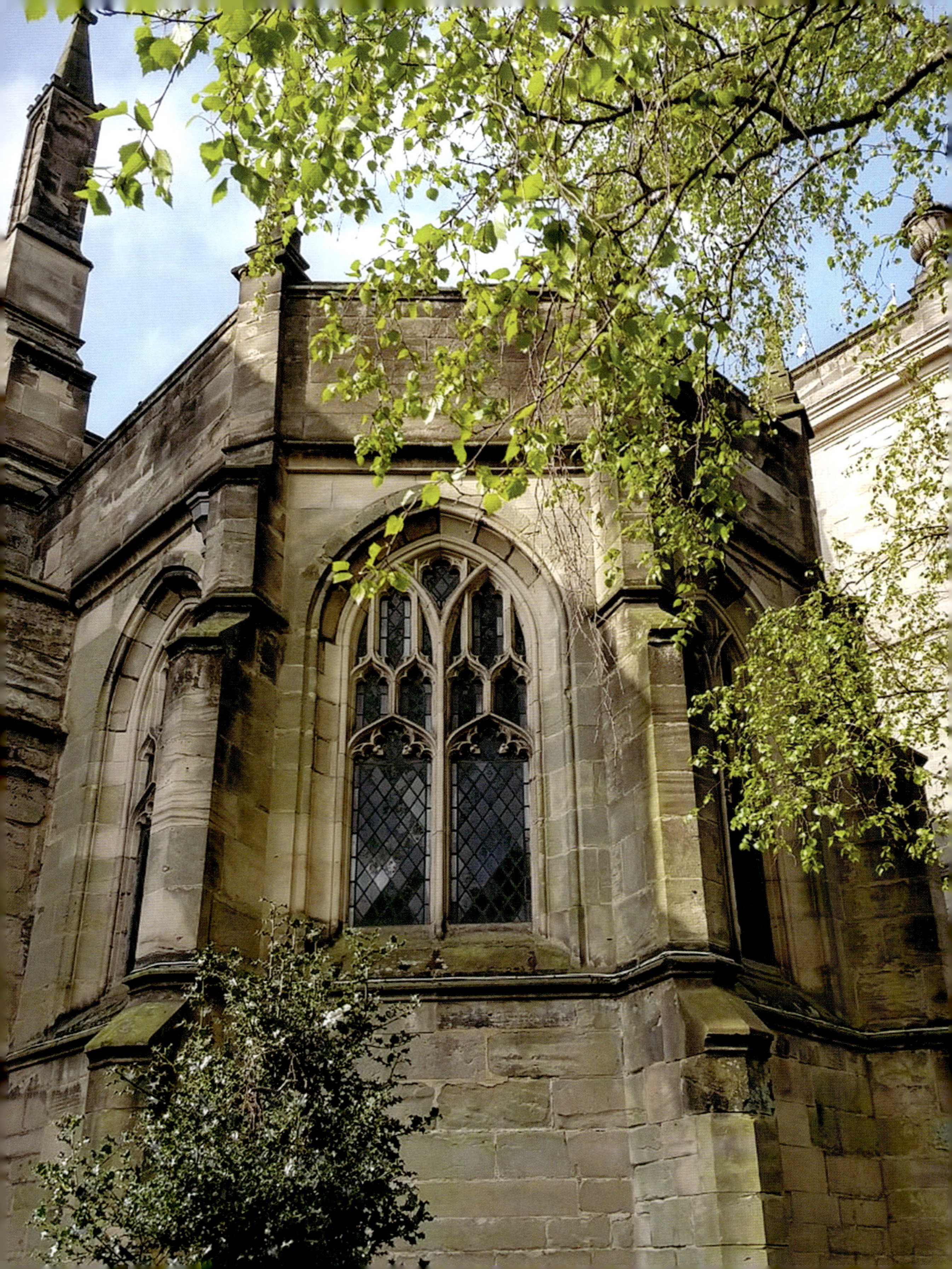

chapel at the church of St. Michael and All Angels, Ledbury (Herefordshire) was built as a chapter house in 1330, but never used as such.

The design of the nave was typical of the fourteenth century. Slightly shorter than it is now, about the same width and, in the centre, about the same height, it had three windows on each side, similar in style to those in the chancel, and above them a clerestory of either five or six windows. There were two arcaded aisles, with, as was usual, vaulted roofs lower than the main body of the nave.

The nave was separated from the chancel by a pulpitum, some twenty feet wide, eight feet thick, between twelve and fourteen feet high, and with a central arch about eight feet wide. Along the top of the pulpitum was a wooden gallery, overhanging the chancel side by some two or three feet, on which the rood was placed, flanked by statues of the Virgin Mary and John the Baptist. It seems that there was a second screen, or low rood, that connected the western ends of the transepts.

Much of the floor space was taken up with altars. The main parish altar was probably in front of the low rood, to the north of its portal. It may have been dedicated to Saint Benedict, or jointly to Saints Katherine and Margaret; St. Mary's had altars to both, but we do not know where they were. There were at least six other altars in the body of the nave, five representing each of the Warwick churches that had been declared redundant by the 1367 statutes, and that of the guild of the Holy Trinity and the Blessed Virgin Mary, which is thought to have been in the north aisle. All would have been screened (except perhaps the parish altar), and orientated so the celebrant faced east, towards the high altar.

The north and south transepts were about six feet narrower and six feet shorter than the present ones. The windows of both were adorned with the arms of Beauchamp, and Beauchamp impaling Ferrers, emphasising the role that the family played in rebuilding the whole church, while displayed in the windows of the south transept were the arms of King Edward III and two of his sons, Edward of Woodstock ('the Black Prince') and John of Gaunt.

The altars between the low rood and the pulpitum, and in the transepts, were semi-private, with access by the parishioners controlled. It is thought

Left: 20. The exterior of St. Mary's chapter house. The detailing of the tracery, compared with that of John of Gaunt's great hall at Kenilworth castle, suggests that they are by the same master builder, Robert Skyllington.

that an altar to Saint Anne, by tradition the mother of Mary and the person who taught Christ to read, was in the north transept. This is commemorated to this day with her image in the transept's window, reading to the infant Jesus. The south transept probably included a Lady chapel from about 1330, but there is no record of this being replicated in the new church until the consecration of the Beauchamp chapel, which is more properly known as the chapel of Our Lady. It seems odd that a chapel dedicated to the church's patronal saint was not retained somewhere. One suggestion is that part of the crypt was repurposed, with its eastward extension, to accommodate it, but the apparent lack of public access suggests otherwise.

An altar reserved for the celebration of mass for the souls of the deceased earls and their families was probably alongside the pulpitum arch. Next to it was a brass chandelier, fixed to the screen, and a sacring bell to be rung at the elevation of the Host. A coffer contained vestments worn by the priest specifically for such masses, which may have been those from the earls' private chapel bequeathed to St. Mary's by Earl Thomas I. They were made of black worsted, finely woven to resemble silk, with white orphreys (borders), perhaps in deliberate imitation of the colours of the earls' emblem, the ragged staff. The arms of the earls of Warwick were sewn on to the chasuble, the poncho-like vestment worn by a priest when celebrating mass.

The chancel, hidden behind the pulpitum, was the domain of the clergy. They bowed towards the dean as they entered the chancel for mass, and again as they left. The dean had his own stall on the south side, with its back towards the pulpitum, so that the dean faced the high altar. The stall was topped by a bishop's mitre; it is not clear why, but we can discount the explanation given to Victorian tourists that what was on display was a survival from the throne of Saint Dubricius, bishop of Warwick. The treasurer's stall was opposite the dean's.

Most of the stalls faced inwards. The canons and vicars sat at the rear, with the prebendaries of the redundant Warwick churches having the names of the relevant saint emblazoned on their stalls, as they were on their seats in the chapter house. The choristers sat on benches at the front, and between them and the canons were a group known as the Clerks of the Blessed Mary: as well as being part of the choir, they probably assisted as sidesmen at the mass, rang the bell to signify the devotional hours, and took care of the altars. Books of psalms, known as psalters, were chained to the stalls.

The high altar, flanked by two latten and two iron candle holders, was surmounted by the canopy donated by Walter Power, probably made of a rich brocade on a wooden frame, from which hung six latten candlesticks. Behind it was a reredos covered in red satin and bearing the image of a cross flanked by the Virgin and John the Baptist.

Traditionally high mass was chanted, rather than spoken, with parts of the service in plainchant, a single line of music sung in unison. However, by 1400 polyphony (two- or three-part harmony) was beginning to be introduced into collegiate churches, and was widespread by the middle of that century. It would have featured in the high mass; in the Lady mass, held at least every Saturday; and in Marian antiphons. Polyphony required a larger and more skilful choir than plainchant, increasing the importance, and numbers, of the Clerks of the Blessed Mary and the boy choristers.

The pulpitum gallery would have been used for readings and solo chant, and it was where the organ was situated, accessed from a spiral staircase built into the wall. The organ had a limited range of up to three octaves, but bellows pumped air into a chamber rather than directly to the pipes, much improving the sound. Even so, with only one keyboard and few stops, it would have made nothing like the volume and swell of a modern instrument.

III

There were no fewer than fifteen executors of Earl Thomas Beauchamp. As one would expect, they included the earl's two surviving sons: his heir and now the twelfth earl, Thomas II, and William, Lord Bergavenny, the co-benefactor of St. Mary's. The wider family was represented by the earl of Stafford, whose son was married to Thomas I's daughter Phillipa, and two more distant Beauchamps.

Executive responsibility for implementing the earl's testamentary wishes lay principally with the four canons of St. Mary's who were also appointed executors, Richard Pirton, John Blake, Albanus del Fen, and William Morton, all members of Earl Thomas II's household. Pirton was particularly close to Thomas II, being one of those who administered his estates during his absence in France for most of the period from 1369 to 1375: a key time in the design of St. Mary's. Thomas II and Lord Bergavenny would have had the final say, but we do not know how much they delegated to their trusted lieutenants, and therefore who was responsible for the very distinctive features that make the chancel unlike any other.

The chancel is a work of outstanding beauty. Too often ignored in favour of its illustrious neighbour, the Beauchamp chapel, it is impressive in its own right. It has been described as being 'of the highest quality and importance for fourteenth century architecture'; 'highly inventive, sophisticated, and influential', and an example of English Perpendicular 'at its most graceful'.[3]

Standing at the chancel steps gives one a sense of its height. This is a feature exaggerated by the Perpendicular style of architecture, prevalent from about 1330, but seen at its extreme at St. Mary's. There are no columns or pilasters, nothing to interrupt the emphasis on the vertical. Liturgical features such as the Easter sepulchre, the sedila, and the piscina, are built into

21. The magnificent chancel at St. Mary's, built ca. 1370 to 1392.

---

3   Morris, 'Architecture of the earls of Warwick', p.161; Monckton, 'Fit for a king', p.33; Jenkins, *England's thousand best churches*, p.715. See *Further reading*.

22. The flying ribs in the chancel vaulting, showing the mouchette work behind them. Their uniqueness begs the question of why the design of the vault is so different from any other church.

the walls to prevent intrusion and distraction, with plain facings. Intricate fan vaulting, another leitmotif of the Perpendicular, is rejected, the usual bosses that decorate the junctions of the ribs absent. No mermaids, imps, or green men here, or even angels. Instead, the eye is drawn to four large octagonal panels, decorated with the arms of the Warwick Beauchamps (eastern-most and westernmost); Beauchamp with Mortimer, representing Earl Thomas I and Countess Katherine; and Beauchamp with Ferrers, for Earl Thomas II and his wife Margaret. Supporting the roof are ten sets of exposed 'flying' or 'skeleton' ribs, braced by mouchettes within the spandrels. Flying ribs are extremely rare in medieval European architecture, and those at St. Mary's are unique in style and scale. Springing straight out of the walls, rather than from a capital or corbel, they are remarkably plain.

It is sometimes said that the absence of elaborate decoration at St. Mary's arose from practicalities, there being a shortage of craft masons following the Black Death. The problem with that argument is the quality and innovation of the architecture. The flying ribs, with the absence of corbels at their junction with the walls, required a high degree of skill to avoid clumsiness. Bosses in the vaulting assist structural integrity and can conceal misalignment, but the masons at St. Mary's had to do without them. There is an unusual amount of decoration on the exterior, and much attention to detail – for example, blind tracery around the inner window jambs. If there was a shortage of craftsmen one would have expected a more conventional approach, but the unfussy and carefully thought-through chancel is a product of intent, not necessity. The overall effect is a space of serenity and beauty, an inner sanctum separated from the hubbub of the nave by the pulpitum, and a prime example of less being more.

IV

The chancel is dominated by the tomb of Earl Thomas and Countess Katherine, but before discussing its design we should say something of what little we know about Countess Katherine. She was godmother to Phillipa, the first granddaughter of King Edward III, so she was held in high regard at court. Her will, dated 4 August 1369 and which is thought to be the date of her death, gives us glimpses of what was precious to her. She left to her husband a goblet of gold, and 'those buckles of gold which I used to carry', and other personal bequests to her children. She also gave twenty pounds each to no fewer than six friars' houses.

It is tempting to dismiss Katherine's role as countess as being confined to wifely domestic duties, but that would be a mistake. First, like all women in her position, she had her own household, separate from her husband's, with a steward and treasurer answerable to her. As already mentioned, her treasurer was William Morton, who was also a canon of St. Mary's and one of her husband's executors.

Secondly, Katherine was probably fully conversant with Earl Thomas's financial affairs. In 1405 the French author Christine de Pisan wrote *The treasure of the city of ladies, or the book of the three virtues*, a conduct manual for women of all ranks, from royalty to prostitutes. She argues that those of high birth should be 'wise and sound administrators' and know the law relating to everything within her husband's jurisdiction, so that she can manage his estate properly and not be deceived by his advisers. Her skills were not to be confined to the times that her husband was away. Rather, she was to play a full part in his business; finances were to be discussed together, and she ought to be able to 'persuade her husband ... by kind words and sensible admonitions'.[4]

---

4   Christine De Pisan (trans. Sarah Lawson), *The treasure of the city of ladies, or the book of the three virtues* (Harmondsworth, 1985), pp.130, 131.

Pisan was the first female professional author in the west, and wrote some twenty books. She was extremely influential across Europe, including in England, where Henry IV invited her to court. Her views were not considered a threat to the established order, and, indeed, we have already seen examples of women exercising power. Countess Gundreda was frequently a witness to Earl Roger's charters, implying that she was closely involved in his affairs. Furthermore her allowing the rebel forces to have access to Warwick castle, while her husband was in London, implies that the commander of the garrison was prepared to accept her instructions. At a more routine level, when the prior of St. Sepulchre's was summoned to the castle in 1396 over his failure to honour the agreement with St. Mary's, something that we shall look at later, he was given a dressing down by the countess, not the earl. Another illustration comes from Katherine herself.

On New Year's Day 1360 Earl Thomas issued a charter that addressed a perennial problem: Warwick's suffering due to lack of trade, by now exacerbated by the Black Death. Reciting how traders from outside the town were no longer visiting it, to the detriment of the inhabitants, it grants them perpetual freedom from tolls and stall rents. What is of particular interest is that the earl expressly states that he is taking this action 'especially on the supplication of my wife'.

Katherine is an exemplar of what Christine de Pisan was advocating, taking on the cause of the townspeople, and persuading her husband 'by sensible admonitions' to forgo a right to taxes in the expectation of making good the shortfall in other ways. Moreover, Earl Thomas not only acknowledged this publicly, but did so in terms that suggest that the charter was made on his wife's initiative. He could easily have avoided any reference to Katherine, but giving credit where credit was due, to a woman, was nothing for him to be ashamed of. He may even have been making clear to the world at large that his wife was taking an active role in the well-being of Warwick, with his blessing, in order to reinforce her authority locally. Even if this is an over-statement, it would be grossly inaccurate to dismiss Katherine as nothing more than a passive wife.

V

Thomas and Katherine lie together in effigy before the high altar. That in itself was unusual, as at that time noble women were not usually buried with their husbands. Some favoured places that they or their natal family had endowed, or shunned their late husband's choice because they were long-widowed, or because their marriage was not one that had engendered a desire to spend their eternity together. Katherine, though, rejected the long-established Mortimer mausoleum at Wigmore abbey, where her father, mother, grandfather, and great-grandfather were all buried, and directed that she be buried 'where my husband shall appoint'. This is not an abrogation of the decision, but a declaration of trust; she does not mind where she is buried, as long as it is with Thomas.

Both effigies are carved in alabaster, a limestone quarried from the Peak District. This was a recent innovation, with the earliest examples dating from the second quarter of the fourteenth century. Alabaster was prized for its relative softness, making it easier to carve fine detail, and enabling a more lifelike appearance than wood or other types of stone. The effigies are not lifelike representations of the deceased, which were rare at this time. This might be because facial features were not normally considered relevant; it was personal qualities and achievements that were valued, virtues to be remembered and honoured by future generations. A bear crouches at Thomas's feet, an emblem of the Warwick Beauchamps and the earliest example of it at St. Mary's. Katherine is supported by a recumbent sheep; it may represent the Mortimers, but it is not associated with the family elsewhere.

Thomas's attire reflects his occupation as a soldier. He wears a short jupon, or tunic, a style that became popular from the 1350s, over a chain suit known as a hauberk and, seemingly, an iron breastplate. His chest is emblazoned with six crosslets: Earl William Beauchamp had added them to his family badge of *gules a fess or* (red with a gold band), possibly as a symbol of pilgrimage. There is an intricately carved camail, or chain mail, around the neck, topped by a basinet, or helmet. The detail of how the camail and basinet were attached is finely rendered, with studs on the edge of the camail projecting through the basinet, and being secured by a lace through holes in the studs. Thomas's forearms are encased in steel, with the left arm wearing a leather gauntlet, and further protection is offered by steel plates. Low on his hips is a belt, or baldric, that was purely decorative. His legs are armoured, with articulated shoes, known as sollerets, on the feet.

Curiously, Thomas does not wear the Order of the Garter, and neither is it shown elsewhere on the tomb. Perhaps membership of the Order did not have

23. The effigies of Thomas Beauchamp and Katherine Mortimer, earl and countess of Warwick, on their tomb in the chancel of St. Mary's. At the time they died, in 1369, it was rare for married couples of the English nobility to be buried together; indeed, Thomas and Katherine may have been the first to be so. It became a little more common later in the fourteenth century. It was also unusual for the nobility to be buried in a parish church.

the cachet it came to have later, but contemporary tombs included it, and it seems odd to ignore an obvious display of chivalric achievement. One possible explanation is that there was a desire not to detract from the personal nature of the effigies, with courtly connections shown in the windows of the south transept (as we have seen), and by other means (as we shall consider shortly).

Katherine is dressed in a tight-fitting kirtle, laced from top to bottom with sleeves fastened by several buttons. Her headdress is made of a fine material, probably linen, that has been crimped and drawn to form a honeycomb pattern around her face. A mantle, or cloak, is pinned to her shoulders with a brooch, the only accessory that she wears.

The effigies were originally coloured, the gold of the crosslets on Thomas's breastplate particularly prominent. Jewels, either gemstones or, more likely, glass, were inserted into his baldric and into Katherine's brooch, which would have glistened in the flickering candlelight. Only bare flesh would have been left uncoloured, as alabaster was prized for its realistic whiteness.

It may sound a rather prosaic way of commissioning a memorial to one of the top-ranking earls of England, but the effigies' design would have been chosen from patterns held by the stonemason, with, no doubt, an element of 'mix and match'. This helps to identify where the tomb was made, and the fact that Thomas and Katherine are shown resting on cushions, with angels stretching an arm towards them, indicates that they were carved at a London workshop. Indeed, the tomb has been described as 'a fairly standard London-made product showing little sign of personal involvement by the client'.[5] There is some truth in this, but there is one glaring exception: Thomas and Katherine are holding hands.

This did not come out of the catalogue. Hand-holding effigies are rare on English tombs, with only twenty or so known from the period *ca.* 1300 to 1465, with about the same number of hand-holding couples on memorial brasses. A more common pose was hands together in prayer, for obvious reasons. By being shown as holding hands, Thomas and Katherine are defying convention and abandoning a display of piety. We do not know who took the decision to do this; it may have been them, or it may have been their family, and specifically Earl Thomas II who, as heir, would have had the final say. The more interesting question is why.

Dispensing with a sign of devotion might be excused on the grounds that it was unnecessary; the tomb is in a glorious chancel that was in itself more than enough evidence of the couple's faith. But that does not explain why they are shown holding hands. One view is that it is a symbol of the power of man over woman, but it is difficult to give this much credence. Apart from anything else, Katherine's hand is dominant, lying over her husband's, and the same arrangement features on several of the other examples. Even where the man's hand is above his wife's, the pose is often one of intimacy. Christine de Pisan saw women as complementary to their husbands, not subservient to them. Katherine herself had sufficient influence over Thomas to procure

---

5   Saul, *Monuments*, p.226; see *Further reading*.

24. *Thomas Beauchamp and Katherine Mortimer holding hands in effigy. The delicacy of the carving is patent.*

the 1360 market charter, and he was not too proud to admit it. Finally, one asks why it was felt appropriate to depict gender superiority before God, in preference to the usual attitude of prayer.

A second theory is that the joining of hands is a political symbol of the uniting of two great families, the Beauchamps and the Mortimers. This explanation is also problematic. First, it implies that the Mortimers were the Beauchamps' equals, and it must be questioned whether the earls of Warwick shared that view by the late fourteenth century. Secondly, marriage to forge a dynastic alliance, or to form part of a wider settlement of disputes, was hardly novel, and not an obvious choice for commemoration fifty years after the event.

There is no need to look beyond the simplest explanation: that holding hands is an expression of Thomas and Katherine's love for each other, a love so strong that they, or their son, felt it appropriate that they be remembered for it. People shown in other hand-holding effigies were known for their mutual affection, including King Richard II and his wife Anne of Bohemia in Westminster abbey. A brass showing hand-holding, that of Richard Hatfield and his wife Ada at Owston, Yorkshire (1409), incorporates an inscription that describes them as being 'fully in right love'.

The sculpting itself supports the conclusion that this is about love. Thomas and Katherine's hands are delicately brushing against each other, palms open, with the mason deliberately leaving a space between them. This is no power grab. The effigies movingly depict a couple who had known each other when they were toddlers, who had lived their life as a partnership, who died within four months of each other, who chose to be buried together, and who were accompanying each other on their journey to Heaven. And the real deciding feature is that, as they do so, Thomas is not looking stoically ahead, as is so often the case, but has tilted his head slightly towards his wife. This is a gesture of affection, protection, and concern: in other words, a gesture of love.

One issue remains to be considered: given that it is so unusual, where did the idea for showing Thomas and Katherine holding hands come from? The possibilities depend on when the tomb was made. Normally this would be within a year of death, in time for the anniversary obit. However, there would have been a practical problem to overcome: the tomb would be in a building site, and great care would have been needed to protect it if the monument were *in situ* from 1370. The alternative is that a stone was laid temporarily over the grave, and that the chest dates from nearer the completion of the chancel in about 1392. Much turns on it when we come to consider the memorial's influences.

If the effigies date from 1370 or thereabouts, then there are no obvious candidates as a precedent, and either Thomas and Katherine, or their family, were being truly innovative. But if it was later, then it might have been influenced by two other tombs with hand-holding effigies, both dating from 1374-80: those of John of Gaunt and Blanche of Lancaster in the old St. Paul's cathedral, and of Richard Fitzalan and Eleanor, Blanche's younger sister, originally in Lewes priory but now in Chichester cathedral.

The tomb of John of Gaunt and Blanche of Lancaster was made by Henry Yevele, the greatest mason of his time, and who was active from the 1350s until the 1390s. Yevele was also the carver of the hand-holding tomb of Richard II and Anne of Bohemia (*ca.* 1395), and possibly the Fitzalan tomb at Lewes, but that is not certain. He was probably responsible for the tomb of Sir John Beauchamp (*ca.* 1361), Earl Thomas's younger brother, also in old St. Paul's. However, despite this chronology and the likely Beauchamp family connection, Yevele has been ruled out of any involvement at St. Mary's. Did the idea for a hand-holding tomb come from, say, that of John of Gaunt and Blanche of Lancaster, or was Thomas and Katherine's tomb the inspiration for the others? We simply do not know.

VI

Around the tomb chest are thirty-six charming statuettes, known as weepers, that have been described, perhaps generously, as 'a superb parade of fourteenth century alabaster carving'.[6] Their nomenclature is inappropriate, as they are certainly not in mourning, and some of them look positively jolly. Some of the men are right on-trend, wearing short tunics and elongated, pointed shoes. Like the effigies above them, the weepers would originally have been highly coloured: their clothes, the niches, and the shields that identified them.

Given that the weepers are not contemplating the mortality of the deceased, what is their purpose? It would help if we knew who the figures represented, but we do not know their names with any degree of certainty, as their accompanying escutcheons have long faded. William Field, the author of a book on the history of Warwick published in 1815, felt able to name most of the weepers along the south side. According to him, they are all family members of the deceased, including four of their daughters, three sons-in-law, and a daughter-in-law. The reliability of his identification is highly questionable, but it is almost certainly correct that most, if not all, of the weepers are relatives.

Thomas and Katherine had at least eleven children, possibly as many as sixteen, of whom ten are known to have married, but these and their spouses cannot account for all the weepers. Thomas had two illegitimate children as well, both of whom were treated as part of the family, so they might be included. There could also be some of the deceaseds' siblings or ancestors; Thomas had one brother and two sisters, and Katherine was one of eleven. Field names one of the weepers as Thomas's grandmother, which is possible,

---
6   Simon Jenkins, *England's thousand best churches* (London, 2002), p.715.

25. Three characterful weepers on the south side of the tomb of Thomas Beauchamp and Katherine Mortimer.

as weepers could represent people who were already dead. Thomas himself was depicted on the tomb of his son-in-law, Sir Ralph Basset of Drayton, in Lichfield cathedral, despite having pre-deceased him by thirty years.

Relatives were shown as weepers to emphasise familial bonds, but weepers might also reflect the deceased's social connections and military achievements. This may be why Thomas was on Basset's tomb: Edward III and his eldest son, the Black Prince, also feature on it, and the context suggests that Thomas is probably shown in a military capacity, rather than his family relationship. It is not impossible that fellow commanders are among the weepers on Thomas's tomb. Thomas' loyalty was noted by a contemporary chronicler, who considered that 'no one had been more faithful to the king and realm in his time', and it would not be surprising to see such fidelity reflected within the weepers. Having said that, none of the weepers are obviously royal.

Weepers can be seen, therefore, as a roll call of those, living or dead, who were important to the deceased, including those who represented values that the deceased wished to portray. As such, they are an integral part of the tomb chest and convey their own message, just as much as the effigies do.

VII

Any significant patron of a church would have been commemorated in it, especially in the chancel windows. Thomas and Katherine were, as one would expect, in the east window, along with arms representing the family's lineage; the Virgin; and an array of saints. Their children were depicted in the windows of the chancel and the north transept. The daughters were kneeling in prayer, dressed in rich gowns embroidered with the Beauchamp crosslet emblem, with those who had married wearing a mantle in their husbands' colours. The one exception is Katherine, who became a nun at Wroxall abbey and was dressed accordingly. A statue of the legendary Guy stood in the chancel, on which the arms of the earls of Warwick were emblazoned: Newburgh and Beauchamp quartered, the former having been appropriated as Guy's arms. This extraordinary display of a secular image within a church, other than on tombs, highlights the importance of Guy to Beauchamp folklore.

The celebration of the patron did not stop with the windows, as both Thomas's public service and his status are embedded in the very design of the chancel. It is comparatively dark, due to its high windows in both the north and south walls. This design accommodates what is now the song school, at first floor level to the north of the chancel, but it enabled the choir to be fitted with high-backed stalls, that would have risen towards the windowsills, and have been canopied. These stalls, which were destroyed by the fire of 1694, imitated those in Edward III's St. George's chapel Windsor, the church of the knights of the Order of the Garter.

There is a second, somewhat unexpected, decorative feature: crenellation around the walls. This is unusual inside a church, but it is something shared with Edward III's St. Stephen's college, Westminster. Both the crenellation and the stalls can thus be seen as symbolic of Thomas's allegiance to his monarch, while the latter also alludes to his membership of England's highest rank of chivalry. This may be why it was not thought necessary to adorn Thomas's effigy with the Order of the Garter.

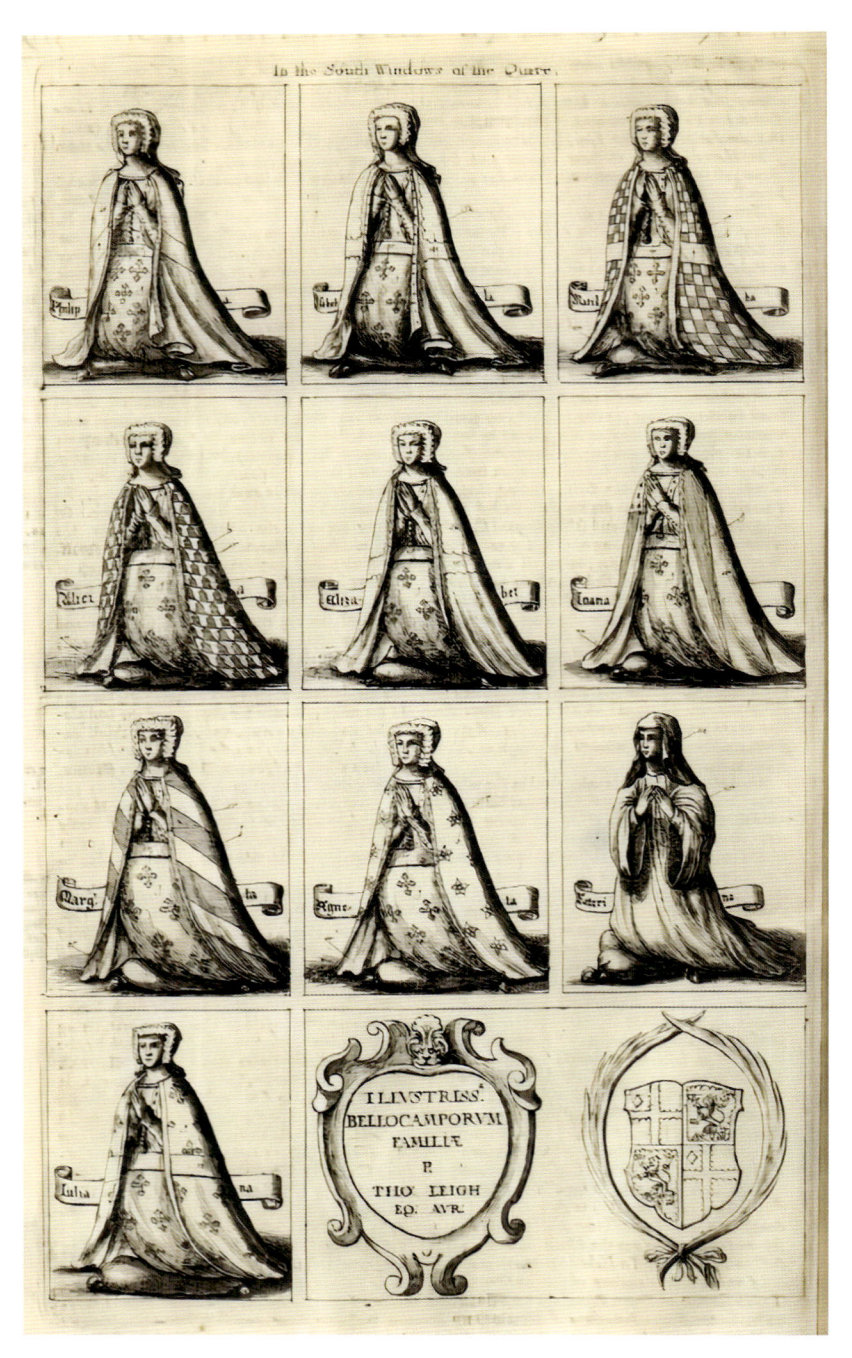

26. Daughters of Thomas Beauchamp and Katherine Mortimer, as shown in the south windows of the chancel. Katherine, third row, far right, is dressed as a nun. The windows were probably destroyed in 1643 by the Parliamentary garrison at Warwick castle.

Aspects of the design of the chancel do, therefore, reflect elements of Thomas's life, but can the same be said of the flying ribs? There are only three other English examples that pre-date the chancel: the Easter sepulchre at Lincoln cathedral (1296); the sacristy to the Berkeley chapel at Bristol cathedral (*ca.* 1330); and the pulpitum at Southwell minster (1335-40). None of these are on anything like the scale of St. Mary's, and none can be considered a precedent for the chancel. But there is one beguiling possibility for their inspiration.

Members of the nobility, with their retinues, were wont to embark on a sort of annual sports tour known as the *Preussenreisen.* They joined with the Teutonic knights (more accurately called the Order of Brothers of the German House of St. Mary in Jerusalem) to crusade against pagans in Prussia – an area straddling present-day Poland, Russia, and Lithuania. There were brutal campaigns in the difficult conditions of a Baltic winter, but that did not preclude copious opportunities for hunting, feasting, tournaments, and general merry-making. Thomas obtained the pope's permission to withdraw from the crusade to the Holy Land that he was to lead in 1364, and was allowed to discharge his vow in Prussia instead. He did so in 1365/66, accompanied by his younger son William, Sir Ralph Basset of Sapcote, and John Blake, his treasurer and a canon at St. Mary's. All three would become executors of his will. Two years later Thomas's eldest son, the future Earl Thomas II, followed in his footsteps, along with Sir Roger Beauchamp of the Bedfordshire branch of the family. Again, both were to be Thomas's executors.

What is significant is the route that Thomas and his retinue would have taken. Although there is no record of the details of their journey, there is of others', and they often sailed to Calais or Flanders and then travelled east overland. That necessitated crossing the River Elbe, and the obvious place to do so was at Magdeburg. While there, they would have attended mass at its cathedral, and prayed for a successful campaign. In the cathedral they would have seen the Portal de Kreuzgangs ('Cloisters Portal'), built about 1340: a small but elegant apse-shaped area that features flying ribs, with mouchettes behind them.

The Portal de Kreuzgangs seems the most likely source of inspiration for the flying ribs at St. Mary's, but there are differences between them – St. Mary's is the more accomplished and daring, with sets of three ribs springing from one same point, without corbels, whereas Magdeburg has single ribs and corbels. And if Magdeburg was where the idea came from, there must have been a sequence of events for which there is no proof: Thomas, or one of his entourage, visiting Magdeburg cathedral; seeing the Portal de Kreuzgangs; and having the idea of reflecting it at St. Mary's. This is by no means implausible. One can go further, and argue that the use of flying ribs at St. Mary's was not simply a matter of aesthetics, but a symbol of Thomas's crusading zeal and achievements. The unprecedented prominence given to the ribs would be worthy of an allusion to a crusade, an act of the highest piety. The ribs might be a visual reminder of this, just as the tall, canopied stalls and the crenellations recall Thomas's chivalry and service to the king.

The chancel is designed to make the tomb the focal point, without competition from elaborate, distracting, and intrusive stonework or fan vaulting. However, within the simplicity of the architecture lie clear indications that the chancel is a commemoration of Thomas's life. It is not so much a chancel, more a mortuary chapel. The idea of being able to read the chancel as a series of representations of Thomas's virtues and accomplishments may seem far-fetched, but its builders, and the canons of St. Mary's, would have been well aware of the references. After all they, their successors, and God, were the intended audience.

VIII

Earl Thomas II died in 1401, his wife, Margaret Ferrers, in 1407. Their canopied monument, thought to have been close to the corner of the nave and the south transept, had a fine quality brass engraving rather than effigies. Although brasses were becoming more popular by the start of the fifteenth century, it was nonetheless an unusual choice for the nobility. The couple are not holding hands. It is as if Thomas II were distancing himself from his parents' tomb, both physically, to preserve the sanctity of their personal space, and stylistically, to avoid any possibility of upstaging them.

Thomas II was taking no chances of his soul being left to rot in purgatory: nine hundred requiem masses were to be said for him with all possible speed after his death, followed by another thousand masses sung on various holy days. He bequeathed six candles to St. Mary's, weighing in total three hundred pounds (about 136 kg), for use on his hearse, and to be kept by the church afterwards. Sixty poor men wore white gowns for his funeral, each carrying

27. The canopied memorial to Earl Thomas Beauchamp II and Countess Margaret, that stood in the south aisle of the nave of St. Mary's, near to the transept. It was destroyed in the 1694 fire, but the brass survived. Note the ragged staff on the end of the tomb chest.

a torch as a symbol of the light of Christ and the banishment of demons. They received alms for their trouble, but there was an ulterior motive: the unwritten deal was that, in return, they would pray avidly for the deceased. It was win-win-win. The prayers of the poor had intrinsic worth for the deceased's soul, with Christ declaring 'blessed are the poor in spirit, for theirs is the kingdom of heaven' (Matthew 5:3). The poor, in turn, would demonstrate their piety before God by praying for the wealthy, and get paid for doing so.

Thomas II was a generous benefactor of St. Mary's. He gave it a cross with a pedestal of silver and gilt enamelled with the story of the Passion; a beryl bound with silver and enamelled to serve as a pyx; his best censer with a chalice; two cruets of silver gilt, used to contain consecrated wine; a basin; and a piece of enamelled silver. By contrast, Elmley received only a vestment – Warwick had

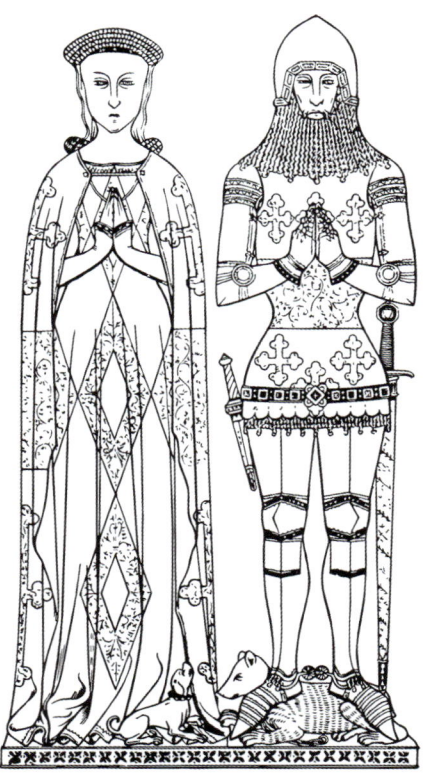

28. This illustration of the brass captures well the detail and quality of the engraving. The brass can be seen on the wall of south transept at St. Mary's.

truly supplanted Worcestershire as the family's spiritual home. But Thomas II's greatest legacy to St. Mary's was the church itself, built on his father's constitutional reforms, and put on a stronger financial footing by them both. In particular, the chancel stood as a fine memorial to his parents, reflecting his father's status and virtues, not just on his tomb, but in its very fabric. It was surely the inspiration for what came to surpass it – the Beauchamp chapel.

After two hundred years of neglect, St. Mary's had been revived by Earls Thomas I and II to become a church that was worthy of their final resting places. Their successor, Earl Richard, was to enhance it beyond measure, and it is to his incomparable chapel-mausoleum that we now turn.

29. *The arms of Earl Thomas Beauchamp II impaled with those of his wife Margaret Ferrers, as depicted in a panel in the chancel vaulting.*

The Beauchamp era earls and their countesses

Earls	Dates	Countesses
William	1268-1298	Matilda FitzGeoffrey
Guy	1298-1315	Alice de Tosny (or Toeni)
Thomas*	1329-1369	Katherine Mortimer*
Thomas II*	1369-1401	Margaret Ferrers*
Richard*	1403-1439	(1) Elizabeth Berkeley (2) Isabella Despenser
Henry†	1439-1446‡	Cecily Neville
Richard Neville	1449-1471	Anne Beauchamp††

Starting dates are when the earl obtained control of his lands after any minority.

* buried at St. Mary's.

† Henry was created duke of Warwick in 1445, the only time that this title has been conferred.

‡ Henry's daughter Anne succeeded to the earldom in her own right, but died in 1449 aged six, so never had control of her lands.

†† Anne became countess by virtue of being Duke Henry's full sister, despite having older half-sisters. Richard Neville became earl by right of marriage.

– 6 –

GLORY

> First, I will ... my body be interred within the Church Collegiate of Our Lady in Warwick where I will, that in such place as I have devised (which is known well) there be made a chapel of Our Lady, well, faire, and goodly built, within the middle of which chapel I will that my tomb be made.

SO DIRECTED the last will and testament of Earl Richard Beauchamp, thirteenth earl of Warwick, made in 1437. His executors were told to 'do faithfully their part and endeavour to execute and perform this my last will, as they all and every one of them will answer afore God at the day of doom'. If, come Judgment Day, they were assessed on the basis of their creation of the Beauchamp chapel, surely they would have been fast-tracked into heaven.

It is difficult to overstate the chapel's reputation. It has been described as 'one of Europe's most lavish funerary buildings',[7] containing 'one of the finest monuments of fifteenth-century England'.[8] John Leland, writing in the 1530s, declared Richard to be 'entombed right princely'. An exhibition entitled *Gothic: Art for England 1400-1547*, held at the Victoria and Albert Museum in 2003, included Richard's effigy, its hearse, the bear and gryphon at his feet, and the statue of Saint Katherine of Alexandria from the east window. When selecting the illustration for the front cover of Sara James's book *Art in England: the Saxons to the Tudors 600-1600*, there was a wealth of treasures to choose from: perhaps an item of exquisite Saxon jewellery;

---

7 Alexandra Buckle, 'Entumbid Right Princely', p.400; see *Further reading*.
8 Ann Payne, 'The Beauchamps and the Nevilles,' in R. Marks and P. Williamson, (eds.), *Gothic: Art for England 1400–1547* (London, 2003), pp.219-221, p.220.

or the intricate Lindisfarne gospels; or the Wilton diptych, that highly symbolic image of the divine status of kingship; or a Hilliard miniature. No, it is Richard Beauchamp's tomb. For good measure, the Beauchamp chapel's statue of Saint Katherine is on the back cover.

30. The Beauchamp chapel from the steps of the west portal.

I

In October 1399 forty-six men were ceremonially bathed, as a sign of purification, and then knighted. It was the forerunner of the creation of the Order of the Bath. The knights then processed together to the coronation of their king, Henry IV, dressed in long green robes trimmed with white fur. One of them was Richard Beauchamp, just seventeen years old.

Richard's qualities had been recognised early, and brought him rapid promotion. He was made earl of Warwick in 1403, almost immediately after he attained his majority at twenty-one. Richard became a Knight of the Garter the same year, after he distinguished himself in the Welsh campaign against Owain Glyndŵr and at the bloody (and close-run) battle of Shrewsbury against the rebellious Henry Percy.

But it was under Henry IV's son, also Henry, that Richard really came to the fore. He enjoyed a particularly close friendship with the prince, four years his junior, and from 1410 was in his pay to the tune of two hundred and fifty marks a year. When Henry succeeded to the throne as Henry V in 1413, his closeness to Richard was demonstrated by Richard's appointment as steward of the coronation, with overall responsibility for the ceremonies.

Richard quickly assumed numerous military and diplomatic roles, including captain of strategically crucial Calais in 1414, but he was not at Agincourt the following year, as he was guarding prisoners from the siege of Harfleur who were being taken to Calais. He returned to England in early 1421 with the king and his bride, Catherine de Valois, and was steward of her coronation as well. Richard was soon back in France, and was at Henry V's side when he died at Vincennes in August 1422. He escorted the king's body back to England, and he was one of Henry's executors.

In 1428 Richard became tutor to the six-year-old Henry VI, and the following year carried him at his coronation at Westminster abbey. Richard was also present when Henry was crowned king of France in Notre Dame in December 1431. Earlier that year, Richard had successfully commanded the English forces at the battle of Savignies, near Beauvais. By now Richard was keeper of Rouen castle, and the gaoler of Jeanne d'Arc, who was burned as a heretic in May 1431 while under his charge.

Richard relinquished his position as the king's tutor in 1436, and was appointed governor and lieutenant-general of France and Normandy the following year. He died in Rouen after a long illness on 30 April 1439, and his body lay in its cathedral for four months before being brought to Warwick, where it arrived on 3 October. Richard was buried, temporarily, in an oak and elm coffin in the south transept of St. Mary's.

Richard had had a distinguished military and diplomatic career, but his reputation was founded on his chivalry. In 1403, the twenty-one-year-old Richard championed Henry IV's second wife, Joan de Navarre, in the jousting tournaments that celebrated her coronation. Six years later, Richard defended the honour of the Order of the Garter itself, in a challenge of personal combat laid down by the Veronese mercenary Pandolf Malatesta.

Richard was not shy in promoting his chivalric persona. In January 1413, at Guînes, near Calais, Richard anonymously challenged noble all-comers to three rounds of combat: the first a joust of ten courses, the second fifteen sword-strokes each on horseback, and the third another joust of ten courses, but without shields. Three French knights accepted the challenge, but there was only ever going to be one winner. After revealing his identity at the start of the third day, to the surprise of no one, Richard entertained the entourages of his challengers, providing a three-course meal for two hundred of their retinue, and food and drink for another one thousand men. It is the stuff of legend, and was stage-managed to be so.

II

This, then, was the man who was to be laid to rest in the Beauchamp chapel, but the chapel had to perform other functions. First, as a Lady chapel, it was a place of especial devotion to the Virgin. Secondly, it was a chantry for Richard's soul, unusually for his alone. No fewer than five thousand masses were to be said as soon as possible after his death, five times the going rate within the English nobility. Furthermore, Richard required that:

> ... there be said every day, during the world ... three masses, whereof one every day of our Lady's God's Mother with note after [*i.e.* with music] ... the second mass to be every day without note of requiem ... the third mass also without note, to be the Sunday of the Trinity, the Monday of the Angels, the Tuesday of St. Thomas of Canterbury, the Wednesday of the Holy Ghost, the Thursday of Corpus Christi, the Friday of the Holy Cross, and the Saturday

of the Annunciation of Our Lady. And to the observances of these masses, in wise as it is expressed, in the said chapel during the world every day to be duly said.

Henry V had also prescribed three masses, every day, for his soul, dedicated similarly.

In case three masses a day at St. Mary's, every day, for eternity, was not enough to ease his passage through purgatory, Richard also directed that a mass be said for his soul daily at Tewkesbury abbey. Further reinforcements were sought: the inscription on Richard's tomb asks for devout prayers for his soul, and around it eighteen angels, intermediaries between God and mankind, each carry a scroll on which is written another invocation for the dead: *sit Deo laus et gloria defunctis misericordia*: 'To God be praise and glory, to the departed mercy'.

The need for the chapel to perform yet another purpose soon became apparent: the preservation of the Beauchamp name. Richard had three daughters from his first marriage to Elizabeth Berkeley, and, with his second wife, Isabella Despenser, a son, Henry, and another daughter, Anne. After succeeding his father to the earldom, Henry had taken advantage of his friendship with the king to lobby for promotion in the social hierarchy, becoming the only duke of Warwick in 1445 and, supposedly, king of the Isle of Wight. However, he died in June 1446, leaving a two-year-old daughter, Anne. So, while construction of the structure of the chapel was underway, but before any of the fittings had been commissioned, the male line of the Warwick Beauchamps had died out.

When the infant Anne died in 1449, the principal heir became Duke Henry's full sister, another Anne, who had been betrothed when she was eight years old to Richard Neville, eldest son of the earl of Salisbury. Neville, somewhat unexpectedly, became the sixteenth earl of Warwick, by virtue of his marriage and the untimely deaths of both his brother-in-law and his niece.

Anne made it her mission to memorialise her father's reputation and that of his ancestors, the Beauchamp name being in danger of being forgotten through want of a male heir, and of being subsumed by the ubiquitous Nevilles. She was a patron of the historian John Rous (born in Warwick *ca.* 1420), a chantry priest at Guy's Cliffe, and whose library was above the south door of St. Mary's porch. Rous's main claim to fame is his notorious *Historia Regnum Angliae*, a history of English kings, published during the reign of

Richard III but rewritten after the king's death to be the first to portray him as a hunchback of unnatural birth, to appease the new Tudor dynasty. But more pertinent to us is his chronicle of the history of the earldom of Warwick, the *Rous Roll* (*ca.* 1483), commissioned by Anne.

The *Rous Roll* is an account of the earls' lineage, unbroken, Rous says, since Guthelinus, the supposed founder of Warwick. Rous sidesteps the problem of the Norman Conquest by declaring Henry de Beaumont, the first Norman earl of Warwick, to have married the daughter of Turchil of Arden, the last Saxon earl. It was pure fiction, but necessary to maintain continuity. Guy of Warwick is, of course, included in the family tree.

Anne Beauchamp also commissioned the *Pageant of the Birth, Life and Death of Richard Beauchamp, earl of Warwick* (1485-90), commonly known as the *Beauchamp Pageant*. It was once thought to be the work of Rous as well, but recent scholarship has questioned this, and its authorship must now be considered as unattributed.

The *Beauchamp Pageant*'s declared aim was to fuel Richard's reputation for 'notable acts of chivalry and knightly demeanour'. It blossomed, the *Pageant* tells us, at the 1403 tournament when Richard championed Joan de Navarre; this 'redounded to [establish] his noble fame and perpetual worship'. More examples of Richard's chivalry follow, most notably the account that, in 1416, the Holy Roman Emperor, Sigismund, said:

> No Christian prince, for wisdom, nurture, and manhood, had such another knight as he had of the earl of Warwick [and] that, if all courtesies were lost, yet might it be found again in him.

'And so ever after', it continues, 'by the Emperor's authority, [Richard] was called the Father of Courtesy'. It was fitting epithet for Guy of Warwick's true heir.

Both the *Rous Roll* and the *Beauchamp Pageant* were keen to record the connection between Richard and a much-respected anchorite, Emma Rawghton of York, and they do so in near-identical terms. According to them, Emma had advised the earl to refound the chantry at Guy's Cliffe, prophesying that if he did, his wish for a male heir would be granted. He did, and it was, with Richard's son Henry born three years later. Emma also endorsed the earl's qualities: Rous reported her as saying that there was:

Here is shewed howe he was baptised, hauyng to his godfadres
kyng Richard the seaund and seynt Richard Scrope then bisshop
of lichefeld, and after in processe of tyme he was Archebisshop
of york.

throughout the realm, no person lord nor other like him in state of grace and true faithfulness, to virtuously nourish and govern his noble person according to his royal estate.

Rous was no doubt laying it on, but he was reflecting society's attitudes to both anchorites and chivalric values, and the desirability of having Richard more than measure up to them.

The *Rous Roll* and the *Beauchamp Pageant* are powerful examples of Countess Anne's desire to immortalise her family and heritage, but they follow an earlier testament to Beauchamp magnificence that she had promoted: the chapel being built for her father. Richard had put the 'oversight and assent' of the executors in the hands of his wife, Countess Isabella, but she died shortly after him, and Countess Anne assumed her mother's role after the death of Duke Henry. Anne's desire to use the chapel to emphasise the Beauchamps' status was so strong that she might have deliberately intended to outdo four contemporary projects of King Henry VI: the college chapels at Eton and at King's, Cambridge, and the mortuary chapels of Henry IV and Henry V at Canterbury and Westminster abbey respectively. Anne's championing of her father demanded that the Beauchamp chapel stand out in a crowded field. It certainly did.

Left: 31. The baptism of Richard Beauchamp, as illustrated in the Beauchamp Pageant. *The ceremony is being performed by the bishop of Worcester, while on the right stand Richard's three godparents: an unidentified lady; Richard Scrope, then bishop of Coventry and Lichfield and a future archbishop of York; and King Richard II himself. The choice of the godfathers explains why Earl Thomas II named his only son Richard, a name not previously associated with the Beauchamps. The illustration exaggerates in showing all three godparents being present; they would normally have been represented by proxies.*

Choosing godparents was a serious business, as they could confer connection and status on the infant. Richard's looked promising, but his father, Earl Thomas II, would later rebel against Richard II, and Scrope was executed in 1405 following his conviction for treason, at a court in which Earl Richard was one of the judges.

III

Anne may have been the one with the 'oversight and assent' of the building of the Beauchamp chapel, but day-to-day responsibility lay with the four executors to whom probate was granted: Thomas Huggeford, John Throgmorton, Nicholas Rody, and William Berkeswell. They were all drawn from Richard Beauchamp's household, they all had close connections both with the Beauchamps and with the town of Warwick, and they were all trusted by Richard implicitly.

Both Huggeford and Throgmorton had acted as Richard's attorneys and had presented new canons to St. Mary's in his absence. Huggeford, from Emscote, was one of at least three generations who served the earldom. His father, Robert, was a lawyer who had been Earl Thomas II's receiver-general, and Thomas had fulfilled the same role for Richard since 1432. We have already met his son John, the constable of Warwick castle and steward of the town. The family also had a close relationship with St. Mary's, and, appropriately, John was granted the right of presentation to St. Mary's by Richard III in 1485.

Throgmorton, also a lawyer, was the son of a retainer of Earl Thomas II, and the son-in-law of Guy Spyne, one of the benefactors of St. Mary's in the early 1400s, and from whom Throgmorton inherited the Coughton estate. He had been Richard's undersheriff of Worcestershire and his appointee as Chamberlain of the Exchequer, following in the footsteps of John de Buckingham and Richard Pirton.

Nicholas Rody was also from a family with strong Warwick connections – his father, John, was a goldsmith in the town, and a Thomas Rody was an affiliate of Earl Thomas II who owned land in Warwick, Myton, and Cubbington. Nicholas had been Richard's steward, is recorded as master of the household to Countess Isabella in 1431-32, and served as an MP for Warwick in nine parliaments between 1413 and 1437. Like Throgmorton, he had been undersheriff of Worcestershire.

William Berkeswell was one of two priests presented to the chantry at Guy's Cliffe on its refoundation by Richard in 1422. He was master of St. Michael's hospital in Saltisford from 1432, became the prebendary of St. Laurence in 1438, and dean of St. Mary's in 1454. He was closely involved in the building of the Beauchamp chapel, particularly after Throgmorton's death in 1445.

There are indications that Richard and his executors had planned the new chapel in some detail before his death. Serious conversations about it may have taken place as early as 1411, when, in an unprecedented move, Richard and others in his household dined twice in one week at the house of Thomas Younge, dean of St. Mary's. Costing St. Mary's the not inconsiderable sum of 34s 4d, it was a significant departure from the convention that those who dined with the nobility went to them, and clearly there was something important on the agenda.

The contract for building the chapel, made in July 1441, required John Mayell, Thomas Kerver, and John Skynner, all of Warwick, to engage the necessary carpenters, masons, workmen, and labourers. They were probably akin to day-to-day project managers, and the identity of the principal builder is unknown. However, there are clues. Architectural similarities with the Divinity School in Oxford suggest that the most likely candidate is Thomas Elkin, who completed it following the death of one Richard Winchcombe in about 1439. Winchcombe is probably the person of that name who undertook work for Earl Richard on a house in Warwick in 1408, so it is plausible that he was involved in the discussions about the earl's proposed chapel at the time of the dinners with Dean Younge. There is also reason to connect Winchcombe with the design of the distinctive pendant vaulting of the Dean's chapel at St. Mary's, built alongside the Beauchamp chapel, as it has similarities with the vault of the Wilcote chantry at North Leigh, Oxfordshire (1438), attributed to him.

Only the best would do: the finest workmen, the finest materials. The glass was by the royal glazier, John Prudde of Westminster, who also worked at Westminster abbey and Eton college. He was obliged to use 'the best, cleanest, and strongest glass of beyond the sea that may be had in England': domestically manufactured glass was not good enough. We do not know where it was made, but it was probably by the Flemish, the leading glassmakers in Europe. Continuing in the same vein, the contract specified the 'finest colours of blue, yellow, red, purple, sanguine, and violet, and of all the other colours that shall be most necessary', but white [*i.e.* clear], green, and black glass was to be used 'as little as shall be needful'. The glass was to be 'finely and strongly set … in lead and solder, as well as any glass in England'.

The glass cost two shillings per square foot, twice the typical rate for good quality English glass, and at least fifty per cent more than the quoted price for

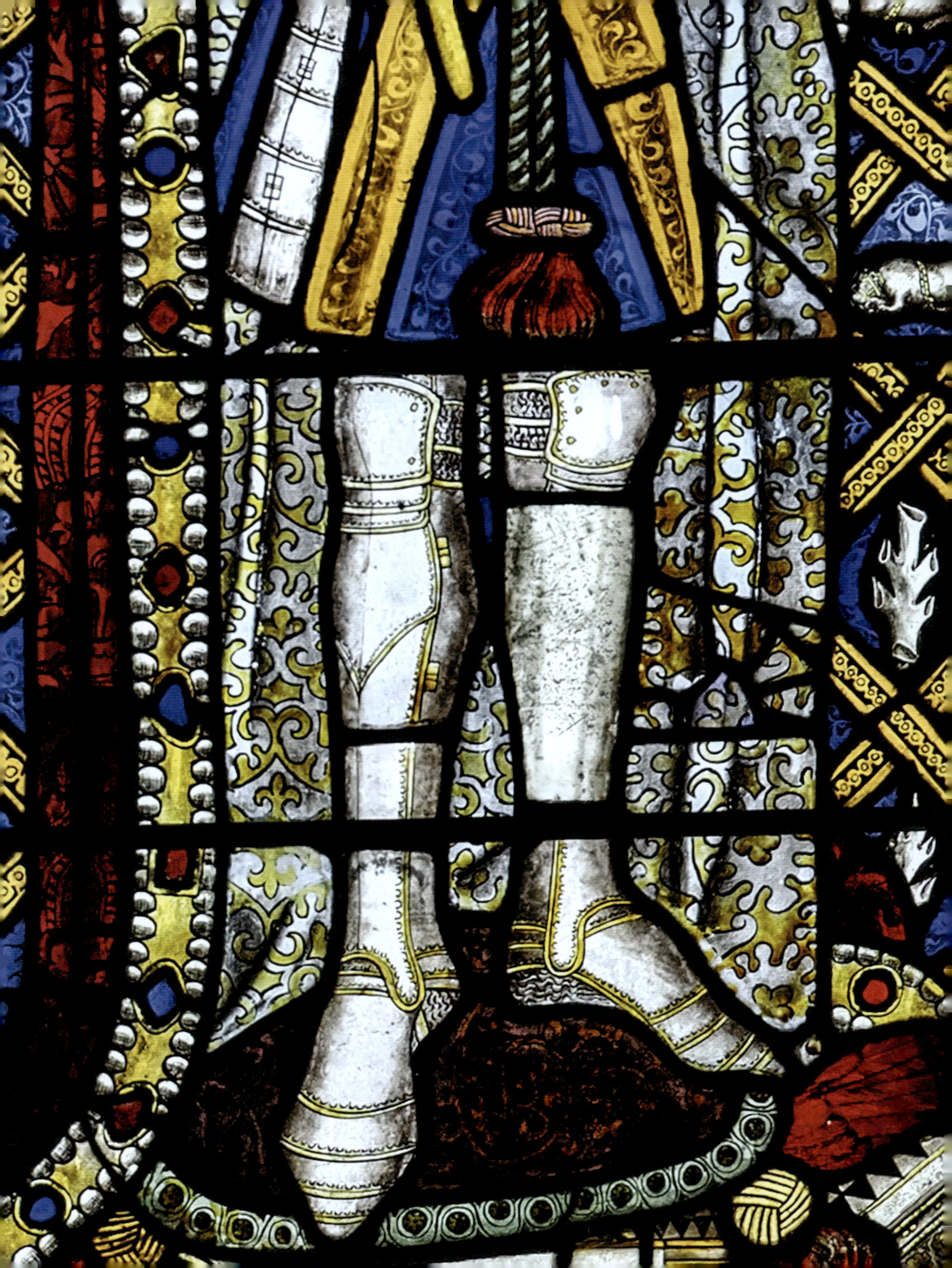

Left: 32. This detail of Saint Alban, in the east window of the Beauchamp chapel, shows the extraordinary craftsmanship of John Prudde, the royal glazier. The depiction of the saint's greave (shin armour) is so fine that it includes its hinges, even though it is virtually invisible to the naked eye from ground level. The inner lining of the cloak is gorgeous. But most extraordinary is the cloak's border, made by inserting glass jewels into holes drilled through the sheet of glass.

that at Henry VI's colleges at Cambridge and Eton. It is clear where the money went. The glass is stained, in its true sense of the base colour being introduced before the first firing, giving the windows a deep, rich, texture. Silver foil or filings were added at the firing stage to produce a sumptuous gold, intense blues were achieved by using cobalt from the Levant, purples came from Italian manganese, reds from copper. Details such as facial features and cloth folds were painted on, shading added by layering, and the finished pane fired again to seal it. Jewels were inserted in the edging on the cloaks of the saints and prophets, rounded glass cut into the principal piece and soldered so finely that it is barely noticeable. It is a technique that demanded considerable skill, and, not surprisingly, it is very rare, with nothing else close to the scale of the Beauchamp chapel.

The specification for Richard's tomb also demanded top quality. The chest is Purbeck 'marble' (actually a polished limestone), valued for its appearance but hard and difficult to carve. Its maker, John Bourde of Corfe, was to use 'a good and fine marble, as well coloured as may be had in England'. The effigy was to be made of the finest latten, and then gilded with gold, and may well have been inspired by Henry V's silver effigy at Westminster abbey, completed in about 1431. Richard's tomb is one of only eight from pre-Reformation England to survive that have effigies made from cast metal, six of which are in Westminster abbey and one in Canterbury cathedral, and is the only one that is non-royal.[9]

The contracts show how the executors were closely involved in the design. The glass was to be made in accordance with drawings that they would

---

[9] The eight tombs are, in chronological order: Henry III (died 1272); Eleanor of Castile (died 1290), wife of Edward I; Edward, prince of Wales ('the Black Prince') (died 1376); Edward III (died 1377); Richard II (died 1400) and his wife Anne of Bohemia (died 1394); Richard Beauchamp; Henry VII (died 1509) and his wife Elizabeth of York (died 1503); Lady Margaret Beaufort (died 1509), mother of Henry VII. The Black Prince's is the one at Canterbury.

supply. Bourde was given the exact dimensions for the tomb chest, and the hearse that embraces the effigy was to be fabricated to a pattern provided by the executors. The executors wanted to know exactly what they were getting, gave precise instructions to the craftsmen, and required any significant decision to be referred to them.

The punctiliousness is extraordinary. In one of the windows an angel is shown playing a pipe, and, not visible from ground level, his cheeks are puffed. The statuettes of angels on the tomb have eyebrows, pupils, and delicately etched toe- and fingernails. But perhaps the most interesting example of the executors' attention to detail is the armour worn by Richard. It is copied so accurately that it must have been made from a suit acquired for the purpose, and the manufacturer of the original can be identified: Antonio Missaglia of Milan, one of the most prestigious armoury workshops of the fifteenth century, supplier to the dukes of Milan, the Medici of Florence, and kings of France but not, at that time, the English Court. The realism is maintained even on the back, hidden unless the effigy is lifted. No compromises, no corners cut, no value-engineering.

IV

The Beauchamp chapel is famed for its imagination as well as its quality. The usual tropes of funerary chapels are here: the deceased's family, his qualities, his status, and a recognition of his role in fashioning it. Richard, his two wives, and four daughters, were depicted in the east window, kneeling in prayer. The garter of the Order of St. George sits below his left knee. At his feet is a bear, with the same emblem used extensively in the glass, as is the ragged staff. So far, so conventional, even if the bears and ragged staves are so numerous in the windows that they imply that the saints are standing in front of a Beauchamp-branded backcloth. Even the Virgin is not immune from them, intruding alongside her halo.

As one would expect, the chapel includes patent references to Richard's reputation for chivalry. Richard's effigy is of a knight armed for the tournament, his head resting on his jousting helm. The crest of the helm is not, as one might expect, a bear or a ragged staff, but a swan gorged (*i.e.* with a collar around its neck, in this case a coronet, as is appropriate for an earl). Like so many images in the Beauchamp chapel, the swan has multiple significance.

At its root is the story of the Swan-Knight – not the better-known German account of Lohengrin, but of Helyas, a similar French version. A damsel in distress is rescued by a mysterious knight arriving on a swan boat. They duly marry, but only on condition that the lady is forbidden to ask the knight's name; if she does, he must leave her. It will come as no surprise to hear that that is what happened, but not before they had a son. Two Norman-English families claimed descent from him: de Tosny (or Toeni) and de Bohun. The latter adopted the swan gorged as their heraldic device.

First, then, the swan is a representation of chivalry through its association with Helyas. Secondly, Richard had both de Tosny and de Bohun blood; Alice de Tosny, the wife of Earl Guy, was his great-grandmother, and her grandmother was a de Bohun. The emblem had been assumed by the Beauchamps, with Earl

33. Richard Beauchamp's Garter stall plate, as illustrated in W H St John Hope's The Stall Plates of the Knights of the Order of the Garter, 1348-1485 *(1901).*

Thomas II bequeathing a swan cup to Richard, and they both used the swan gorged on their Garter plates in St. George's chapel, Windsor. Richard bore the swan gorged to reveal his true identity to his challengers at Guînes in 1413.

The image of the swan gorged is, therefore, a reference to a chivalric and prestigious heritage, but it is more than that. The de Bohun male line had died out in 1373, but a daughter, Mary, married Henry Bolingbroke in 1380, and he adopted the de Bohun device as his own. With Bolingbroke becoming King Henry IV in 1399, the swan gorged became a symbol of the royal house of Lancaster, and its use on Richard's tomb alludes not only to his chivalry and to a noble line of his ancestry, but also to his loyalty to the Crown.

The helm is not the only intimation of Lancastrian affinity on Richard's tomb. Bolingbroke had favoured Milanese armour for a series of jousting tournaments in 1391, and he also wore it for the duel between himself and Thomas Mowbray, duke of Norfolk, that was to be held on Gosford Green, Coventry, in 1398. Richard II, having demanded the duel in the first place, called it off at the last minute, and sent Bolingbroke into exile. The armour that Bolingbroke wore at Coventry was a gift from his friend Gian Galeazzo Visconti, duke of Milan, and the Missaglia workshop supplied the Visconti family. We cannot be certain that Missaglia made Bolingbroke's armour, but the fact that Richard wears a suit by that workshop seems too much of a coincidence for it not to be a testament to Bolingbroke's honour before exile.

Richard's support for Lancaster can also be seen, at least in part, in the choice of four English saints in the east window of the Beauchamp chapel: Thomas of Canterbury, Alban, Winifred, and John of Bridlington. A case can be made for including two of them on grounds other than politics. Images of Thomas Becket were common, but he was also associated with the Black Prince and with Henry IV, both of whom rest in the Trinity chapel at Canterbury, alongside Becket's shrine. The cult of Saint Alban was particularly strong in the early fifteenth century, the saint having been promoted as a patron of chivalry by self-serving monks at St. Albans looking to bolster their abbey's finances. Moreover, Richard had spent two months recuperating at the abbey in 1428, so an attachment to Saint Alban in gratitude for his recovery would not be surprising.

Right: 34. Saint John of Bridlington, one of four English saints shown in the east window of the Beauchamp chapel.

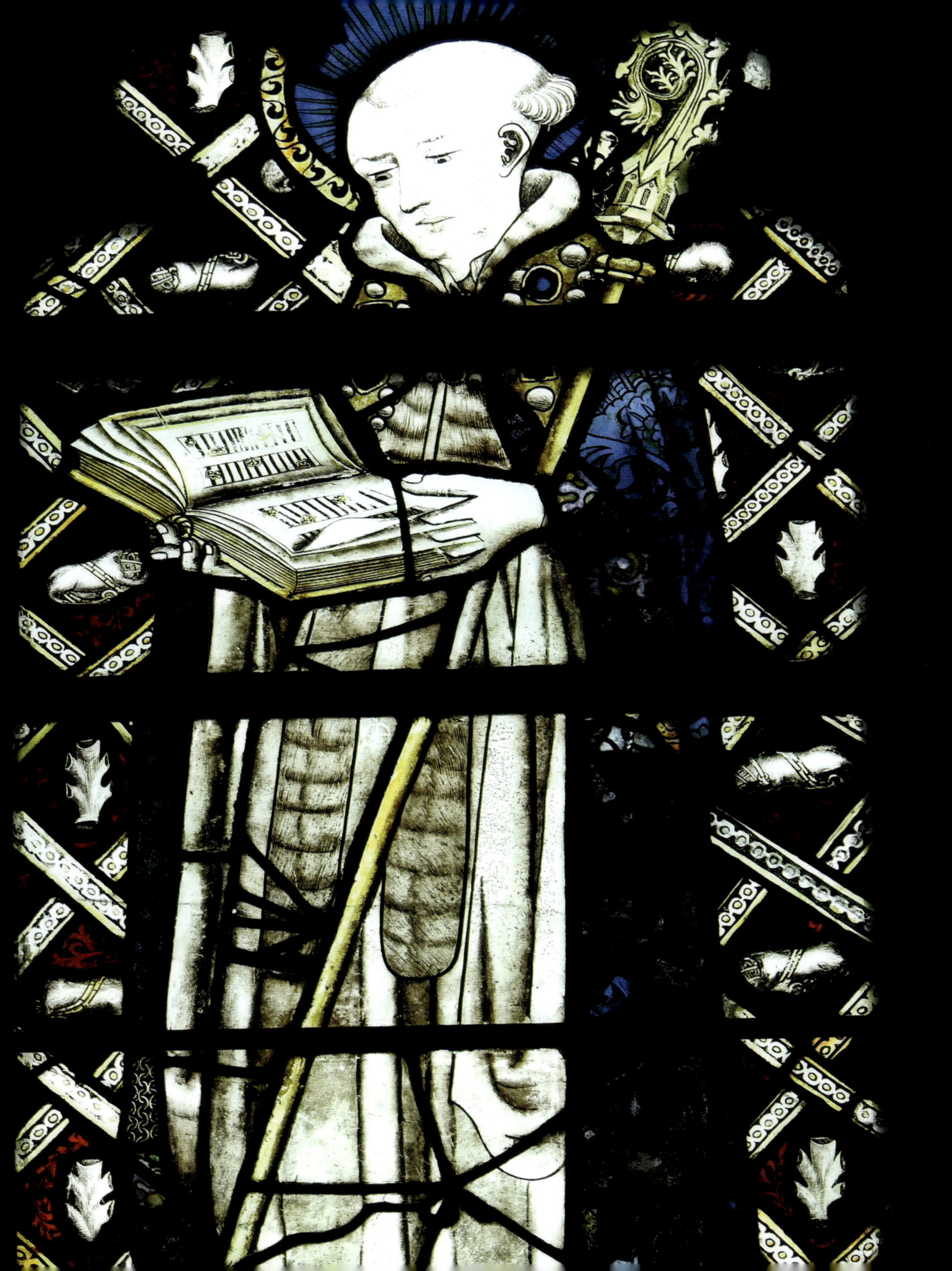

The presence of Saints Winifred and John of Bridlington is less easy to explain, other than through a Lancastrian association. Like Alban, Winifred was a product of monastic marketing, this time by Shrewsbury abbey, where her bones were kept as relics. She was credited with intervening at the battle of Shrewsbury in 1403, which secured the rule of the house of Lancaster, and to have saved the then Prince Henry (later Henry V) from a near-fatal wound sustained at the battle. An arrow lodged in his cheek, narrowly missing his eye. Winifred was also held to have assisted Henry V at Agincourt. The prince's devotion to Winifred was such that he intended to establish a chantry in her name, though he died before doing so. And, in 1449, Henry VI made financial provision for a chaplain at Shrewsbury to pray for the souls of kings, past and present.

John of Bridlington had died as recently as 1379, and was fast-tracked to canonisation in 1404. Henry Bolingbroke was particularly devoted to him. When Bolingbroke returned from a *Preussenreisen* in 1391, he immediately made for John's shrine to offer thanks; he prayed at it in 1398, before telling Richard II of a plot against the king; and he landed at Bridlington on his return from exile in 1399, at the start of his campaign for the reinstatement of his lands, which led to him seizing the crown. Prior to that, Bolingbroke reportedly swore 'on the relics of Bridlington' that his ambitions were limited to claiming his inheritance, and some contemporaries believed that John of Bridlington had prophesized Bolingbroke's disposition of Richard II.

Lancastrian devotion to John of Bridlington was continued by Henry V, who visited his shrine in 1408 and again in 1421, with Richard Beauchamp accompanying him on the former occasion. Like Winifred, John was credited with interceding at Agincourt. Bridlington priory would later give two relics of Saint John to Henry VI, in recognition of the royal association, that were delivered to the king by none other than Richard's son, Duke Henry.

Some have implied that Alban, Winifred, and John of Bridlington owe their very presence in the Beauchamp chapel to a demonstration of Lancastrian allegiance. That may be going too far. Richard bequeathed gold statues of himself, each weighing a hefty twenty pounds (nine kilos), to the shrines of these three saints, plus that of Thomas Becket. He therefore had a spiritual relationship with all the saints depicted in the east window, and he may have identified more with Alban than the house of Lancaster did. Richard may also have felt a particular affinity with Winifred, as he too had reason to be grateful for her intercession at the attritional battle of Shrewsbury, which he survived, and was made a Knight of the Garter immediately after it. Nonetheless, contemporaries would have been well aware of these saints' connections with the house of Lancaster, along with the image of Richard as a knight ready to defend Lancastrian honour, dressed in Missaglia and sporting a helm with a symbol of de Bohun.

V

Memorialising chivalry and fidelity to the royal house was not in itself unusual, but depicting one's own funeral was. The higher echelons of society were taken to their burial on a cart, and a wooden structure, the hearse, was constructed over the coffin to support the pall. This can clearly be seen on an illustration

35. *Richard Beauchamp's tomb. On one level, it depicts Richard's funeral, with the body arriving beneath a hearse and his family shown as weepers around the tomb chest.*

36. *This illustration, made in 1468 by an unidentified artist, is based on one in the chronicle of Jean Froissart (died ca. 1404). It shows the body of Richard II being taken from Pontefract castle, where he died in 1400, with his funeral effigy (made of wood and wax or plaster, and dressed in royal robes) on display. There is a clear resemblance between the hearse and that on Earl Richard Beauchamp's tomb. It gives a good impression of how Earl Richard's body would have been transported from Rouen, where he died, to St. Mary's.*

of Richard II's funeral cortège as it leaves Pontefract castle (*see image 36*). The metal frame over Richard Beauchamp's effigy is identical in design to that over the king's coffin, and there is no doubt that Richard's tomb shows his body being transported to his own funeral.

This narrative is reinforced by the fourteen weepers around the tomb chest, also made from latten and gilded, a precedent set by Edward III's tomb. In contrast to that and to Earl Thomas I's, here they are shown in mourning, carrying bibles, rosaries, or scrolls, and looking suitably solemn. The distinctly monkish air of the men is heavily influenced by the *pleurants*

37. A pleurant (weeper) from the tomb of Philip the Bold of Burgundy (died 1404), attributed to Claus de Werve. Sluter and de Werve were pioneers in their ability to convey a sense of grief merely through their treatment of drapery and the posture of their figures, with faces often concealed.

38. Compare this with the image of a weeper on Earl Richard's tomb, in this case John Talbot, earl of Shrewsbury. The styles are similar, though it must be admitted that de Werve's is the more successful.

on the tomb of Duke Philip the Bold of Burgundy, by Claus Sluter and his former apprentice Claus de Werve (died 1406 and 1439 respectively). It is difficult to see the executors, resourceful as they were, imitating Sluter and de Werve on their own initiative, so the implication is that the style reflects Richard's personal wish.

Richard's weepers can be identified from the escutcheons beneath each one: his son, his four daughters, and their spouses account for ten of them, while the others emphasise the Neville connection: Earl Richard Neville's parents, his aunt, and her husband.[10] There is no doubt that the Nevilles were keen to demonstrate their association with the Beauchamp dynasty; after all, they had paid enough to be so – four thousand seven hundred marks for the double marriage of Richard Neville to Anne Beauchamp and of his sister Cecily to Richard Beauchamp's heir, Henry. That was more than the cost of the Beauchamp chapel, with almost enough left over for the tomb. A third link between the two families, the marriage between Richard Beauchamp's third daughter, Elizabeth, and Richard Neville's uncle, George, Lord Latimer, would also have involved a handsome payment.

Audaciously, the imagery of the chapel graduates beyond Richard's death to represent his afterlife, for the central theme of the chapel is his entry from purgatory into heaven. The day of judgment, visualised by a doom painting of the 'finest colours and fine gold', was not in its usual position on the west face of a wall, but above the west door. It was both literally and figuratively behind Richard, while acting as a reminder to visitors leaving the chapel of what they faced.

Richard's head, resting on his helm, is raised higher than normal, to bring his eyes – wide open – raised upwards, where he can see God, enthroned in gold above the east window, holding the world in his hand, and flanked by the royal arms and the cross of Saint George. Close by, in a panel on the centre line of the vault, is the Virgin crowned as Queen of Heaven. Richard's hands are not in the customary position of prayer, but are open in awe at the sight

---

10   The weepers are: east end – George Neville (Lord Latimer) and his wife, Elizabeth Beauchamp; north end – Richard's son Henry, and his wife Cecily Neville; south side, east to west – Richard Neville (earl of Warwick); John Talbot (earl of Shrewsbury); Humphrey Stafford (duke of Buckingham); Edmund Beaufort (duke of Somerset); and Richard Neville (earl of Salisbury, father of Richard Neville, earl of Warwick). On the north side and in corresponding position, are their respective spouses, namely: Anne Beauchamp, Margaret Beauchamp, Anne Neville, Eleanor Beauchamp, and Alice Montacute.

of God and the Virgin. The drama is a testament to the meticulous planning of the executors, as it depends upon the precise placing of the effigy, and the angle of the head in conjunction with the images of God and Mary.

Blood pulsates through Richard's temples and hands, a clear indication that he is reborn. The accuracy of the veins is thanks to Roger Webbe, warden of the Worshipful Company of Barber-Surgeons in 1449, who was consulted on the making of the effigy. Richard is shown much younger than he was when he died, perhaps reflecting Thomas Aquinas's belief that the soul passed from purgatory into heaven in a state of perfection that extended to physical appearance. The now youthful Richard's smile is captured at the point of breaking: not for him the agonies of a struggle between Christ and the Devil for his soul, despite this being a popular theme of the time.

Richard's communion with God is witnessed by prophets and saints in glass, and by no fewer than thirty-eight angels carved into the mullions and hoodmould of the east window. The angels are joined by four of the most

39. Richard Beauchamp's head and open hands. It is not the usual supplicant pose of a man facing his maker.

popular saints of the Middle Ages – Katherine of Alexandria, Barbara, Margaret of Antioch, and Mary Magdalene. Katherine is shown, not with the familiar wheel on which she was tortured, but with a book, signifying learning and wisdom. Barbara was invoked to avoid sudden death. She was believed to be a protector against thunder and lightning, and, more recently, against firearms and gunpowder, both of which were emerging in European weaponry in the 1400s. The significance of both saints to a late-medieval knight is obvious.

Margaret of Antioch was normally associated with survival of childbirth. However, she promised those who honoured her would receive an unfading crown in heaven, and an appeal to her on one's death-bed would protect against devils. She is, therefore, particularly apposite for a chantry chapel.

Mary Magdalene might also seem an odd choice, given her (false) reputation as a fallen woman, but she symbolises redemption through repentance, and Richard's second wife, Countess Isabella, was particularly devoted to her, to the extent that her will directed that she be shown at the head of her effigy.

Most of the angels are dressed neck-to-ankle in feathers, a feature closely associated with the representation of angels in mystery plays, but unusual in medieval English statuary. Those on the outer course of the hoodmould bear arms associated with the Beauchamps, including the cross of Saint George. Not all the angels can be identified, but among them are Saint Michael the Archangel, who slew the Devil, and Uriel, the angel of the Expulsion, his sword held erect to prevent the return of Adam and Eve to the Garden of Eden.

Welcoming Richard into paradise is the celestial choir and orchestra, ethereal against the gorgeous deep blue glass in the

40. Statues around the east window. Left top: Saint Barbara; left bottom: Saint Katherine of Alexandria; right centre: Uriel, the angel of the Expulsion and, beneath him, a censing angel. All the statues in the east window are original, with very little restoration done on them, and, arguably, form the finest collection of late medieval statues in an English church.

41. Two members of the heavenly orchestra in the south-easternmost window of the Beauchamp chapel. They are playing crwths (anglicised to 'cruths'), a type of violin of Welsh origin, which seems to need a lot of concentration. It is an image full of animation, and even the brown of the feather-suits is vibrant.

tracery of the north and south windows. Acclaimed though the east window is for its technical accomplishment, arguably these are more beautiful. Many of the angels here are also feathered, some with peacock, and there are a variety of colours for the wings: white, red, blue, pink, orange, gold, green, brown. Most have white bodies, but others are red or blue, usually associated with seraphim and cherubim respectively.

The choir is singing from scores of chants, polyphonies, and antiphons associated with the Virgin. Two of the pieces were sung on the eve of, or at, the feast of the Assumption, complementing the purpose of the chapel as a Lady chapel, and the depiction of Mary as Queen of Heaven. The music of the window comes from the Use of Sarum, and would have been sung in the

42. *Members of the heavenly choir, south side, Beauchamp chapel.*

chapel, accompanied by an organ situated in the gallery that was above the west door, and amplified by sound boxes built into the base of the stalls.

Thirty-two musical instruments are shown in the orchestra, twenty-two of them different, ranging from portable organs to the cups, all drawn in considerable detail. They include a very early illustration of a harpsichord, which evolved in Flanders in the early 1400s, the casing of which is in the Burgundian style: another example of the duchy's influence on the art of the Beauchamp chapel. The organs accurately represent the number of pipes usual for this type of instrument. As with the armour, the designers must have been working from actual examples.

As well as being part of the narrative of the entry into heaven, the prominence given to music reflects Richard's patronage of it. His household had included eighteen clerics, nine choristers, and two known composers, Robert Chirbury and John Sousby. The former was dean of St. Mary's during most of the construction of the Beauchamp chapel, from 1443 until his death in 1454, while the latter was the choir master between at least 1432 and 1448. The extraordinary number of musical instruments shown in the glass reflects, not only the concept that all would have been present in heaven, but also that they were familiar to Richard through his love of music.

VI

The Beauchamp chapel was completed by 1455, yet it was not consecrated for another twenty years. There is no simple explanation for this delay. In part it was because the endowments required to fund the chapel's chantry priests were not made until about 1469, by when St. Mary's had received the manors of Wolverton and Baginton (both Warwickshire), and Preston Capes (Northamptonshire), plus land and three tenements in Warwick. The reason that this took so long may be connected with a feud between Richard Neville and his wife's half-sisters, particularly Eleanor, duchess of Somerset, over their entitlement to Richard Beauchamp's assets following the death of the infant Countess Anne in 1449. It was a complicated, ugly, and messy affair, but suffice to say that it originated in the question of whether the lands of Richard Beauchamp's first wife, Elizabeth Berkeley, passed to the children of that marriage, or whether they formed part of her husband's estate and thus fell to be inherited by Richard Neville's wife, Anne. It was probably because of this that work on the Beauchamp chapel stalled between the springs of 1450 and 1452, and continued slowly thereafter.

The inheritance dispute became embroiled in the power struggle occasioned by Henry VI's breakdown in August 1453, possibly due to catatonic schizophrenia, after which he was incapacitated for eighteen months. The resulting vacuum was the beginning of what would become known, inaccurately, as the Wars of the Roses. Richard Neville was at this time part of the faction that favoured Richard, duke of York, professing the usual excuse of rebels that they were merely protecting the king from treacherous advisers. Eleanor Beauchamp's husband, the duke of Somerset, was in the opposite camp, and found himself in the Tower of London, accused of treason. He was released, without trial, over a year later.

Matters came to a head in May 1455 when the rival forces met at the first battle of St. Albans, a Yorkist triumph at which Somerset was killed – according to rumour by his brother-in-law, the earl of Warwick, himself. A degree of reconciliation followed, and, in November 1456, Henry VI made offerings at St. Mary's with Neville and Countess Anne. However, the two sides again became polarised as Queen Margaret strengthened her position, and in November 1458 Neville was stripped of the captaincy of Calais. His assets were confiscated a year later, making it a propitious time for Eleanor to reassert her claims to her mother's estate.

With all this going on, no wonder the Beauchamp chapel was mothballed, its endowment still pending. And another problem had arisen: the embarrassment of the chapel's Lancastrian iconography. Henry VI was deposed in March 1461 to be replaced by the duke of York's eldest son, Edward IV, for whom Richard Neville secured the north of England. In January 1464 the new king, accompanied by Neville and Countess Anne, attended St. Mary's, and he must have been shown the Beauchamp chapel. In 1468 he even renewed the fiscal concessions that had been given to Bridlington priory by both Henry V and Henry VI, perhaps as an attempt to avoid devotion to its saint being solely associated with the house of Lancaster. Even so, with a Yorkist king, a Yorkist (*pro tem*) earl of Warwick, and the earl's sister-in-law Eleanor deprived of control of her estates on the grounds that her sons were pro-Lancaster, this may not have been the best time to reveal to the world a chapel displaying the swan gorged, Missaglia armour, and images of Saints Winifred and John of Bridlington.

Henry VI was restored to the throne in October 1470, but in name only. With the king mentally unstable, the crown was effectively controlled by a renegade Richard Neville. Neville had deposed Henry VI to put Edward IV on the throne, and then deposed Edward IV to restore Henry VI, hence the sobriquet by which he is best known, 'Warwick the Kingmaker'. Armed conflict was inevitable, and Neville was killed at the battle of Barnet on 14 April 1471. The Lancastrian forces were routed three weeks later at Tewkesbury, and Henry VI died shortly afterwards. Edward IV was back, and a period of relative stability followed, until his death in 1483.

Rous would have us believe that Richard Neville wished to be buried in the Beauchamp chapel. That is not beyond the realms of possibility, as Neville would not have been a passive spectator in the building of the chapel, and, at least until he deserted Edward IV, he had a reputation of being particularly courteous, generous, and chivalrous. One can see how the portrayal of his father-in-law in the Beauchamp chapel would chime with Neville as something that he would wish to be associated with and, arguably, Neville was responsible for exaggerating Richard Beauchamp's image as a chivalrous knight to bolster his own reputation. As it was, Neville was laid to rest at his family's mausoleum at Bisham priory, Berkshire, his grave lost with the dissolution of the monasteries under Henry VIII. St. Mary's does, however, have his image, as he is one of the weepers on Richard Beauchamp's tomb; it is thought to be the only extant image of him made during his lifetime.

With no male heir, Neville's death triggered another inheritance dispute, complicated by the fact that, as a traitor, his lands were liable to forfeiture. Subject to that, the best claim to his estate seemed to lie with his widow, the redoubtable Anne Beauchamp, but this was challenged by her two sons-in-law, George, duke of Clarence, and Richard, duke of Gloucester (later Richard III), both brothers of Edward IV. It was not in the dukes' interests to see Neville posthumously attainted for treason, which would defeat both their claims, and he was not. Their path was cleared in 1474 when Edward IV, aided and abetted by a supine parliament, disinherited Anne Beauchamp as if she 'were now naturally dead'. Neville's estates were duly divided between Clarence and Gloucester, and the Warwick honour and earldom granted to Clarence, by right of his marriage.

Clarence respected the earldom's heritage and embraced its prestige. He made Warwick castle his principal residence, he worshipped regularly at St. Mary's, and John Huggeford, the son of one of Richard Beauchamp's executors, became his loyal servant. Clarence even followed his predecessors by supporting the college in yet another dispute with the archdeacon of Worcester over visitation fees. But, most importantly, he fulfilled the testamentary wishes of Richard Beauchamp. Ironically, it was a son of Richard, duke of York, and a brother of a Yorkist king, who opened up to the world the Lancastrian imagery of the Beauchamp chapel.

VII

The consecration of the Beauchamp chapel finally took place on 27 December 1475, on the anniversary of Countess Isabella Despenser's death. The date may have been chosen deliberately, as Clarence's wife was the countess's granddaughter, and prayers would have been said for Isabella's soul. The bishop of Worcester was too ill to preside, and the consecration service was conducted by John Hales, bishop of Coventry and Lichfield.

A copy of the order of service for the reburial has, uniquely, survived. The rites resembled those of the funeral itself, with additional prayers and ceremonies relating to the reinterment of the bones. Three masses were said, the last of them, the requiem, held in the Beauchamp chapel, probably after most of the laity had left. There was much accompanying music: seven psalms, six antiphons, and several other choral works, probably requiring the full choir of six vicars and six choristers, plus the four priests and two vicars attached to the Beauchamp chapel. We do not know who else attended, but presumably Clarence did, along with, possibly, the queen, Elizabeth Woodville, and her two young sons, Richard and Edward, the future 'Princes in the Tower', who are known to have been at St. Mary's at around this time.

The reburial began by opening Richard's grave, sprinkling his coffin with holy water, and censing it. The coffin was then covered and carried to the high altar in the chancel, to be sprinkled and censed again. From there, possibly on the following day, it was taken in procession from the chancel to the Beauchamp chapel, and finally laid to rest in a burial chamber beneath the tomb-chest, which extends westwards to enable it to be entered. The crown of the vault lies some two feet below floor level, and is six feet six inches deep, so the coffin-bearers could stand upright as they laid the body in it, aligned with the effigy. The reburial and consecration services, including the usual cycle of daily masses, would have lasted over twelve hours.

The chapel looked splendid. Brightly lit, the flickering candles highlighted the tomb, and accentuated the beauty of statues of the Virgin, Saint Anne, Saint Gabriel, and Saint George that were of:

> the finest oil colours, in the richest, finest, and freshest clothings that may be made of fine gold, azure, of fine purple, of fine white and other finest colours necessary, garnished, bordered, and powdered in the finest and curiousest (*sic*) wise.

These statues were, presumably, placed in the now-vacant niches in the north-east and south-east corners of the chapel, and on the north and south walls.

A statue of the Virgin cradling the infant Christ, bequeathed to St. Mary's by Richard Beauchamp, was probably beside the altar. It was twenty inches high, weighed ninety-five and a half ounces (2.7 kg), and was mounted on a gold plinth which, like the Virgin's crown, was richly garnished with pearls, rubies, and sapphires. Jesus was holding a branch made of a ruby and four pearls, with a green stone at the centre of the pearls.

Items which had been used for Richard's funeral were displayed in the chapel. They included:

- A sword with a scabbard of black velvet and a girdle of black silk, garnished with five studs, a buckle, a pendant, and a silver gilt triangle.
- A full suit of armour.
- The body armour of a horse, its trappings embroidered with the arms of the earls of Warwick. It is possible that it would have been worn by a real horse at the ceremony.
- Eighteen banners of different lords' arms made of tartan (then meaning simply a wool cloth, without the connotation of pattern that it has now), all of the same size and with silk fringes.
- No fewer than sixty-two small pennons displaying white ragged staves on a black background.
- Three small black banners, each with a ragged staff on them.
- Four small banners bearing mermaids, symbols of pride and lust, and reminders to avoid temptation.
- Two banners of black tartan bearing the arms of the earls of Warwick.

- Two banners of purple satin each with three gold crosslets, the arms of the college of St. Mary.
- A great standard, three yards long, of red double satin, embroidered with bears and gryphons (the emblem of Countess Isabella) holding a branch between them, and with additional bears and ragged staves.

The prevalence of the ragged staff, passed down from the valiant Guy, is unmistakable, and while the arms of the earls of Warwick are represented, with their heraldic reference to Guy, no prominence is given to the Beauchamps' six gold crosslets on a red background. It is as though romance had surpassed genealogy.

There we have it: Richard Beauchamp resting in a chapel fit for royalty, a paean to duty and heroism, to a life so virtuous that the soul is on the threshold of heaven, and to the culmination of almost two hundred years of family honour and tradition born of legend. And, unlike that of his grandfather in the chancel, this tomb was to be admired by the public, with the language of the tomb's inscription switched from the Latin specified in the contract to English, making it intelligible to the laity. The area known as the Dean's chapel, built between the walls of the chancel and the Beauchamp chapel, was probably where most of the masses were said for Earl Richard's soul. With only Lady mass and high mass being celebrated in the Beauchamp chapel itself, it could be freed up for public access. The cult of Earl Richard Beauchamp was in the making.

The Beauchamp chapel brims with superlatives: the effigy, the weepers, the glass, the celestial music, the workmanship, the quest for perfection, the imagination, the innovation, the intricacies, the very concept, the cost. It boasts the best collection of late medieval sculpture inside an English church; the most extensive use of musical notation in medieval glass; the best contemporary illustration of late-medieval musical instruments in England in any medium. The glass was, per square foot, the most expensive in England of the fifteenth century, bar a now-lost window at Henry IV's extravagantly

Right: 43. A drawing of the Dean's chapel taken from a book published in 1847. At that time four helms were on display, that are assumed to have formed part of the earls' funereal achievements. The extravagance of the (then rare) pendant vaulting emphasises the chapel's intimate connection with the Beauchamp chapel.

T. Scandrett

rebuilt Eltham palace. John Flaxman, best known for his work with Josiah Wedgwood, thought John Massingham, who carved Richard's effigy and, probably, the weepers on his tomb and the statues of the east window, the equal of the great Italian sculptors Donatello and Ghiberti. The tomb may have been the most expensive made in England before the Tudor era, those of kings not excepted, though it probably did not match the £950 cost of the double tomb of Richard II and Anne of Bohemia (another with cast effigies). Never mind that this was precisely the time of the 'Great Slump', which brought crippling economic hardship to the population from 1440 to 1480.

There is one weeper with a markedly different pose from the rest, her chin resting in the crook of her right hand, her thoughts drifting. It is Anne Beauchamp, who seems to be contemplating not so much the life of her father, but the chapel she has built in his memory. But centre stage, of course, is Richard himself, in shining gold, wearing Europe's finest tournament armour, his broadening smile smug and self-satisfied as he enters the Promised Land. It is as though he is ready to champion the Virgin herself – and that is a role customarily assigned to none other than the patron saint of the Order of the Garter, Saint George.

44. A thoughtful Anne Beauchamp, as shown on her father's tomb.

There is an arrogance to the Beauchamp chapel, a whiff of narcissism, an invasion of monarchical privilege, a gnawing sense that it outranks its founder, illustrious as he was. Yet all can be forgiven; St. Mary's is truly blessed with what has been described as 'one of the most spectacular funerary ensemble of its day [that] can stand comparison with the finest mortuary chapels in Europe'.[11] It is that astonishingly, jaw-droppingly, good.

---

11   Richard Marks, 'Entumbid right princly', p.163; see *Further reading*.

The bear and ragged staff

Bears and ragged staves are shown, separately, throughout the Beauchamp chapel. They were in every large window, and are used as spacers on the inscription of Richard Beauchamp's tomb.

The bear is probably an allusion to Beauchamp's ancestor Urse d'Abetot, ursus being Latin for bear, though Rous, ever keen to emphasise the longevity of the earldom, claims that its origins lie with a past earl of Warwick, Arthgallus, and arth is Welsh for bear. The staff may derive from another Saxon earl, Morvidius, who was said to have killed a giant with a branch of a tree.

The bear, then, was a Beauchamp family badge, while the staff represented the earldom. The chaining of the bear to the staff represents the conjoining of the family and the earldom, and, contrary to popular belief, has nothing to do with bearbaiting.

The only place in the Beauchamp chapel where they are used as a united emblem, before the advent of the Dudleys, is on the finials of the stalls. The bear and ragged staff is used today in the emblems of Warwickshire County Council, Warwickshire Cricket Club, and numerous other organisations.

45. Richard Beauchamp's seal is an early example of the bear and ragged staff being used together. It also features a swan gorged, and a reference to Guy through the depiction of the arms of the earls of Warwick.

– 7 –

REFORMATION

THE COLLEGE of St. Mary was dissolved in 1544. The exact date is not known, but the last entry in its accounts was for Tuesday 25 July. It went not with a bang but a whimper, a voluntary surrender in the face of an impossible future. The political tide had turned against colleges, but, more immediately, the college was broke yet again, and dissolution was the only possible outcome.

I

Any optimism engendered by the reforms of the late 1300s proved to be misplaced. Earls Thomas I and II had reorganised the administration of the college, imposed new disciplines upon the canons, introduced a resident treasurer to take control of St. Mary's finances, and added endowments to bolster its income. Later, the Beauchamp chapel had boosted both the church's prestige and its revenue stream, as pilgrims came to honour the memory of Earl Richard. But by 1544 Richard had been dead for over a hundred years, the Warwick Beauchamps were extinct, and their reputation faded.

The very earldom had also gone, and with it the church's patron. With the execution of the duke of Clarence in 1478, rumoured to have been drowned in a butt of malmsey, it passed to his infant son Edward. He never took possession of his estates; they were vested in the Crown during his minority, and there they stayed. He was only ten years old when he followed his father to the Tower of London, seen by Richard III as a rival to the throne, and he did not leave it alive. Fourteen years later Richard's victor, Henry VII, executed Edward as the last legitimate male Plantagenet, and an alleged co-conspirator in the Perkin Warbeck plot to depose the king.

The earldom was not all that went adrift. The administrative and financial structure created by Earl Thomas Beauchamp I in 1367 began to unravel as early as 1400, when the chapter met with all of the prebendaries present. This was a rare event, but self-interest was at stake. Considering that the low rate of pay for non-resident canons was a disincentive to attend, which had resulted in an embarrassing level of absence at services, the chapter decided that the remedy was to change the stipend to ten pounds a year for all canons, resident or not. This was the year after Thomas Beauchamp II had obtained a mortmain licence to increase the church's endowment on the grounds that it could not cover the costs of its vicars and choristers.

If any prebendary thought it necessary to seek diocesan approval, given that this change to their remuneration was contrary to the statutes promulgated by Bishop Whittlesey, he did not persuade his colleagues. The chapter got away with it in the short term, no doubt protected by the earls, but within two years of Richard Beauchamp's death Bishop Bourchier reversed the 1400 decision on the grounds that it was made without authority, and had resulted in the canons receiving more than the church could afford. Indeed, the pay increase had caused expenditure to exceed income, and the chapter sold off assets to meet the deficit. One can imagine how that must have looked while embarking on the most expensive chantry chapel in England.

Clearly the appointment of a treasurer had not been enough to ensure financial discipline, especially as since 1415 he was appointed from among the canons for one year in rotation, and any canon refusing to serve would have five pounds deducted from his prebend. It must have been difficult for any treasurer to resist the majority view, no matter how imprudent he thought it, assuming that he overcame his own vested interests in the first place. Even if he did, his decision might quickly be reversed by his successor.

Several measures were put in place by Bourchier to counter this loophole. Stricter controls were imposed on the ability of the chapter to dispose of property. All church expenses were to be met before paying the prebendaries, who would now receive an amount per day of residence up to a maximum of twenty marks a year, the figure set in 1367. Stipends would be reduced if there were insufficient funds to meet them in full, with canons resident for fewer than two hundred and sixty days suffering disproportionately. Bourchier also prevented qualification through token attendance, because to get paid a canon had to be present at both matins and either the Eucharist or vespers (sunset), unless away on church business.

Before considering the college's financial situation in the years immediately prior to its dissolution, we should pick up some themes that we looked at before the rebuilding. Problems that had surfaced two hundred years earlier had not gone away. In 1395 the prior of St. Sepulchre's tendered only 1s 9½d of the 2s 6d annual pension due to St. Mary's, and the next year he refused to pay any of it. He also claimed a share of St. Mary's revenue from the churches that had been appropriated to it by Thomas Beauchamp II, even though the earl had declared publicly in St. Mary's churchyard that St. Sepulchre's was not to benefit from them. The prior was summoned to the castle to appear before the countess herself and members of the college, and his obduracy resulted in the bishop of Worcester expelling him from the chapter of St. Mary's, an *ex officio* position that had been held by his predecessors for over two hundred and fifty years.

Five years later St. Mary's faced another dispute over burials, this time with the Dominican friars. Alice Russell, a parishioner of St. Mary's, had been buried at the friary. The arrangement between the church and the friary over interments does not seem to have been as well established as it had been with St. Sepulchre's, but St. Mary's claimed a quarter of Alice's funereal offerings and those of all future funerals at the friary. It seems to have been a test case, and this time the forum was an arbitration conducted jointly by a Dominican professor of theology, and an archdeacon of St. Paul's cathedral. This suggests that the parties were prepared to resolve the issue amicably, appealing to the wisdom of higher authorities.

St. Mary's claim was upheld, and, unlike their counterparts at St. Sepulchre's, the Dominicans complied with the decision. St. Mary's received a quarter of the value of Alice's offerings to the friary, which were a wax candle weighing two pounds, a gold coin worth 7s 8d, a brass pot (4s 4d), a 'Parisian' handkerchief that Alice had inherited (8s), and offerings amounting to 10d. It may not seem much, but the brass pot alone was comfortably worth more than a vicar would have earned in a week.

Meanwhile, another source of competition for funds had emerged, the guild. Although commonly associated with the protection and regulation of trade in places like Coventry, guilds were, at heart, religious and charitable organisations. They were a sort of savings club for the soul; members paid a subscription in return for which the guild would provide a priest to pray for deceased members and members' ancestors. Guilds were, therefore, chantry foundations. They would also make payments to members who had fallen on hard times, to members' widows, and to the poor at large. Their popularity was such that one historian has described them as 'the most important vehicle for the expression of late medieval lay piety'.[12] In other words, increasingly wealthy artisans and merchants were likely to be benefactors of guilds, possibly at the expense of the church.

Warwick is known to have had two guilds. One was dedicated to Saint George, its foundation being authorised by King Richard II in 1383, though almost certainly it had been in existence before then. The guild's members paid a not inconsiderable eighty marks to the king for the privilege of establishing it. One of the founders, William Russell, might well be related to the Alice who was buried at the Dominican friary. That same year Earl Thomas II gave the disused St. James's church to the guild to have as a chapel for the provision of divine service, for which two chaplains were appointed.

The other guild was that of the Holy Trinity and Blessed Virgin Mary, possibly older than St. George's, but also licensed by the king in 1383. It provided three chaplains to say a daily mass at an altar in St. Mary's. Of the guild's thirteen founder members, at least eight were within the earl's retinue, including Robert Walden, who, as we have seen, was a generous benefactor to St. Mary's. Four of them had been, or would become, MPs for Warwick. These were powerful men.

Support for guild and church was by no means mutually exclusive, far from it, as Earl Thomas II and Robert Walden demonstrate. Nicholas de Southam, who was dean of St. Mary's from 1361 to 1395, seems to have been a member of the Guild of the Holy Trinity, and one of his successors, John Alestre (died 1517), left money to the canons, vicars, and choristers at St. Mary's, and to the guild priests of Warwick, in each case dependent upon them saying masses for his soul on each of the seven days after his death.

To a large extent, the guilds' functions were complementary to St. Mary's rather than antagonistic, but they quickly became wealthy, and must have

---

12   William Jones, 'English religious brotherhoods and medieval lay piety: the enquiry of 1388-89', *The Historian* 34:4 (1974) pp.646-659, p.646.

received endowments that might otherwise have been given to St. Mary's. In 1393/94 the Holy Trinity guild alone had seven houses, three tofts (homesteads), twelve cottages, eight shops, almost forty acres of land, four acres of meadow, and rents amounting to thirty shillings per annum. In all these properties were worth twenty pounds a year, only a little less than the value of St. Mary's holdings. The guild of St. George was authorised to have property to the same value as Holy Trinity. The two guilds had merged by 1401 to form the Guild of the Holy Trinity and St. George, or simply the Guild of Warwick. They became rich enough to be able to build, between 1392 and 1430, a surprisingly large complex adjacent to the guild chapel of St. James, comprising a great hall, master's house, and lodgings. These buildings have survived to form part of the Lord Leycester hospital.

At the same time, St. Mary's income from its existing endowments remained under pressure. There were practical difficulties in managing distant holdings. St. Mary's had property in four counties. Both Spelsbury and Chaddesley Corbett were at least a day's journey from Warwick, and an official travelling from St. Mary's to Whittlesford was unlikely to get there within three. There were other problems. Sluggish demand meant that the college was unable to increase urban rents, particularly in Warwick, which remained relatively poor beyond a small elite. Furthermore, there had been a fall in population, and hence revenue, at some of St. Mary's rural possessions, most notably at Compton Mordak and Wolfhampcote, both of which had been deserted for decades, and the rectory barns abandoned. To make matters worse, the Lucys of Compton reneged on an agreement with Richard Beauchamp to assist with the funding of his chapel by transferring to St. Mary's the manor of Kingston (Chesterton). It was not all bad news; the manors of Baginton and Haselor became particularly valuable because of their woodland, as did the pasture held at Beausale and Fulbrook, but it was not enough to compensate for losses elsewhere.

By 1501, and with the earldom extinguished, the college's patron was the king, Henry VII. Pleading poverty, the college successfully petitioned him for the grant of the ruined and abandoned chapel of St. John the Baptist at Cuckow (or Cuckoo) in Beausale. The attraction was its endowment, and St. Mary's received an annual rent of two pounds in lieu, subject to a mass being said at St. Mary's every Friday for the soul of the king, with a yearly obit after his death.

The college's seemingly perpetual impecuniosity made the quality of the clergy, particularly the vicars, a matter of general concern, and many were poorly educated. They received no formal training, and usually learned on the job. It was hardly well-paid. An assessment conducted in 1535 showed that Robert Hoole, a curate, was paid £6 13s 4d a year, about the going rate but not much more than an unskilled agricultural labourer earned. Ten vicars got £7 6s 8d each, and six choristers two pounds each, the same amount that they received in 1367. Some ten years later, one of the priests, John Blythe, was being paid a mere £6 4s 4d, less than Hoole had received as a curate, though one year he received a generous bonus of twenty shillings for helping to hear confessions at Lent.

The prebendaries fared better, but even they were not generously remunerated. The dean in 1535, John Carvanel, received a stipend of £26 13s 4d, and two resident canons were both paid £13 6s 8d. The other three canons were non-resident, and received two pounds each. Naturally, they all had other sources of income. However, despite their modest pay from St. Mary's, the prebendaries were of a high calibre with, at the time of the dissolution, four of the six being university graduates.

There was one other item of regular expenditure disclosed in 1535: an annuity of forty shillings to Henry Grey, marquess of Dorset, the 'high steward' of the college. As Grey was only eighteen at the time, this looks like a fabricated sinecure by the hand of Henry VIII. It is a curious link between St. Mary's and a man whose daughter would soon have her nine days of fame.

II

The 1535 assessment was made in the wake of the Act of Supremacy, passed the previous year, that made Henry VIII, not the pope, the supreme head of the Church of England. On 20 August 1534 the college met in the chapter house to sign and seal a declaration accepting that the pope 'had not any greater jurisdiction bestowed upon him by God in this kingdom of England, than any other foreign bishop whatsoever'. It was a pivotal moment.

The dispute over control of the English church was not simply a product of the question of the king's divorce from Queen Katherine of Aragon, as the identity of the ultimate arbiter of ecclesiastical law in England had long been an area of debate. Thomas Becket's murder in 1170 had its roots in his resisting royal interference in the privileges of the clergy, and the Crown's claim to have jurisdiction over clerics accused of a crime had been hotly contested as recently as 1515. And there were more fundamental elements of the Reformation – an attack on abuses thought endemic within the church, and disagreement over what was the true faith, and hence the correct liturgy. It was far more complex than a conflict between conservative Catholicism and radical Protestantism: committed Catholics called for church reform, and there was nothing inconsistent in believing that Henry's marriage to Katherine was invalid, yet accepting control from Rome, or in supporting the marriage and opposing the pope.

The Act of Supremacy is a classic example of regime change without planning what was to replace it, allowing an outcome in which tenets of belief that had held sway for centuries would first be challenged, and then criminalised, within a period of twenty years. Some of the persons close to the Crown, notably Thomas Cranmer, archbishop of Canterbury, and Thomas Cromwell, took advantage of the Act to pursue a reformist agenda.

The doctrine of purgatory was an early casualty, and, in truth, it had got out of hand. One couple, who died in 1506, felt able to offer remission of no less than twenty-six thousand years plus, oddly, twenty-six days, in return for prayers for their souls. It is not surprising that condemnation of the entire concept of purgatory was forthcoming, with Martin Luther calling it the biggest lie on earth. Even a loyal Catholic could write that purgatory was based on a fiction driven by priests being paid to say masses. A primer, written in English rather than the traditional Latin, described prayers for the dead as 'lies and vanities'. If they were considered useless, relics and indulgences had to go with them. The cult of the Virgin Mary, and the intercessory power of saints, were being questioned with increasing voraciousness.

In 1535 monks were forbidden to accept money for the display of relics, with pilgrims encouraged to give their offerings to the poor instead. The following year Cranmer delivered a sermon advocating the giving of money to charity rather than spending it on masses for the souls of the dead, while Hugh Latimer, bishop of Worcester, accused the clergy of supporting fraudulent relics, exploiting images, and extorting money in the name of an 'ancient purgatory pick-purse'. He also linked the existence of monasteries to purgatory, implying that if purgatory were contrary to scripture, there was no point in having them. The same could be said of chantries such as the

46. The sale of indulgences, as shown in an etching by Lucas Cranach the elder for Martin Luther's book Passional Christi und Antichristi *(1521). The pope is sitting on his throne, with a pile of pre-printed indulgence certificates ready to be filled in with the names of paying customers. The queue has turned its back to the altar, and a dog, representing true faith, has turned its back to the pope.*

Beauchamp chapel and of collegiate churches like St. Mary's. It must have been uncomfortable for the canons, to see their institution under fire from their own bishop.

By 1538 images and relics were being removed from churches, with the enthusiastic Latimer going so far as to describe a celebrated image of the Virgin at Worcester, his own cathedral, as 'the devil's instrument'. The statue of Our Lady of Walsingham in Norfolk, the greatest of the English shrines to her, was taken to London and burned as if it were a heretic. The use of candles was heavily restricted, now allowed only on the rood screen, altar, and at the Easter sepulchre. Saint Thomas Becket was declared *persona non grata* for the obvious reason that he suffered his martyrdom through challenging the authority of the king over the church. All images of him had to go, even (or especially) at Canterbury, where his shrine was dismantled and his bones burnt. Once ubiquitous, few pre-Reformation images of him survive, that in the east window of the Beauchamp chapel being a rare example.

The proponents of the new faith did not have it all their own way. Rituals that they considered displays of superstition, such as Candlemas and creeping to the Cross, were still permitted, with the king himself observing the latter in

1538. The Act of Six Articles, passed the following year, continued the fudge, remaining silent on purgatory, on the efficacy of prayers for the dead, and on the presence of images. It also took a conservative line on another issue that was emerging as a battleground, transubstantiation: whether bread and wine were truly transformed into the body and blood of Christ at the Eucharist. Denying it became punishable by burning at the stake, and Latimer either resigned his bishopric in protest or jumped before he was pushed. He was replaced at Worcester by a Henrician loyalist, John Bell, who back-pedalled on his predecessor's reforms and ejected his supporters from the diocese, some of whom were described as 'disorderly and colourable [of doubtful loyalty to official doctrine]'. Others, including some of his own ministers, had accused Latimer of infecting the diocese with heresy. They were turbulent times.

The remainder of Henry VIII's reign was characterised by inconsistency, a consequence of personal uncertainties and diplomatic considerations. The most powerful ruler in Europe was Queen Katherine's nephew, the Holy Roman Emperor Charles V, and provoking him with more radical change would not have been politic. Overall, Henry was reluctant to depart too far from tradition. The seemingly innocent and light-hearted practice of appointing boy bishops was outlawed in 1541 as childish and contrary to the true faith, but other measures tended to support Catholic principles. Instructions issued to churches in 1543 continued to accept the true presence at mass, and images were tolerated on the grounds that they could 'provoke, kindle, and stir' devotion to God, if they were not themselves worshipped. Praying for individual souls was prohibited, but doing so for all souls was not.

The changing times were reflected in two wills made in Warwick, one made in 1545, the other a year later. The former is that of a canon, David Vaughan. He requested that prayers be said for his soul, for those of his parents, and for all Christian souls, a common way of side-stepping the injunction against prayers for individuals. He also asked that a hearse be placed over his grave with two candles on it, to be lit daily at mass. The other will was made by Richard Howe, who left money for a priest to say masses for a year for his soul, that of his late wife, and, again, all Christian souls. Both men were coming to terms with the new order, while clinging to the notion that purgatory might yet exist.

Henry VIII's will, made about a month before his death in January 1547, also reflected spiritual ambiguity, but was less subtle than Vaughan's or

Howe's. It provided for two priests to say daily masses for him for the rest of time at St. George's chapel Windsor, and he left one thousand marks to paupers who were to pray for his soul.

Perhaps Henry died a Catholic after all, but even so his reign had resulted in seismic change for St. Mary's. Its clergy and parishioners had to adjust to liturgical reform, and there were disastrous consequences for its finances. They were fragile anyway; the dean of St. Mary's was one of the richer men in Warwick, but that was of no benefit to the church's funds. Stunted economic growth meant that the population of the parish was probably below one thousand five hundred, not much more than it had been in 1086, and few of them were wealthy. Almost three quarters of those assessed for tax in 1543 had assets of five pounds or less, and the poverty of the town meant little to spare for offerings to the church.

Other sources of income dwindled to little or nothing as the Reformation took hold. Testators would no longer request – and pay for – masses to be said for their souls. Indulgences, once a virtual currency and, as we have seen, an important source of funds for the rebuilding of St. Mary's, had been abolished. With veneration of images falling foul of the new order, sales of candles to worshippers suffered, and even the candles themselves came to be considered idolatrous. The disparaging of relics must have hit St. Mary's badly; it is hard to resist the thought that the acquisition of so many of them was not unconnected with the financial difficulties of the fourteenth and fifteenth centuries. By 1538 the bubble had been pricked and they had to go, and with them the revenue that they attracted.

Reduced income was not the only reason for St. Mary's plight, as mismanagement and downright theft played their part. John Watwood, prebendary of St. Peter's since 1523, was singled out for blame. He was, it was said, a lecher, a fighter, and a disruptive influence; not qualities that a canon should aspire to. At Newarke college in Leicester, where he was also a prebendary, he had settled an argument with another canon by throwing beer into his face. In 1536 he was locked up in Warwick castle, on Bishop Latimer's orders and perhaps maliciously, for ringing the church bells on the feast day of St. Laurence, at a time when such commemorations were frowned upon. Watwood later managed to gain access to St. Mary's treasure chest, despite the requirement that its three keys were to be held by different persons, and decided that an advantageous way of spending the church's funds was for him to stay in London at its expense. Latimer's instruction that he return to Warwick was ignored. Summoned to Thomas Cromwell at Latimer's behest, Watwood was at first belligerent but calmed down later. By 1539 the loose canon had become reconciled with his fellow prebendaries, but he had died by 1542.

In 1538 Latimer wrote that St. Mary's was so poor that the vicars and other ministers had not been paid – a direct echo of 1367 – and he felt obliged to waive his visitation fees. He asked Cromwell for financial support for St. Mary's, perhaps 'some piece of some broken abbey', in other words, a grant of ex-monastery land. This is not as fanciful as it sounds, as an early justification for dissolving monasteries was to redirect their resources within the wider church, where they could be put to better use. St. Mary's had already lost what was described as its 'chief jewel', the statue of the Virgin Mary that had been bequeathed to it by Earl Richard, and given by Watwood to the king in an act of appeasement. Latimer asked that the gift of this magnificent piece be taken into account, but his plea fell on deaf ears, and his prediction that the college 'would grow shortly to nought' proved correct. In 1540 the king appointed John Reay, the lay sub-treasurer of St. Mary's, to be the receiver-general of its income, effectively taking financial responsibility away from the chapter.

47. Hans Holbein the younger's portrait of Thomas Cromwell, dating from 1532-33, captures well the ruthlessness of its subject. One can see that John Watwood would quickly have been put in his place.

The then dean, John Carvanel, resigned by 1542, and the vacancy was filled by John Knyghtley, one of Henry VIII's chaplains. Whether he had been appointed to try and turn the college round or to procure its dissolution matters not, for a little over two years later the chapter agreed to its own demise, seemingly without dissent. The college's assets were valued at a modest £58 14s 4d.

The downfall of the college saw the dean, five canons, and ten vicars-choral made redundant. The vicars had to make do the best they could. The prebendaries, on the other hand, all received pensions of between ten and twelve pounds a year, except the dean, Knyghtley, who got £23 6s 8d – not far short of his salary – even though they all had livings elsewhere. One of them, William Wall, the prebendary of St. Michael since 1540, became the first post-college vicar of St. Mary's, but kept his pension.

The history of the college had been a chequered one. Some periods were less than successful, a struggle to keep going through the times of uninterested and impecunious earls, compounded by lax controls and distracting arguments with their own bishop over jurisdiction. One may frown at the pluralism and absenteeism that was rife among the college, but that was commonplace and did not in itself imply dereliction of duty. Besides, the hard truth was that none of the prebends was particularly valuable, and it was inevitable that they were used, not just as an opportunity for patronage, but as a way of rewarding those whose principal source of income lay elsewhere. This was not necessarily to St. Mary's disadvantage, especially during the earldoms of Earl Thomas I, his son, and grandson, when its prebendaries included men of ability and foresight: John de Buckingham, Robert Mile, Richard Pirton, Thomas Younge, and William Berkeswell to name but five. It is no coincidence that they all enjoyed close relationships with their earl, and we owe them our gratitude for making St. Mary's as impressive as it is today.

In the four hundred years after its foundation as a collegiate church, St. Mary's had been enriched not only by its building but also with its fittings: jewelled tombs and statues; paintings; sumptuous vestments; silver chalices; finely worked cloths and hangings; Walter Power's canopy above the high altar, hung with chandeliers. The church would have looked splendid, and bustled with worshippers venerating images and relics, moving from one altar to another. Yet it was cash poor, exacerbated by the inability of successive chapters to preserve the church's holdings and to keep control of expenditure.

There was no patron to bail it out again, and besides, sentiment had turned against such institutions. The dissolution of the college became inevitable.

In 1544 the Crown took possession of St. Mary's and its satellite churches. The following year they all passed to the corporation of Warwick on its formation, in its capacity as trustee of the King Henry VIII charity, though the nave and tower of St. Mary's became the responsibility of the parish. The deal had been facilitated by the Guild of Warwick, which bought the college's assets from the Crown and then granted them to the corporation.

The corporation was granted tithes worth fifty-eight pounds a year, which was insufficient to meet its outgoings, and the shortfall had to be borne by the townspeople. The vicar of St. Mary's was to be paid twenty pounds, that of St. Nicholas ten marks, and at Budbrooke a paltry £5 3s 3d. St. Mary's also employed two chaplains, a clerk, and a sexton, who was a caretaker as well as grave-digger ('sexton' comes from 'sacristan', the person who looked after church plate and valuables). The chapter house, no longer required for its original purpose, was used as a meeting chamber for the corporation, and was described as the 'council house' in the minutes, which may have helped to ensure its immediate survival; the Beauchamp chapel was also used.

III

William Wall resigned as vicar of St. Mary's on 19 November 1558, just two days after the death of the Catholic Queen Mary. This may be too quick to conclude that her death was the reason for his resignation, but she had been ill for several months, so it would not have come as a surprise. If Wall was a Marian sympathiser, he must have been deeply troubled during the earlier part of his ministry. The reformers made little progress towards the end of Henry VIII's reign, but his death in January 1547 left a nine-year-old boy as king, and a wave of new assaults on tradition was unleashed by his advisers. A *Book of Homilies* was published within six months, along with a direction that every parish should have a copy, to be read from to the congregation every Sunday. Its texts devastated the old way. Predictably, purgatory, relics, images, candles, and bells were condemned, though doing so by describing them as 'by Antichrist invented' must have put many in fear as to what retribution they would face, in this world or the next, for their past devotion. Parish processions were banned, including those around the church before communion. Images were to be destroyed or obliterated, whether painted on the walls and screens, or appearing within windows. Even crucifixes and images of Christ, found in every home, had to go.

What followed has been described as 'a festival of destruction, a performance of gleeful triumph of the new ways over the old'.[13] In December 1547 the Chantries Act made endowed prayers for the dead illegal, with surprisingly little opposition. It well and truly put the final nail into the coffin of purgatory by declaring that:

> a great part of the superstition and errors in the Christian religion hath been brought into the minds and estimations of men ... by devising and sanctifying vain opinions of purgatory and masses satisfactory to be done for them which be departed.

The whole *raison d'être* of both guilds and the Beauchamp chapel was swept aside.

A few weeks later Candlemas was abolished, quickly followed by creeping to the Cross. A new Book of Common Prayer, issued in 1549, required the entire service to be conducted in English, stopped communion anywhere but at the high altar, and banned the elevation of the Host. The following year the bishop of London demanded that all altars be removed from churches on the grounds that they were a symbol of sacrifice; they were to be replaced by wooden communion tables, to better reflect the Eucharistic representation of the Last Supper. His stance was taken up throughout the country, and it duly became law. Ordinary bread was to be used for the communion, rather than consecrated wafers, and kneeling for it became controversial, on the ground that it could be seen as the worship of bread and wine.

Church interiors were being transformed. In 1547 St. Nicholas's removed its timber rood loft, sold its sepulchre and hangings, and replaced its altar with a communion table. The Paschal candle, lit at Easter to represent the light of Christ and weighing a hefty thirty-one pounds (fourteen kilos), was removed from St. Mary's in January 1549. The following year Thomas Fisher, who we shall meet later, paid 13s 4d for the stone of the high altar at St. Mary's, and Richard Oughton bought the timber around the altar for 5s 4d. Four pounds

---

13 Marshall, p.310; see *Further reading*.

of iron around the high altar and the altar in the Beauchamp chapel was sold for 7s 6d. It was something of a fire sale.

Images were removed and paintings covered up across the land, and St. Mary's chancel was whitened as a cost of 18s. In 1552, any goods and vestments considered non-essential were confiscated by the Crown, though much was sold or hidden before the commissioners arrived. There is no contemporary inventory for St. Mary's, but in 1465 it had five processional crosses, three of which were silver, nine silver chalices, four silver basins, six silver cruets, and four silver candlesticks. Countess Margaret Ferrers had given a sacring bell, a censer, and a pax – a plate engraved with the crucifixion that was blessed by the priest at mass and then passed to the congregation. They, too, were silver. There was also a silver gilt tabernacle – a box in which holy bread and wine were kept – with a jewel set upon it, given by Richard Beauchamp. They all disappeared, with a box used to put the pyx in during the Rogation Week sold for 8d.

Many parishes vandalised or removed monuments. Because their inscriptions usually began 'pray for the soul of …', or words to that effect, as Richard Beauchamp's does, they were seen to be a direct endorsement of the concept of purgatory, and therefore were to be eradicated. Brass memorials were sold off, with St. Martin's church in Leicester, later to become a cathedral, removing a staggering nine hundredweight (about four hundred and fifty kilos) of them. It may have been at this time that brasses in the nave of St. Mary's were defaced, including those of William Berkeswell and John Rous.

The miracle is that the fabric of the Beauchamp chapel survived largely intact: the image of Thomas Becket and other saints in the glass, the statues of saints around the east window, Richard Beauchamp's tomb. There are three possible reasons for this. First, there is evidence that the mood of both vicar and congregation tended towards the conservative, and would have covered up anything the new regime considered offensive, rather than destroy it. Secondly, Nicholas Heath, Bell's successor as bishop of Worcester, continued a policy of toleration and stayed out of the limelight until 1551, when he was sacked for refusing to enforce the removal of altars and images. And, thirdly, St. Mary's may have been protected by a man who saw St. Mary's as the church of his ancestors, and had no desire to see it vandalised: John Dudley. The Dudleys' involvement with Warwick in general, and St. Mary's in particular, is where our story takes us next.

– 8 –

TWO TAILS

I

WITH HENRY VIII's successor, Edward VI, a minor, the government was in the hands of a cabal of nobles led by Edward Seymour, earl of Hertford, and John Dudley, Viscount Lisle. Another prominent member was William Parr, the brother of Henry VIII's last queen, Catherine, who we shall meet again. One of their first acts was to grant themselves elevated titles, on the questionable ground that Henry VIII had intended to do so but had never got round to it. Seymour became duke of Somerset, Parr marquess of Northampton, and Dudley earl of Warwick.

Dudley's choice of title was no accident. He had been constable of Warwick castle since 1532, having requested the appointment on the basis that 'because of the name, I am the more desirous to have the thing, and also I came of one of the daughters of the right and not defiled line'. In other words, he saw himself as the true heir of the Beauchamp legacy, conferring prestige on the relatively inferior Dudleys. John Dudley was indeed Richard Beauchamp's great-great-great grandson, descended from Richard's daughter Margaret, countess of Shrewsbury, but whether he was the rightful heir was debatable. Nonetheless, it would have been unfortunate, to say the least, if Dudley's religious programme had resulted in the desecration of the church of the illustrious forebears he was so keen to be associated with.

Dudley's influence increased in 1549 when, following the downfall of Somerset, he became Lord President, the premier member of the council advising the king. In 1551 he secured his own promotion to duke of

Northumberland, and two years later he surrendered the Warwick earldom to enable Parliament to grant it to his eldest son, John. However, John died soon afterwards, and the title with him.

By 1553 Edward VI was ailing, and under the terms of his father's will his successor was to be his elder sister, Mary. There were two problems with that: her unwavering Catholicism, and her antagonism towards Northumberland and his associates. Edward, unlawfully, declared that on his death the Crown would pass, not to Mary, but to a future son of Frances, Henry VIII's niece who was married to Henry Grey, the former 'high steward' of St. Mary's. If Frances had no son, then any son of her daughters would become king. There were none, and Edward's declaration was amended, possibly through Northumberland's influence, specifically to name Frances's eldest daughter Jane as his heir.

48. An allegory of the Reformation, painted by an unknown English artist in about 1575. Henry VIII is on his death-bed, with Edward VI sitting beside him. The pope collapses under the weight of 'The word of the Lord [that] eduret[h] for ever', a reference to the Bible being the only path to truth. Images are being destroyed, top right. John Dudley is centre-right, alongside Somerset (to his right) and Archbishop Cranmer (to his left).

Jane Grey had three qualifications for being a suitable candidate for queen, but genealogy and legal entitlement were not two of them. She was a staunch Protestant; she was sixteen years old, and so a minor who could not rule in her own name; and she was Northumberland's daughter-in-law, following her marriage to his son Guildford. Nobody bothered about Jane's opinion, and the fact that she considered Princess Mary to be the legitimate heir was brushed aside.

It was a desperate attempt to preserve the new religion, and it failed miserably. Jane was destined to become known to history as the Nine Days' Queen, Mary took her rightful crown, and Northumberland had his head severed. Jane and Guildford were imprisoned in the Tower of London, as were Guildford's four brothers, John, Ambrose, Robert, and Henry. With delicious irony, these four were housed in the Beauchamp Tower, bearing the name of the family they were so keen to associate themselves with due to Earl Thomas II having experienced its hospitality in 1397. Jane and Guildford were executed in 1554, after her father had unwisely supported a pathetic attempt at rebellion. The other brothers were spared and released, with both Ambrose and Robert being pardoned in January 1555.

The Dudley brothers outwardly conformed to Mary's Catholic regime, and put pragmatism above faith by joining a force to support Mary's consort, Philip II of Spain, against the French. Meanwhile Mary swiftly ordered a return to the liturgy of the last year of Henry VIII's reign, though Edward VI's Chantries Act was not repealed, probably for the practical reason that to do so would have involved unscrambling property transactions.

At St. Nicholas's new images were painted and the rood loft re-installed, having been bought back from the widow of the man to whom it had originally been sold. Richard Oughton, who had bought the timber from around St. Mary's high altar for 5s 4d, sold it back for the same amount. The altar stones returned. These very much look like sham transactions, with the redundant items put safe and out of sight, preserved should they be needed again.

But Mary died in November 1558, barely five years after her accession. Childless, she was succeeded by her half-sister, the Protestant Elizabeth I. Ambrose and Robert were favoured immediately, with the former appointed Master of the Ordnance, the latter Master of the Horse. An illustration of Elizabeth's coronation procession, held by the College of Arms, shows

Ambrose leading the second litter horse (bearing the queen's litter) and, immediately behind him, Robert has charge of the palfrey of honour.

What the brothers really wanted though, was, as Robert himself put it, the restoration of the Dudleys to the name of Warwick. It finally came when Ambrose was created earl of Warwick in December 1561, with Elizabeth granting him the titular castle three months later. Robert had been appointed a Knight of the Garter in 1559, but he had to wait for his earldom, perhaps because of rumours that his relationship with the new queen was closer than thought proper for a married man. It became worse when his wife, Amy Robsart, died in mysterious circumstances in September 1560. He did, though, regain Kenilworth castle for the family in 1563 (his father had obtained it shortly before his death), and became earl of Leicester the following year. The Dudleys had become the dominant force locally, and Warwick soon found itself under their influence.

II

William Wall, who, coincidentally or not, had resigned as vicar of St. Mary's immediately after Queen Mary's death, was succeeded by John Leche. Little is known about Leche, or of how he came to be appointed to St. Mary's, but he was probably no radical. Although the advowson was now vested in the Crown, it may then have been exercisable by the bishop of Worcester, the Marian sympathiser Richard Pate.

Indeed, Warwick was not ready to shed all vestiges of the old religion. One of Warwick's two MPs in 1559 was the religiously conservative Thomas Fisher, the man who had bought St. Mary's high altar in 1550. His career began in John Dudley's household, but he then attached himself to the earl of Somerset, through whose influence he was appointed constable of Warwick castle in 1545. A year later Fisher acquired St Sepulchre's, which had been dissolved in 1538, and built on its site a house that became known simply as the Priory – the grandest in Warwick, bar the castle. He was imprisoned following the ousting of Somerset, but the wealth that he had accumulated remained intact, and he reinvented himself as a loyal servant of Queen Mary. He represented Warwick in four parliaments, the one in 1559 his last.

The other Warwick MP was Thomas Throckmorton of Coughton, the great-great-great grandson of John, one of Richard Beauchamp's executors, and a resolute Catholic. He had been an MP for Warwickshire in 1558, switching seats to Warwick the following year, possibly because he had sufficient influence in the borough to secure his election despite his beliefs. After all, his father, and no fewer than four of his uncles, had served as a Warwick MP since 1542. Generally boroughs thought it prudent to avoid sending Catholics to the 1559 Parliament, called to restore royal supremacy over the Church of England, but Warwick was an exception.

Wherever Leche's sympathies lay, his appointment was short-lived, as Edward Moseley succeeded him in 1563. By now the influence of the Throckmortons in Warwick had waned, and one of the town's MPs for the 1562 Parliament, Walter Haddon, was a committed Protestant. A Cambridge academic and lawyer, Haddon had no connection with the town or county, and is an early example of the local influence of Ambrose Dudley, with whom he was friendly. Whether Moseley too had reason to be grateful to the earl is a moot point, as the corporation did not yet share the Dudleys' enthusiasm for reform. In 1564 Edwin Sandys, an ally of Robert Dudley who had replaced Pate as bishop of Worcester, considered the mayor of Warwick (Thomas Fisher's brother, John) and six of the principal burgesses to be 'adversaries of the true religion'. However, such beliefs would come under pressure as the Dudleys came to dominate the area.

Mary's reign had seen dissatisfied and fearful Protestants flee to self-imposed exile on the Continent, particularly to Geneva, a city-state controlled by the controversial reformer, Jean Calvin. They started to return after the accession of Elizabeth I, and the Dudleys were quick to select their household chaplains from within their ranks. One was William Whittingham, who became a chaplain to Ambrose, and accompanied him to Le Havre in 1562, where Ambrose was leading an expeditionary force to support the Protestant French Huguenots. It was Robert Dudley who had encouraged Elizabeth to provide the Huguenots with military assistance in their struggle against the Catholic king of France. Ambrose not only allowed Whittingham to preach to the Le Havre garrison and to use the more extreme Genevan form of worship rather than the English Prayer Book, but he refused to stop when ordered to, ostensibly on the grounds that to do so would be offensive to his Huguenot hosts. On his return, Ambrose procured Whittingham's appointment as dean of Durham; Whittingham had not been ordained as a priest, but that was not an insurmountable problem.

Elizabeth I may have been a Protestant, but for some she was not Protestant enough, especially the returnees from Geneva. The queen had refused to be drawn to extremism, and even retained a silver crucifix and candles in her private chapel. Twice the cross was vandalised, and twice it was replaced. Instructions issued to churches in 1559 were riddled with compromise: bells were permitted, and though the Eucharist was to be performed at a communion table, it was to be dressed permanently with 'fair linen' with a covering of silk or buckram (a stiffened cotton): in other words, it was an altar, except for the consecrated stone. Three years later even a stone altar was ruled to be acceptable, though not compulsory; images were allowed provided that they were not idolised; and prayers could be said for the souls of the deceased generally, but not for individuals. Music was tolerated up to a point, but had to be 'modest and distinct', and therefore intelligible to the congregation. It was normally confined to anthems at the end of the service and during communion, which people attended only three or four times a year at most. On the other hand, transubstantiation and purgatory had gone for good, and, particularly pertinent to the iconography of the Beauchamp chapel, the Assumption of the Virgin and her coronation as Queen of Heaven were condemned.

A new word was entering the English language: puritan. At first it was derogatory, meaning an evangelical obsessed with purity both as an individual and as a foundation of church governance. As Elizabethan humour had it, a puritan was 'a Protestant frayed out of his wits'. King James I is said to have described them in terms that we recognise as the stereotype: pests, fanatics, and hypocrites. Puritans were never a coherent group, but, as one contemporary neatly put it, they can be characterised as ministers who 'seek reformation of some ceremonies and some part of the ecclesiastical discipline', and their followers as those who 'do hear sermons, talk of the scriptures, [and] sing psalms in private houses etc.' One could add to that list *ad hoc* fasting, called on the initiative of local ministers, and, especially after 1600, strict observance of the Sabbath.

There was, by now, a Protestant consensus that individuals were predestined by God to be, or not to be, saved, but there was debate over whether one could identify who was one of the elect. The establishment view was that one could not, and that it was necessary to conform to the Church of England to achieve salvation. Puritans, on the other hand, stressed the need for personal responsibility, believing that the godly could be identified by their unyielding obedience to the word of God as set out in the scriptures. Those who failed to meet the required standard should be excluded from the sacrament, in effect banished from the church and forfeiting their election. The role of the minister was to teach and encourage, to help the godly know and interpret God's will, and to support their faith. The trappings of ceremony were at best irrelevant, at worst a dangerous distraction.

It followed that puritans emphasised the value of preaching by trained men, and promoted the holding of *classis*, gatherings where preachers would meet to discuss the Bible and improve their own understanding of the scriptures. Both Ambrose and Robert supported them, despite opposition from the queen, who unsuccessfully tried to ban preaching and *classis*. She much preferred that ministers read to congregations from approved homilies. Nonetheless, *classis* flourished in the mid-1570s, and Southam, under its extremist minister, John Oxenbridge, became one of their leading locations, with Robert sometimes attending there personally. Robert even considered the establishment of a preaching centre at St. Mary's in the late 1560s, and one, possibly two, of his itinerant chaplains preached there in 1568. Quite how Robert was going to bring about such a centre is unclear.

Some puritans, but by no means all, rejected the need for an episcopacy. Pointing out that bishops are not to be found anywhere in the bible, they believed that bishops were unscriptural, unnecessary, and an obstruction to the true teachings of God. It became known as presbyterianism, a doctrine considered highly corrosive by Elizabeth I and most of her nobility. As the sovereign was the supreme head of the Church of England, which was administered through her appointed bishops, presbyterianism could be seen as a direct attack on her authority, and on the very fabric of society.

This was too radical for the Dudleys, who never supported presbyterianism, though they acted as patrons to those who did. Neither would they tolerate any criticism of their personal behaviour or lifestyle, accusing those who dared to of ingratitude. Overall, the Dudleys were committed promoters of preaching, but did not adopt for themselves the more extreme elements of puritanism. Despite these limits, Robert wrote that 'there is no man in this realm … that has shown a better mind to the furthering of true religion that I have done'. He was, arguably, right, but placing himself in the vanguard of puritanism did not preclude him from putting on a lavish display at St. Mary's.

III

On Saturday 29 September 1571, the feast day of St. Michael, Robert Dudley attended St. Mary's to commemorate his award of the Order of St. Michel, France's order of chivalry. He had been granted the honour in January 1566, as part of a diplomatic manoeuvre intended to rebuild relationships following the 1562 Le Havre campaign led by his brother Ambrose. Charles IX of France had been made a Knight of the Garter in 1564, but he could not reciprocate as the French Order did not admit women; it would have to be conferred on one of Queen Elizabeth's male subjects instead. Unsurprisingly, Elizabeth seems to have had reservations about nominating Dudley, not just because of his involvement with the Huguenots, but receive it he did. If Dudley had qualms about accepting the highest honour France could bestow from a Catholic king, to improve relationships that he himself had done much to jeopardise, he did not show it. No doubt the act of reconciliation salved his conscience, aided by the swelling of his ego.

49. Robert Dudley was very conscious of his image, and commissioned at least twenty portraits of himself, carefully constructed to convey the impression he wanted. This one, by an unknown artist, dates from ca. 1564. The insignia of the order of St. Michel, above his right shoulder, was added later, which explains the rather awkward composition. His jerkin resembles the one he wore for the ceremony at St. Mary's in 1571, and this picture gives a good impression of how Dudley would have appeared for the occasion.

It was quite a spectacle at St. Mary's. Dudley was dressed all in white, with velvet shoes lined with silver cloth, a silver doublet, and a white velvet jerkin embroidered with silver and gold that sparkled with jewels. His white satin robe was embroidered with gold a foot wide, and he wore a black velvet cap with a white feather. His collar was also gold, set with gemstones, and around his leg was the garter of the Order of St. George.

The procession started on foot from the Priory, where Robert was staying. It was led by gentlemen of Robert's retinue, who were followed by the burgesses of Warwick, two heralds, Robert himself, the earl of Hertford, and other dignitaries. Ambrose was absent, for reasons that are unknown.

The chancel of St. Mary's was resplendent. Set over the vicar's stall, on the right-hand side of the chancel, was a 'cloth of estate' – a hanging that formed a canopy over and a backdrop to a seat, and a symbol of high status. It was probably made of velvet, and it bore the arms of the king of France. On the other side of the chancel was a seat for Robert, adorned by his own arms encircled by the garter of the Order of St. George, and by a golden wreath formed of knots of scallop shells, symbolising the Order of St. Michel. The other stalls were hung with rich cloth or leather of gold. The communion table was draped with a tapestry, and positioned at the eastern end of the church where the altar had been, moved from what had become its usual position in front of the tomb of Earl Thomas and Countess Katherine on the grounds that the pulpit had been placed there. One wonders if any of those present remembered Walter Power's canopy above the high altar with a wry smile.

Robert bowed towards the French king's arms as he entered the chancel, and was escorted to his seat by the heralds. A sermon was followed by communion. As Robert approached the communion table to make his offering of a piece of gold, two gentlemen laid out a Turkish carpet in front of it. Robert knelt before the table on a rich cushion of white tissue (a delicate cloth, often woven with silver or gold). He returned to his place, bowed before his own arms, and was brought back to the table by the heralds, where he offered more gold. It was a far cry from the humble representation of the Last Supper that communion was meant to be, but demonstrations of rank and munificence took precedence over purity.

There is no doubt that Robert chose St. Mary's as the venue for the service due to its association with the Beauchamps, underlying the validity of the Dudley lineage at the very time that he was constructing a new building at

Kenilworth castle that was to be fit for a queen. Here at St. Mary's, the church of his ancestors, he could parade the glory of not one but two prestigious chivalric honours, and demonstrate that he was indeed a true descendant of Guy of Warwick.

IV

It was during this visit to Warwick that Robert considered the location of the hospital he was to establish for the relief of the poor and needy. He was accompanied by the elderly John Butler, who had been mayor of Warwick in 1555/56[14] and one of the town's MPs in 1558. Butler had a foot firmly in each camp, as he was not only still one of the town's burgesses, but also a Dudley retainer and, indeed, the keeper of Kenilworth castle. They inspected a site by St. Mary's churchyard on the Tuesday after the Order of St. Michel ceremony, but Robert did not consider it suitable. Butler then offered Robert the former guild buildings, including St. James's chapel. He did so, apparently, without the knowledge of the mayor or his fellow burgesses, but no matter: the arrangement would, Butler said, save Dudley five hundred marks. The deal was done, amid much confusion and embarrassment on the part of the corporation, already wrong-footed by a breach of etiquette in its greeting of the earl. Indeed, the corporation might well have been set up from the start by Butler, with there being no true intention to select the churchyard site. Be that as it may, the Lord Leycester hospital was duly founded by the end of 1571.

A second grand event took place at St. Mary's some six weeks after the St. Michel ceremony. William Parr, marquess of Northampton, had travelled to Warwick to attend the service, but was stricken by gout and could not leave the Priory. He died there on 28 October 1571.

Parr's fortune had nosedived since he was at the centre of government during Edward VI's minority. Convicted of treason at the same time as John Dudley, he audaciously denied his support for Lady Jane Grey, but his defence was undermined when it was pointed out that he was caught, armed, alongside Dudley when he was trying to secure Cambridge for the rebels.

---

14   Warwick's 'mayor' was known as the 'bailiff' until 1664 but, to avoid confusion, the term 'mayor' will be used throughout.

Parr was duly condemned to death and, like Dudley, tried to improve his chances by taking the sacrament according to Catholic rites. Parr was spared, but he was stripped of his title and lands.

A rehabilitation of sorts followed under both Mary and Elizabeth, including the restoration of his title, but Parr never regained his former position at Court, or his wealth. By the time of his death, Parr's widow claimed that he was so poor that she could not afford to pay for the funeral. Parr's nephew and nearest blood relative, the earl of Pembroke, offered to contribute a stingy one hundred pounds, wholly insufficient for a ceremony appropriate for a marquess, a Knight of the Garter, and the brother of a queen of England. Parr remained unburied until Elizabeth I agreed to foot the bill, and the funeral duly took place on 5 December.

The cortège was led by some twenty priests, followed by a gentleman carrying the marquess's standard, another his banner, and a herald dressed in his arms and bearing his coat of armour. Next came his achievements, with one herald carrying his sword and shield, another, the chief herald, his helm and crest. Behind them was the coffin, borne by eight gentlemen and covered with a pall of cloth of silver and bandekin (silk interwoven with gold thread) hung with escutcheons. Four other gentlemen in black gowns carried the banner rolls of descent, displaying Parr's ancestry. Bringing up the rear were the mourners and their entourage. The earl of Pembroke was expected to be the chief mourner, and the bishop of Worcester was to perform the funeral rites, but neither of them came.

A hearse had been placed in the nave, standing on four pillars about twelve feet high, covered with black cloth, and decorated with twelve escutcheons bearing the marquess's arms. His arms were also displayed on the canopy, again of black cloth, and on the valance. There were forty pennons of fine silk, each of which bore a metal escutcheon. The coffin was placed within the hearse, with Parr's achievements upon it.

A psalm was sung, followed by a sermon, and then the heralds led the carrying of the coffin into the chancel for communion. Offerings were made by the chief mourners, and Parr's were presented to the table. Each item was borne separately by a mourner led by a herald, who returned to his place before the next was brought up. Then came his banner and standard, and more offerings were given, accompanied by psalms. Finally, the coffin was taken from the hearse, and laid into a grave in the chancel.

After the service, all returned to the Priory for 'a very great feast', paid for by Elizabeth. The next day, Parr's achievements were hung above his grave, but there was a final indignity to be suffered. The heralds claimed the hearse and its cloths as their fee, but John Fisher, the brother of Thomas of the Priory, paid them eight pounds so, it was said, 'the country people resorting to the town might see the honourable order of part of the said funeral which standing is also benefiting of the church'. The achievements were still above Parr's grave seventy years or so later, but there was no memorial stone.

Despite the impecuniosity of the deceased and the seeming reluctance of the great and the good to attend, the funeral had the pomp appropriate for a person of distinguished rank, with its emphasis on achievements and lineage echoing medieval ceremony. Yet there were elements of modernity. Offerings were made for the benefit of the poor rather than for the saying of mass for the departed's soul, and the sermon was given not by the vicar of St. Mary's but by Rafe Griffin, a protégé of Robert Dudley, who had been master of the grammar school from 1565 to 1568. If preaching had been a novelty for St. Mary's it would soon get used to it, thanks to the Dudleys.

V

Ambrose and Robert had contrasting personalities, but remained close and often acted in concert. Robert had, and still has, the higher profile, not least because of his relationship with Queen Elizabeth. Ambrose was known as the 'good earl', a nomenclature bestowed upon him by a puritan in 1574 and earned through his religious views rather than any obvious sympathy with his comital subjects. He led a quieter life than his younger brother, not in the best of health through gout and a troublesome leg injured on the Le Havre campaign. He spent most of his time at his houses in Hertfordshire and London rather than at Warwick; indeed, it is doubtful if much of the castle was habitable during his tenure, and this may explain why Robert stayed at the Priory for the Order of St. Michel ceremony.

The brothers' absence from Warwick was no bar to their involvement in the town's affairs. For example, Robert successfully pressed the corporation to grant the tithes of Budbrooke to one of his followers. Conversely, the burgesses were not averse to seeking the Dudleys' financial help, and they took the opportunity of Robert being in Warwick for the ceremony of St.

Michel to ask for money. The salaries payable to the vicars were, they said, barely sufficient when set in 1545, but now inflation meant that they were not enough to support 'learned men' and their families. In their view, the vicar of St. Mary's ought to be paid thirty or thirty-five pounds, but they could not afford the increase. It seems that their plea fell on deaf ears. Two years later, the corporation sold two chalices and a silver and gilt crucifix that had somehow survived and been kept in the parish chest, raising £7 15s. Presumably they were melted down, the fate of much of England's medieval church treasure. The proceeds were used, not to benefit St. Mary's, but to repay a debt.

The corporation thought it prudent to add to their request to Dudley that the town was too poor to be able to pay for someone who could 'better instruct the people': in other words, a lecturer. Robert was more receptive to this, and agreed to provide one with a handsome annual pension of fifty pounds, compared to the twenty earned by the vicar. The man appointed was the preacher at Parr's funeral, Rafe Griffin, who had also become the first master of the Lord Leycester hospital. He was now also, officially, a preacher at St. Mary's.

Griffin seems to have been welcome in Warwick. On her visit to Warwick in 1572, the year after Griffin's appointment to St. Mary's, Queen Elizabeth was told that, without him, the townspeople 'should lack the heavenly food of their souls by want of preaching', adding, none too subtly, that the town was too poor to be able to have afforded him itself. Even the irascible and religiously conservative John Fisher, town clerk for twenty-seven years, twice mayor, and MP for three parliaments, praised Griffin for 'his great learning and rare life'. And Griffin was present for the final hours of Thomas Oken, a wealthy mercer who died in 1573. Oken specified that Griffin should preach at his funeral – the funeral sermon was itself a puritan innovation – 'to declare God's word to the people'.

But, as with Parr's funeral, there were echoes of past times; not surprisingly, given that Oken was born before the Reformation and was the last master of the Warwick Guild. Six poor men and six poor women were to carry Oken's body to St. Mary's, dressed in black cloth provided by him, and each to be paid 4d. The church bells were to be rung, and after the service a dinner was to be held, at the end of which those present were to 'praise God for the soul of [Oken and his wife, Joan] and all Christian souls

50. The memorial brass of Thomas Oken and his wife Joan on the wall of the north transept of St. Mary's, close to where they were buried. The inscription is finely balanced between what was, and was not, acceptable.

departed out of this transitory world'. The invocation to pray for the souls of specific persons was, by now, off-message, but Oken used the same formula that David Vaughan and Richard Howe had, almost thirty years beforehand. Oken's will also specified that his memorial should depict himself and Joan with the plea 'Jesu have mercy upon me' beneath each of them. That went too far, and the inscription reads instead '… give thanks for the souls of [Thomas and Joan] on whose souls hath mercy. Jesus hath mercy …'. Even that wording had become rare by then.

Within six years of Oken's death came allegations that money belonging to the charity that was founded under the terms of his will had been appropriated by members of the corporation for personal gain. Appeal was made to Ambrose Dudley, who called for an investigation. It resulted in court proceedings, and the dispute escalated into claims that accounts had not been produced and elections to the corporation not held. Another complaint was made about the corporation's finances in 1583, this time to Robert, and it is an example of how he was considered a suitable arbiter, despite him not being the earl of Warwick. Robert appointed none other than Griffin to investigate.

Griffin had clearly become a prominent member of the community, and the indications are that the vicars of St. Mary's were beginning to show more sympathy towards the new religion. William Bolton replaced Moseley in 1572 but resigned after only a year; it is not known why, but it may have always been intended to be a temporary appointment. Bolton was also rector of Beaudesert, to which Ambrose held the advowson, and where he stayed until his death in 1580. His successor at St. Mary's, Martin Delene, also owed his position to the patronage of Ambrose, and initial impressions were favourable. Shortly after his appointment the corporation recorded that his sermon had shown 'very learnedly the office of a good magistrate', but he would later become embroiled in controversy.

VI

If Warwick had been warmed by puritanism through Griffin's lectures, it became positively hot by 1585. The government had requested that the nominations for the Parliament of that year should be the same persons as those who had sat in 1584. One of those had been John Fisher, and the other was Thomas Dudley, a distant relative of the earls. Dudley's position was confirmed, but Fisher was challenged by the puritan Job Throckmorton, son of former Warwick MP Clement. The Dudleys had expressed themselves to be neutral, but it is difficult to believe that they were not backing Throckmorton; he certainly had influential sponsors among the local gentry, including John Harington of Combe abbey, near Coventry, who was elected for Warwickshire that same year, and Fulke Greville of Alcester. They were both Dudley clients, and Robert had knighted Greville at Kenilworth in 1566. Throckmorton also garnered support from 'the meaner sort' and the husbandmen of Bridge End and West Street, and a 'sober' dinner at the Swan Inn for between sixty and eighty of his followers may have been anything but, despite puritan dislike of excess. Bowing to pressure and alarmed at the prospect of a contest for which Throckmorton had stirred up the lower strata of society, the burgesses backed down and nominated him.

Throckmorton was not just of the 'hotter sort', as enthusiastic puritans became known, he was positively fiery. He wasted no time in using his position in Parliament to launch a viperous attack on Catholics and on the queen's foreign policy. Elizabeth's chief adviser, William Cecil, considered Throckmorton's remarks to be 'lewd and blasphemous', but Warwick's MP had not finished yet. Three months later Throckmorton gave a speech that championed puritanism and presbyterianism, and then turned on the leaders of Catholic nations, including James VI of Scotland. That crossed the line, and Throckmorton avoided the Tower only by going into hiding and writing a grovelling apology to Cecil. Throckmorton's parliamentary career was over, though he remained an outspoken advocate of puritanism until ill-health forced his retirement.

If having a puritan hothead stir up the town's meaner sorts was not bad enough, in January 1585 Rafe Griffin had been promoted, or kicked upstairs, by the Dudleys, to become dean of Lincoln. The suspicion is that he was moved on to create a vacancy for a man who, arguably, was the most notorious puritan of Elizabeth's reign (though Job Throckmorton could run him a close second): Thomas Cartwright.

Cartwright had been appointed a professor of divinity at Cambridge in 1570, only to be deprived of his chair a few months later for supporting presbyterianism. He fled to Heidelberg following the publication of several radical tracts that he either wrote or was associated with, including *An Admonition to the Parliament* (1572). It described the Book of Common

51. Thomas Cartwright, shown in a line engraving made in 1683, after an unknown artist.

Prayer, to which all ministers had to subscribe, as being 'culled and picked out of [a] popish dunghill', while bishops were called antichristian tyrants. The authors found themselves in Newgate prison, but were quickly moved to more congenial accommodation, probably due to the Dudleys' intervention. Cartwright, meanwhile, remained on the Continent until Robert Dudley procured first his return to England, despite Elizabeth I's objections, and then his position as master of the Lord Leycester hospital – but not without Cartwright paying a brief visit to the Tower for his beliefs.

The new arrival's fearsome reputation was put to good use, if we are to believe this account:

> There was one Mr. Chaplin, a woollen draper in Warwick, who made a profession of religion, but many times broke out into scandalous practices [possibly drunkenness]; Mr. Cartwright on a time walking with him in his garden [*i.e.* at the Lord Leycester hospital] dealt plainly and faithfully with him, rebuking him for his miscarriages, and showing him the dishonour that he brought to God and the gospel thereby; this so wrought upon Chaplin that he recently sunk down, and being carried home, died within a few hours after.

It may be apocryphal, but it was told approvingly almost sixty years after Cartwright's death by a supporter, Samuel Clarke, whom we shall come cross again soon.

Clarke's explanation for Chaplin's swift demise was that the Lord rewarded Cartwright's labours in his ministry with success in the conversion of many, and the 'terror and restraint' of others. That was not a universally accepted point of view. Matthew Sutcliffe, dean of Exeter and virulently anti-presbyterian, exchanged polemics with Cartwright in the 1590s, accusing Cartwright of delivering a sermon (presumably at St. Mary's) soon after Chaplin's death on the subject of Ananias and Sapphira, who were struck down for lying before God (Acts 5:4). Sutcliffe was implying that Cartwright could call on divine powers, and not just on this occasion. A man called Harris, he said, was threatened with God's wrath by Cartwright, and died soon afterwards, while one Browne died after Cartwright had delivered God's judgment on him for refusing to admit that he had got his maid pregnant. The verdict on Browne was passed even though his wife gave testament that he was 'impotent and unable to do it', evidence that was, intriguingly, said to be supported by others. Cartwright, of course, denied that he was able to summon up God's retribution on sinners; 'woe should be unto me if I should vainly boast of miraculous works', he said.

Sutcliffe was pursuing his own agenda, but there is no doubt that Cartwright was a controversial figure. He had been refused a licence to preach by Elizabeth I, despite pressure on her from Robert Dudley, but that did not stop him. On top of his stipend of fifty pounds for the mastership, Cartwright received another fifty pounds – as Griffin had done – from Dudley for his duties as a preacher. He regularly lectured at St. Mary's on Saturday afternoons, and on Sundays he preached at St. Nicholas's at seven am, and at St. Mary's in the afternoon.

Condemning the ungodly to hell was one thing, but preaching, as Cartwright did, against the law, government, and the liturgy of the Church of England, was quite another. Worse, he invited others of like mind to St. Mary's pulpit. Cartwright was duly summoned to appear before the bishop of Worcester, Edmund Freake, accused of 'disturbing the peace and quietness of the church by innovations and obtruding fancies and devices'.

There are differing accounts as to what happened. On one version, Cartwright was treated with calmness and courtesy by Freake, but he refused to answer the charges and left abruptly without taking his leave – despite the bishop having invited him to dine that evening. A different spin was put on events by Benjamin Brook, Cartwright's nineteenth-century biographer. More sympathetic to his subject, Brook claimed that Freake was an elderly, feeble, man who wanted a quiet life, and that he merely censured Cartwright, warning him that:

> You had best take heed that you run not upon the same rock on which the papists split, and draw upon yourself the same penalty that is ordained for those who alienate the hearts of the subjects both from their prince and religion.

If that was what Freake had advised, Cartwright ignored it.

Cartwright may have been reported to Freake by the vicar of St. Mary's, Martin Delene. Certainly, if Brook is to be believed, there was no love lost between them. According to him, Cartwright's lectures in Warwick were 'exceedingly offensive to men of severe principles and worldly ambition, who seldom or never preached, but who stigmatised them as innovations of ecclesiastical order and disobedience to the laws'. There is no doubt that Delene was one of the offended men he was referring to.

But Cartwright's position was becoming precarious. By 1590 his patrons and protectors, the Dudleys, were both dead. In that year Cartwright wrote to John Puckering, a self-made lawyer from Yorkshire who had risen to become a serjeant-at-arms, a small and select band of attorneys that represented the Crown. Puckering had acquired the Priory in 1582, even though he had no obvious connection with Warwickshire. He became Speaker of the House of Commons in the Parliaments of 1584 and 1586, the latter being that in which Warwick's MP, Job Throckmorton, had thought it necessary to give the queen the benefit of his advice on foreign policy.

Brook tells us that Cartwright was seeking Puckering's support for the 'poor church in Warwick, that likely enough may be deprived of all manner of tolerable ministry … in regard to the poor souls there'. It was hardly a ringing endorsement of the vicar of St. Mary's, but the appeal has the air of desperation. Puckering was not a natural ally of Cartwright (though Cartwright addressed him as if he were), and, indeed, may have been encouraged by the moderate and influential Sir Christopher Hatton to acquire the Priory to act as a bulwark against the growth of puritanism in Warwick, and, by implication, as a check against the Dudleys' local power.

Cartwright had good reason to be nervous; four months later charges were laid against him by the archbishop of Canterbury. They ranged from a refusal to kneel at communion, his alleged authorship of the presbyterian *Book of Discipline*,[15] and:

> that since his settlement in Warwick, he and others had agreed to hold, and had holden, divers public fasts, without the Queen's authority, and had invited sundry persons to be present to preach three, four, or five in succession, all of whom were noted for disliking sundry points in the Church of England … And since his abode at Warwick, he had nourished faction and heart-burning of one inhabitant against another, by distinguishing them as godly and profane.

Meanwhile Delene had been succeeded as vicar of St. Mary's by Leonard Fetherston. Fetherston would have been an ally of Cartwright, having attended conferences of puritan preachers, signed the *Book of Discipline*, and being described in a puritan survey of ministers in 1586, when still at Long Itchington, as 'diligent and honest'. However, he was deprived of the living of St. Mary's in January 1591 for unknown reasons, and replaced by Andrew Bordman. Bordman was anything but sympathetic, and, according to Brook, accused Cartwright of being:

> … so confident and implacable against the Church of England that he could not endure Mr. Bordman and others preaching at sundry times at Warwick to speak in defence thereof

Moreover, it was said that Cartwright:

> took upon him to confute … those things which Mr. Bordman had truly and dutifully preached. In his sermons, at Warwick and elsewhere, he had delivered many frivolous, strange, and indiscreet positions; that it was requisite that hearers of the word, who were able, do stand up during sermons …

---

15 Authorship of the *Book of Discipline* is now generally attributed to Walter Travers, a long-standing associate of Cartwright's.

The animosity was mutual, with Cartwright complaining that Bordman was inviting to St. Mary's preachers whose sermons were entirely composed of invective against him. He also feared that Bordman was not content with the livings of St. Mary's and Alvechurch, which he held in plurality, and wanted to add the mastership of the Lord Leycester to his portfolio. If true, discrediting Cartwright would be a good way to further that end.

In a quirk of fate, when Cartwright's case came before the court of the Star Chamber the prosecuting counsel was none other than John Puckering. Cartwright, having previously sampled Newgate and the Tower, was now sent to the Fleet prison pending the verdict. However, he was released, unsentenced, in 1592, and then spent six years in Guernsey, not returning to Warwick until 1601. He preached at St. Mary's for the last time on Sunday 21 December 1603 on the prescient text 'the then dust shall return to the earth, and the spirit shall return to God who gave it' (Eccles. 12:7). On 27 December he spent two hours praying on his knees in his rooms at the Lord Leycester, and told his wife that he had 'found wonderful and unutterable joy and comfort', God having given him a glimpse of heaven before he came to it. He died later that day, and was buried in St. Mary's churchyard. As a parting shot his funeral sermon was preached by his friend John Dod, a popular hardliner who he had called 'the fittest man in England for a pastoral office'.

VII

Robert Dudley died at his house at Cornbury, Oxfordshire, in September 1588. His will expressed a desire for a 'convenient tomb or monument ... at Warwick where sundry [of] my ancestors do lie'. He meant the Beauchamps, not his father and grandfather, who were both executed as traitors and rest, headless, in the graveyards of Blackfriars priory and St. Peter ad Vincula in the Tower of London respectively.

Robert also asked that his funeral 'be done with as little pomp or vain expense ... as may be, being persuaded that there is no more vain expense than that is'. No chance. On 10 October a procession of his banner, achievements, horse, two trumpeters, and some four hundred people, including one hundred poor, began at Kenilworth castle and made its way to St. Mary's. Ambrose was due to attend, but did not, presumably due to ill-health. The funeral sermon was preached by the bishop of Salisbury, a favourite of Elizabeth I who, the following month, was chosen by her to deliver a sermon at a thanksgiving service at St Paul's for the defeat of the Spanish Armada. The chief mourner was Robert's stepson, the earl of Essex, and others included his brother-in-law, the earl of Huntingdon, and Henry Clinton, earl of Lincoln, who was from a family of long-standing Dudley allies. At the other end of the social scale were Robert the fisherman, Abraham Campion, a brewer, and Ann Crowe, a laundress at Kenilworth. The 'without vain expense' funeral cost a staggering three thousand pounds, despite Robert Dudley's legacy of fifty thousand pounds of debt.

Ambrose died less than eighteen months later, in February 1590. He lies in the Beauchamp chapel with Robert, according to the inscription on his tomb to be near his 'noble ancestors' and his brother. It has been suggested, unconvincingly, that his desire to show his affinity with the Beauchamps explains the colouring of his armour, in imitation of latten.

The Dudleys' contrasting public personae is reflected in their tombs. Ambrose has a memorial with an almost apologetically medieval air, while Robert's is fashionably garish. One Victorian writer was unimpressed, comparing Robert's monument to a mountain of confectionery, though, in Robert's defence, several of his contemporaries' tombs were far more outlandish. And while Robert rests his head on two plump tasselled pillows, Ambrose lies in humility on a rush mat.

Both monuments are of high quality. Ambrose's has been attributed to the Cure workshop in Southwark, either Cornelius, a Dutchman who had settled in London to become Elizabeth I's master mason, or his son William. The Cures are known to have made the tomb of Ambrose's widow, Anne Russell, the daughter of the earl of Bedford, but they are most famous for the tomb of Mary, Queen of Scots, at Westminster abbey. Robert's was almost certainly made in the Midlands, perhaps by another man of Dutch descent, Jasper Hollemans, at Burton-on-Trent. Both the Dudley tombs display their connections, not only with the Beauchamps, but with many of the great families of the past. They are a dazzling demonstration of status and entitlement, a clear attempt to bypass the misfortunes of their immediate predecessors and to rebut forcefully the contemporary rumour – false – that their great-grandfather had been a mere carpenter.

The first Dudley display of rank in the Beauchamp chapel was, in fact, on the memorial to Robert, Lord Denbigh, the son of Robert and his second wife

Lettice Knollys. He was nicknamed 'the Noble Impe' – 'impe' then meaning a child (usually of noble descent), without the implication of devilment that the word later acquired. The size of his effigy belies his age, as he had just turned three when he died in 1584. It is a very rare effigy of an infant, the lad unbreeched and wearing his reins (or 'leading strings'), a poignant testimony to his parents' anguish.

Denbigh's monument, which may well also be by Cornelius Cure, records the descent from the Beauchamps, something repeated on Ambrose's tomb. However, his parents' tomb goes way beyond this. Behind their effigies is a collage of sixteen banners that associate the Dudleys with many of the noble families of the Middle Ages, some of whom are also represented in a coat of arms on the front of the monument. To reinforce the message of Robert's accomplishments, status, and chivalric credentials, the Order of the Garter is shown no fewer than five times, along with the garland of the Order of St. Michel, twice. Never mind that, less than a year after the ceremony in St. Mary's, Charles IX had unleashed the massacre of thousands of Huguenots, who Robert had defended in 1562.

The responsibility for the design of Robert's tomb lay with Lettice, buried alongside him even though she quickly remarried and outlived him by forty years. She too wanted her place in the Beauchamp chapel, and the tomb – as well as the cost and pageantry of her late husband's funeral – says as much about what she considered to be her rightful place in the social hierarchy as his: the wife of the most famous earl in England and, probably, the granddaughter of Henry VIII through his relationship with Anne Boleyn's sister, Mary. There is certainly a remarkable resemblance between Lettice, as shown on her portraits and effigy, and Elizabeth I.

There is one emblem that, more than any other, connects the Dudleys with their Warwick past, and shows their determination to be associated with the Beauchamps: the bear and ragged staff. Used sparingly on Ambrose's tomb, though a bear lies at his feet, the badge is prominent on the Noble Impe's, and prolific on Robert's. Outshining the Dudley device of a lion with two tails, it was blatant appropriation of an emblem to underline the Dudleys' prestigious ancestry. The ragged staff was used to form the stem of Robert's initials, as at a fire surround at Kenilworth, and the family tree in the sixteenth-century manuscript *Descents of the earls of Warwick and Essex* (*see image 13*). And there is a further significance to the young Denbigh's moniker of Noble Impe, for

The Dudley tombs in the Beauchamp chapel:

Left: 52. Robert Dudley, 'the Noble Impe'. The effigy is of a figure much larger than the Nobel Impe would have been when he died. This may have contributed to the erroneous belief that a child's suit of armour on display at Warwick castle had belonged to him. The inscription on the tablet beneath the effigy sets out the line of descent of the Dudleys from Richard Beauchamp.

Below: 53. Ambrose Dudley, earl of Warwick, with his younger brother's behind him.

Right: 54. Robert Dudley, earl of Leicester, and Countess Lettice.

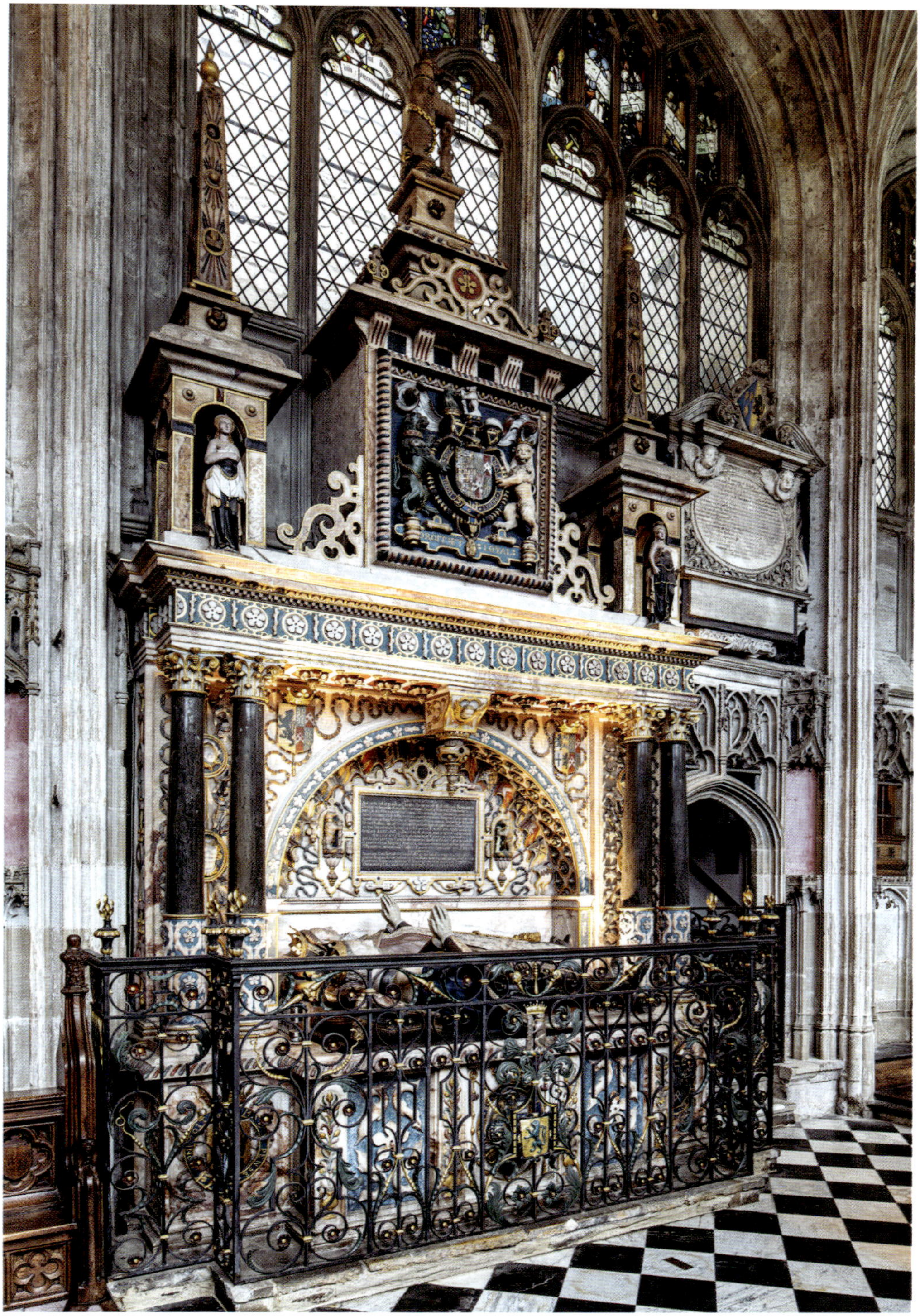

'impe' also meant a sprig or shoot; in other words, he was Dudley's long-awaited heir, and the plant that he was sprouting from was the ragged staff.

Some were unimpressed with the Dudleys' use of the bear and ragged staff. 'The bear wants a tail and cannot be a lion' became a local proverb that alluded to the Beauchamp and Dudley badges, directed at people who aspire to a status above their worth.

* * *

The Reformation put paid to the benefits that St. Mary's had received from the kind of patronage shown by the Beauchamps. The earls of Warwick would no longer enrich the church by gifting valuable artefacts, by directing masses to be said for their souls at one of its many altars, or by constructing buildings of stunning beauty. St. Mary's had become duller, with side altars, statues,

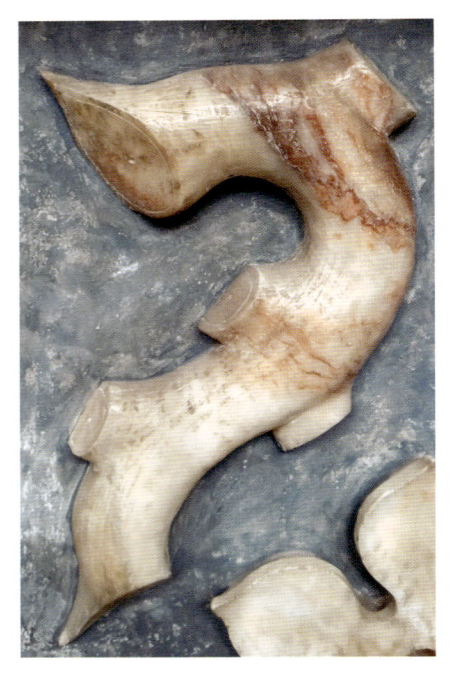

Robert Dudley wasted no opportunity to display the bear and ragged staff as a reminder of his lineage.

Above left: 55. This historiated 'T' is the first letter of the founding charter of the Lord Leycester hospital in Warwick.

Above right: 56. The ragged staff features heavily on Robert Dudley's tomb, including, as shown here, in the form of a mouchette.

jewels, and images gone; much fewer candles; the colour and sociability of processions and feast days abolished; the mystique of a Latin high mass superseded by Genevan functionality. The crucifix on the rood loft had been replaced with the royal arms. Yet proponents of the new religion, bolstered by the Dudleys, would say that St. Mary's was now a purer place. Religion had become more understandable and relevant to worshippers, who could now communicate with God directly without the impediments of saints and theatrical ritual, aided by lecturers who explained and exhorted.

The parishioners of St. Mary's had been exposed by Cartwright to extremist preachers who challenged the Church of England head-on, against the views of their vicar. Most probably ignored him, but, as the charges against Cartwright and the objections of Delene reveal, it was a distressing and divisive time. After a period of calm, it would get worse.

– 9 –

GODLINESS

I

AMBROSE DUDLEY had no children, and on his death the earldom lapsed again. Warwick castle had fallen into a dire state on his watch. It was riddled with rot, lead from the roof had slipped or had been stolen, and the stone walls of its chapel were barely standing. According to Thomas Spencer, the lecturer at St. Mary's between 1633 and 1635, it had become 'a habitation of night-monsters, a court of satyrs, a house of hags, a dwelling of the screech owl, and of the flying mouse'. Caesar's Tower was used, he said, as 'an uncouth prison of felonious persons, clogged with fetters and bolts of iron'. Fulke Greville, he who had supported Job Throckmorton in his bid to become a Warwick MP, wanted to use stone from the castle to rebuild the family seat of Beauchamp's Court, Alcester. Thankfully, Queen Elizabeth did not agree, and in 1604 King James I granted the castle to Greville's son, also Fulke. Rather than demolish it, Fulke rebuilt the castle to create a modern and comfortable residence, at a reputed cost of over twenty thousand pounds, though that is probably an exaggeration. Like the Beauchamps before them, the Grevilles abandoned tradition in favour of Warwick: it was Beauchamp's Court, which the family had held since 1266, that soon fell into disuse.

Although Greville was a long-standing member of Elizabeth's court, he was never one of her inner circle, and the highest office he reached was Navy Treasurer. He was ousted from government when James I came to the throne, to be recalled ten years later as an outside choice as chancellor, with a remit to restore the Crown's finances. He had some success, but could neither overcome widespread corruption at Court nor rise above shifts in the political fortunes of others. To his disappointment he was cast aside again in 1620. His elevation to the baronetcy the following year, as Lord Brooke of Beauchamp's Court, was something of a consolation. The earldom of Warwick, meanwhile, had been granted to Robert Rich of Essex, severing the connection between it and the castle until 1759.

Greville enjoyed a friendship with Sir Philip Sidney that dated from childhood. They were the same age, and they started school at Shrewsbury on the same day. Sidney's father, Sir Henry, was the Dudleys' brother-in-law, and always closer to the centre of power than Greville. Indeed, it is likely that Greville was introduced at Court by Sir Henry, and that he was dependent on his influence to obtain various offices under Elizabeth. After Philip was killed at Zutphen in 1586, serving under his uncle, Robert Dudley, Greville was determined to ensure that a book of his friend's poetry was worthy of his memory and, almost certainly, oversaw its publication himself. Sidney was buried, without a memorial, in St Paul's cathedral, and Greville had the bizarre idea of erecting a pathos-charged double tomb for them both, Sidney elevated above him. It never happened, but had it been made, Greville would have been put to rest where he had spent much of his life: in Sidney's shadow.

Fulke Greville was a moderate puritan, though his faith intensified later in life. He was never the fount of patronage that the Dudleys were, and, even when the opportunity arose, he did not favour the hotter sort. Lancelot Andrewes was preferred to the deanery of Westminster on Greville's recommendation, and was far from radical. Neither did Greville involve himself in the affairs of Warwick; indeed the town clerk wrote, probably harshly, of his 'private and obscure manner [that] caused him to be disregarded [and] … would neither by purse nor power be seen in the affairs of the corporation'.

Greville's lack of interest in local religion, in stark contrast to Robert Dudley, coincided with a hiatus in radical preaching and demands for presbyterianism generally. The position of lecturer at St. Mary's had been left vacant after Cartwright's death, and it was not until 1611 that the corporation appointed Richard Roe. And, in 1620, a sermon was preached in Warwick supporting conformity with the Church of England.

On 1 September 1628, at his house in Holborn, London, Greville was stabbed twice by his servant Ralph Haywood, who then fatally turned the knife on himself. Greville was seriously wounded in the back and stomach, but survived until his surgeons decided to replace damaged tissue around his intestine with pig fat. He died in agony from putrefaction, thirty days after his wounding.

Rather than to St. Paul's, Greville's body was carried to Warwick castle and then to St. Mary's, where it was laid in a vault in the crypt. Directly above it, in the chapter house and far too big for the space, is the monument that he had installed some seven years beforehand, made by the London carver Thomas Ashby at a cost of two hundred and eighty pounds. On it were placed his achievements – helm, crest, shield, sword, gauntlet, and spurs – and his banners and pennons hung from the walls. Medieval traditions lived on.

Sombre and brooding, made largely of black marble relieved by white alabaster insets now brown with grime, Greville's memorial needs to be considered in the contexts of his life, values, and the monuments of his contemporaries. The popularity of heraldry on tombs was fading, and the brashness of memorials such as Robert Dudley's, pre-dating Greville's by less than thirty years, was falling out of fashion. It was an era of freedom of expression for funerary architecture, with a penchant for extravagance and pomposity. Sir Francis Vere's tomb in Westminster abbey (*ca.* 1609) depicts Vere lying on a rush mat, like Ambrose Dudley, but there the reference to humility ends. The effigy lies beneath a marble slab, borne by four strapping knights, on which Vere's armour is laid out. This two-tier design was also used in the more classically influenced tomb of Robert Cecil (died 1612) in St. Etheldreda's church, Hatfield. It shows the kneeling Faith, Justice, Fortitude, and Prudence, effortlessly bearing a slab on their shoulders on which lies Cecil's effigy, beneath which is a cadaver.

Greville's monument rejects the ostentation of Vere's and Cecil's. The principal message is found in the simple epitaph that encircles the sepulchre: 'Fulke Greville, servant to Queen Elizabeth, chancellor to King James, and friend to Sir Philip Sidney'. This has been seen as referencing the chivalric virtues of honour and loyalty, and certainly the display of his achievements suggests that these were valued, but there is no need to draw this comparison. The epitaph lived in the present, not the medieval past, and reflects those aspects of his life of which he was most proud – service and friendship.

There is another inscription on Greville's memorial. On its north side, barely visible in the poor light, are the enigmatic words 'Trophaeum Peccati': 'sin's trophy', or 'sin's monument'. It is a declaration of humility; an

Left: 57. The brooding memorial to Fulke Greville, by Thomas Ashby. Little is known about Ashby, and this is the only monument that can be attributed to him.

Below: 58. The tomb of Sir Francis Vere (died 1609) in Westminster abbey. It reflects Vere's career as a soldier, including serving under Robert Dudley in the Netherlands campaign of 1585.

awareness of his shortcomings; an admission that, no matter how great his qualities, he was a sinner; an acceptance of unfulfilled potential and of falling short of what God had predestined for him. It is an expression of failure, of apology, of self-examination, of dignity, a plea for the Lord's forgiveness. As a *memento mori*, it negates any suggestion of vanity that the tomb might otherwise invoke far more successfully than Robert Cecil's cadaver or Vere's rush mat. Greville's memorial stands in stark contrast to the egotism exuded by the likes of Vere's and Cecil's, and, for that matter, Richard Beauchamp's.

Some have interpreted 'Trophaeum Peccati' as a coded message. One suggestion is that it is a reference to Greville being homosexual, for which there is no evidence (any suggestion that he and Sidney were lovers is baseless), and even if he was, it is not something to be admitted on a Jacobean tomb. Others have interpreted it as meaning that Greville was concealing some other secret, such as his supposed authorship of Shakespeare's *Antony and Cleopatra*. The chatter surrounding this became so intense that in 2010 an endoscopy was performed on the monument to see if it revealed any clues, or even, as some thought it might, the bones of Sidney. It didn't.

II

Fulke Greville's heir was his cousin's son Robert, who was about twenty-one years old when Fulke died. It was some step up, from minor Lincolnshire gentry to the title of Lord Brooke and possession of Warwick castle. Brooke was the most enthusiastic of puritans, and fiercely presbyterian. He considered bishops to be anti-Christian usurpers of the power of God, and, in a particularly extreme comment, that they were worse than Anabaptists – schismatics who had become associated with anarchy. Bishops were also, of course, institutionally papist: 'if any man please to survey episcopacy with an impartial eye', he wrote, 'he shall find [it] and popery to be all one in re'. That was as insulting as it could get.

The accession of Charles I in 1625, three years before Brooke's arrival in Warwick, was a catalyst for heightened religious tensions. The uneasy peace enjoyed during his father's reign was threatened by the new king's apparent sympathy with papists, fuelled by his marriage to the openly Catholic Henrietta Maria. Worse, William Laud was a controversial choice for archbishop of Canterbury in 1633. Believing strongly in conformity, Laud was hostile towards puritans, and wished to see a Church of England that was nearer to that at the time of Henry VIII's death. In doing so, he alienated those puritans who had come to terms with the *status quo* during the reign of James I.

The vicar at St. Mary's was now the long-serving Thomas Hall, who had been appointed in 1596. He, like Laud, was a traditionalist, and so had a very different outlook to Brooke. Tension was inevitable. Brooke promoted the puritan cause by encouraging a programme of lectures, that could now be heard at St. Mary's every Tuesday morning. There were also lectures on Sundays at St. Mary's, St. Nicholas's, and at the castle chapel, the timing of which was deliberately staggered so that people could go to all three. They attracted large congregations drawn from a wide area, with the practice of going to other parishes to hear sermons being known as 'gadding', hence 'gadding about'. It was an intensely social occasion, as people on their way to St. Mary's or one of the other venues walked in groups, singing psalms, and discussing the merits of the preacher as they returned.

Among the lecturers that could be heard in Warwick were Richard Roe, one time lecturer at St. Mary's but who had been vicar of St. Nicholas's since 1616; John Bryan, the rector of Barford; Thomas Spencer, lecturer at St. Mary's and later minister of Budbrooke, and whose colourful prose we have already experienced; the itinerant John Poynter; Ephraim Huitt, minister of Wroxall; Richard Vines, a very popular preacher and minister of Caldecote and Weddington, near Nuneaton; and Simeon Ashe and Peter Sterry, both chaplains at the castle. Poynter had been ejected from a lectureship at Wootton Wawen in 1632 (presumably because of his views) and moved to Warwick for short time; Huitt would flee to New England in 1639 to avoid prosecution for his beliefs and was lauded as a martyr to tyranny; Vines was appointed an 'orthodox divine' by Parliament, to be consulted by it on religious matters; Ashe quickly took up arms to fight for Parliament when civil war loomed; and Sterry would become chaplain to Oliver Cromwell. They all had solid puritan credentials, but they were not all of like mind: for example Brooke's chaplains, Ashe and Sterry, did not share their patron's opinions on presbyterianism.

Two men on the lecture circuit were particularly noteworthy. One was Thomas Dugard, who was appointed master of the school in Warwick in 1633 at the age of twenty-five. Despite owing his appointment to Brooke's patronage, he was a moderate, and even enjoyed a close friendship with Thomas Hall. Dugard was well regarded in the town, and when Charles I came to Warwick in August 1636, attending a service in the chancel of St. Mary's on Sunday 24th, Dugard proudly gave the welcome oration. It was conventional and uncontentious – and in Latin. Brooke, on the other hand, publicly snubbed the king by openly leaving for London five days before his arrival.

The other notable lecturer was Samuel Clarke, who was appointed to St. Mary's in 1628 as a deliberate attempt on the part of the burgesses to present more 'godly' views than those held by the conservative vicar, Hall. According to Clarke's own account he was 'sought for' by the corporation of Warwick, despite him having recently been barred from the pulpit of both St. Michael's and Holy Trinity in Coventry, and banned from preaching anywhere there by the bishop – an injunction that he defied. Not surprisingly, Hall objected to Clarke's arrival, and the town appealed to Brooke, who wrote to Hall. The minister of St. Mary's was, in Clarke's words, 'overawed', and backed down.

Relations between Hall and the corporation were clearly fractious. He first appears in the records in 1594, when, as the master of the school, he asked to be relieved of his obligation to say prayers at St. Mary's because to

59. Samuel Clarke, as shown in an etching made some sixteen years after he left St. Mary's. Like many of his radical contemporaries, he was to welcome the restoration of Charles II, but he could never come to terms with demands to reject presbyterianism.

do so conflicted with his other duties, which he was accused of neglecting. His request was refused. He also complained that there were too many rival teachers in the town, which 'ensured diversity of opinion and prejudiced the good education of young scholars'. Clearly, thirty years before his objections to Clarke, he was not one to tolerate competing views. Hall's pugnacious character was revealed again in 1618, when the burgesses asked the mayor to speak to him about his 'invective sermons and reproachful and scandalous speeches' against them, threatening to report him to the ecclesiastical authorities unless he desisted.

It is possible that the cause of the dispute was his pay, and, if it were, it surfaced again 1631. Hall threatened legal proceedings unless he received an increase to his stipend, now fifty pounds per annum. The corporation's response was to tell Hall that if he proceeded with the lawsuit his stipend would revert to twenty pounds, the amount fixed in 1545. A compromise of a ten pounds increase was reached due to his age, his increased expenses, the way he performed his duties in visiting and comforting the sick, and his hospitality and charity in relieving the poor. Hall may have been dogmatic and cantankerous, but he seems to have had redeeming qualities, and it must be admitted that arguments between ministers and their paymasters were far from unusual.

Duly appointed as Hall's assistant, Clarke preached at St. Mary's every Sunday and Tuesday for over four years, and, he said, achieved 'much room in the hearts of all the godly in the town'. But Hall did not see it that way; Clarke accused him of always looking to pick a quarrel, and thought that this arose from Hall's envy of Clarke's relationship with Brooke. Certainly Hall, unlike Roe at St. Nicholas's, was never invited to preach at the castle.

In 1633 Hall complained about Clarke to John Thornborough, bishop of Worcester, an act that Clarke would have attributed to the hand of Satan. We do not know precisely what the grounds were, but according to Clarke it was for 'the omission of ceremonies' – perhaps refusing to make the sign of the cross, or not kneeling at communion. He had faced similar complaints in Chester and Coventry. The final straw may have been Clarke's refusal to read to the congregation, as he was obliged to do, the *Declaration of Sports*, an edict originally issued by James I and reissued by Charles I in 1633. It was highly contentious because, contrary to puritan beliefs, it encouraged 'lawful recreation' on Sundays, such as archery and dancing.

Dugard supported his friend Hall against Clarke, but Clarke escaped without punishment due, he said, to Bishop Thornborough being 'an old man, and peaceable'. It has echoes of Bishop Freake's treatment of Thomas Cartwright. Thornborough certainly had no appetite for confrontation; he was probably sympathetic to Clarke, yet he implemented Laudian reforms. An indignant Hall was, according to Clarke, reduced to 'pull[ing] me out of the pulpit, and by his clamours and noise so interrupt[ing] me that I was forced to give over'. Hall then went over his bishop's head by travelling to London to complain directly to Archbishop Laud, though nothing came of it. Nonetheless, Clarke was sacked from St. Mary's to avoid further trouble, a detail omitted from his autobiographical note. Brooke swiftly preferred Clarke to the vacancy at Alcester, where he held the advowson, and Clarke was replaced at St. Mary's by Spencer. But Hall had not seen the back of Clarke, who, despite his dismissal, regularly returned to preach at Warwick.

James Cole, who moved to Warwick in 1634, was 'amazed' by the godliness of the town, though that may be either an exaggeration, or a reflection of the enthusiasm of a dedicated puritan. He wrote that there were 'two great congregations', neither of them using the Book of Common Prayer, crosses, or surplices, as they should have been, and no-one knelt at the sacrament. There was only, he said, a puritan service of 'reading the Word, singing of psalms, [and] prayer before and after sermon with catechism'.

The two congregations that Cole was referring to must have been St. Mary's and St. Nicholas's, but it is very doubtful that he was accurately portraying any service led by Hall, given the grounds upon which Hall had reported Clarke the previous year. Cole's account is also called into question by the findings of a visitation to Warwick shortly afterwards to assess compliance with Laudian policy. Not surprisingly it found Hall to be 'conformable', and so was his assistant, Spencer. However, there were unsubstantiated doubts about Roe. Spencer and Roe must have been on their best behaviour.

The message of the puritan lecturers was far from comfortable. As well as regular reminders of the evils of popery, the congregation at St. Mary's would have been implored to observe a strict moral code, especially the Ten Commandments. They were to eschew the evils of drunkenness, brawling, and swearing. Dancing and music were condemned as distractions from the true path and opportunities for temptation. The Devil constantly lay in ambush. Meticulous observance of the Sabbath was essential, which is why men like Clarke could never accept the *Declaration of Sports*.

While at Alcester, Clarke went so far as to say that life was a perpetual war with the world, and Huitt at Wroxall spoke of a daily fight with inward fears and outward troubles. The battle had to be fought with self-examination of one's soul, utilising frequent prayer and bible reading. If the torment of hell were to be avoided, one had to acknowledge one's sins and seek redemption through prayer and repentance. A state of grace could only be attained through introspection; there were no shortcuts through outward conformity, and the ritual of the communion service was at best a distraction. The route to redemption was solitary and desolate, a message delivered bluntly by Richard Vines when he said that 'if we cannot know ourselves to be miserable, we cannot know God to be merciful'. No wonder puritan preachers earned the epithet 'painful', and that Fulke Greville could write of the 'dark desolation' of his soul and memorialise his suffering by dedicating his monument to sin.

III

Puritan fanaticism could lead to conflict. There are no accounts of civil unrest in Warwick, if one discounts Hall's manhandling of Clarke out of the pulpit of St. Mary's, but it cannot be ruled out. There was elsewhere in the Midlands. In Wolverhampton, anti-Laudians vandalised the altar rails, moved the communion table back to the nave, and threatened violence against a moderate curate. When the churchwardens of Ellastone, Staffordshire, took the table out of the chancel, the vicar immediately put it back, and was indicted before the Quarter Sessions for his trouble. The removal of a cross from a Kidderminster churchyard caused a minor riot. Closer to Warwick, the vicar of Napton was assaulted in the chancel of his own church, and Francis Holyoake, the minister of Southam, left no doubt where his sympathies lay by publishing a dictionary that defined the core Calvinist belief of predestination as heresy. He was poles apart from his *classis* holding predecessor, John Oxenbridge.

Nationally, most people were content to conform to official policy, and would not have been unduly bothered if their minister made the sign of the cross or gave the sacrament to a congregation that was kneeling. Painful ministers were wont to complain of apathy, though their definition of it was wide enough to include those who disagreed with them. The presence of so many committed godly lecturers in Warwick must have had some effect, but they may literally have been preaching to the converted, and most of the townspeople probably ignored them. The puritan manifesto was not one that was likely to have universal appeal, and puritans were gaining a reputation as hypocritical killjoys. The archdeacon of Gloucester, preaching in Warwick in 1619, reflected this and, referring to the first issue of the *Declaration of Sports* the previous year, said:

> I could wish that these zealous and painful preachers ... would for a time forbear these maypoles and Morris dances, and other such trifles, upon which they spend too much of their strength.

Those who paid attention to the sermons at St. Mary's would have heard conflicting messages. In 1630, in a barbed reference to the likes of Thomas Hall, his own vicar, Clarke complained of those who:

> ... preach[ed] frequently ... but profit not the people [or] preach mercy to the benefit [of the] broken hearted and discourage them in the way of godliness [or] preach peace to those against whom judgment is to be denounced.

Hall would have had no difficulty with maypoles and Morris dancing, notwithstanding their pagan overtones, nor with playing football after church on Sundays. He would have emphasised the benefits of churchgoing and participation in communal worship and ceremony as against introspection and anguish: the church would help you in your quest for eternal peace. It was more comforting, more inclusive, and frankly more attractive to most. And there is evidence that one social tradition from the past, walking the boundaries of the parish, was still performed at St. Nicholas's as late as 1640, with the churchwardens providing beer and bread for the participants. Puritans disapproved, not only because of the festivity and the opportunity for excess that it offered, but because of its overtones of paganism.

There are two people from Warwick, both puritans, for whom we have a record of their religious experiences. Abiezer Coppe was born on 30 May 1619, the son of a reasonably prosperous tailor, and baptized two days later at St. Mary's. He became a pupil at the school under Dugard, and attended godly lectures in town. At one, perhaps unwisely in view of future events, he was told that the thought of adultery was worse than the act itself.

According to his own account of his life in Warwick as a teenager, Coppe prayed every evening and at midnight, read the bible each day, memorised large parts of scripture, frequently fasted, and confessed his sins 'with grief of soul, sighs and groans, and frequently with tears'. He added:

> Tears were my drink: dust and ashes my meat … sackcloth my clothing. Zeal, devotion, and exceeding strictness of life, and conversation, my life.

Fearing that his soul had become 'besmeared over with filth and uncleanness', he kept a ledger of his sins and, taking literally the words of Matthew 5:37 – 'let your communication be yay, yay, nay, nay; for whatsoever is more than these cometh of evil' – he wrote these words on a band around his wrist, raised the appropriate hand in response to any question, and bridled his mouth. He was still only thirteen.

Four years later, in 1636, Coppe went up to Merton College Oxford, where, apparently, he compromised his puritan credentials by having an affair with a married woman. He failed to graduate, and returned to Warwick in 1641. He preached at one Sunday and five Tuesday lectures that year, even though he was almost certainly unlicensed to do so. At first, he was probably a more-or-less orthodox presbyterian, but the outbreak of the first Civil War unleashed a wave of radicalism which Coppe was swept up in. He embraced Anabaptism, claiming to have baptised seven thousand adults, mainly in Warwickshire, and then joined the Ranters, a sect that denied the authority of God and scripture and held life to be a moral free-for-all. The puritan minister Richard Baxter, who was in Coventry from 1642 and himself no stranger to controversy, accused Coppe of swearing 'most hideously' while preaching, and of 'filthy, lascivious practices'.

Coppe's unpalatable behaviour landed him in Coventry gaol, probably in 1646, but it did not curb his ranting. He continued to preach that social constraint inhibited a state of purity, and that no law, man-made or moral, could stand between man and God. This was tantamount to anarchy. 'I can, if it be my will,' Coppe wrote, 'kiss and hug ladies, and love my neighbour's wife as myself, without sin' and practised what he preached. He was said to be 'living very loosely … spreading blasphemies and committing base lewd sins', and to be preaching stark naked by day, and lying stark naked and drunk with a harlot at night. Presumably it was less sinful than merely thinking about doing so. Coppe was lambasted by cartoonists, who revelled in the opportunity afforded by a 'puritan' who endorsed merry-making and sexual licence.

In January 1650 Coppe published the notorious *A fiery flying roll: a word from the Lord to all the Great Ones of the Earth*, that, besides promoting his extreme views on personal behaviour, criticised both the privilege of royalists and the hypocrisy of parliamentarians, in far from measured terms. Parliament immediately condemned *A fiery flying roll* for its 'many horrid blasphemies and damnable opinions' and ordered that every copy in the realm be found, and burnt 'by the hands of the hangman'. Coppe was arrested for blasphemy and treason, and imprisoned again, this time in Warwick, before being moved to Coventry and then Newgate. Eventually he was released, and, horrifyingly, in 1667, under the assumed name of Higham, he was granted a licence to practice medicine and surgery, which he did in Barnes, south-west London. He died there in 1678, reputedly (and not surprisingly) of syphilis.

The second of our Warwick puritans was infinitely more chaste but provides an equally tragic story. Cecily, or Cecilia, was the second daughter of Sir Thomas Puckering. Puckering had inherited the Priory from his father John (he to whom Thomas Cartwright had unsuccessfully appealed for protection), and made it his principal residence. It was widely believed that Sir Thomas had converted to Catholicism in his early twenties, and his wife was the daughter of a suspected papist, though there can be no doubt about the puritanism of his later years.

Cecily was just thirteen when she died on 9 April 1636. Her funeral sermon at St. Mary's was preached by John Bryan of Barford, an example of how the relationship with a minister could now be a personal one that transcended parish boundaries.

Funerals were often used by painful preachers as an opportunity to reinforce a strict puritan message, but Bryan was comparatively restrained. Taking as his text Proverbs 31:29: 'Many daughters have done virtuously, but thou excellest them all,' he categorised virtue as:

> … a gift of God's spirit, and a part of regeneration whereby man is apt and able to deny all ungodliness and worldly lusts, and to live soberly, righteously, and godly in this present world.

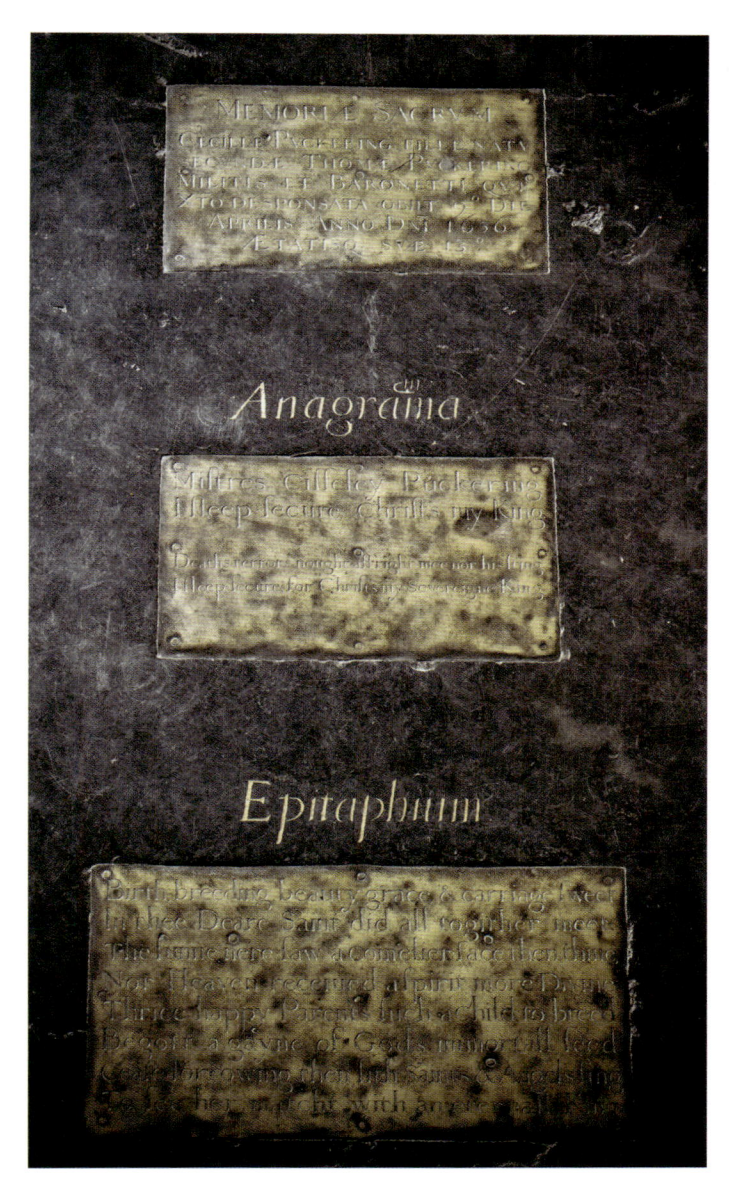

60. The badly worn ledger stone of Cecily Puckering (1636), the work of either Nicholas Stone the elder of Westminster or his son, also Nicholas. As it is relatively simple, it might be an apprentice piece by the latter. Its inscription implores the reader to rejoice in Cecily being in a better place, the anagrama beginning 'Death's terrors nought affright me, nor his sting / I sleep secure, for Christ's my sovereign King'.

It was a classic formulation of the puritan message, and Bryan expanded the theme through constant reference to relevant scripture, emphasising that the word of God was central to one's life and was to be found through personal study of the Bible. The virtuous not only knew the difference between good and evil, Bryan said, but they put it into practice. They were motivated by an inner virtue, because 'a corrupt tree cannot bring forth good fruit' (Matthew 7:18).

Bryan spoke of how Cecily had earned the right to be judged virtuous. He made it clear that, in doing so, he would not flatter her, as that would both 'rob her of her due honour' and be untrue before God and his audience. Virtue, he said, was a combination of knowledge, piety, and patience. He gave several examples of how Cecily had been imbued with 'knowledge', which we might equate with faith. But it is his exposition of the components of piety – self-denial, sanctification, and devotion – that tell us most about Cecily's life as a sickly, deeply religious, child.

When Bryan had asked Cecily if she would rather suffer pain, or commit a sin to be released of it, she opted for the former. She loved her parents, but not as much as she loved Christ. She could find no good in her life, only a great deal of evil. Bryan only saw Cecily smile twice, he said, and, on both occasions, she was expressing a preference for death over life. However, she feared that she was laden with more sin than sickness, and had neglected her scriptures. She bore her illness with fortitude, and when Bryan asked her if she felt that God had dealt her harshly, she said 'no, truly I do not, but I think he deals with me very well, because I have been so wretched a sinner'.

Bryan concluded by addressing Cecily's parents directly. Her piety had set them a good example, revealing to them the true meaning of virtue. Her death had drawn them closer to God, and it was a matter of rejoicing because 'the day of their death is better than the day of their birth' (Ecclesiastes 7:1). The ability of godly ministers to find a biblical quotation for anything knew no bounds.

Such was the message to the parents of a girl, barely a teenager, who had died not a week beforehand after a long and painful illness, and who was the second daughter they had lost: Cecily's older sister Frances had also died while young. Their comfort was their rejoicing for Cecily's gain, which overcame their sorrow. There was no cause for them to 'overmuch lament' her death, Bryan wrote in the dedication of the printed sermon to her parents, because 'God has blessed you with many children, though one but be living'. He was referring to their third daughter, fourteen year-old Jane, but she was also sickly and not expected to live.[16]

It would be wrong to dismiss Cecily as a too-good-to-be-true prig, and Bryan as a callous preacher with no sense of compassion. Bryan knew the

---

16 The prognosis was unduly pessimistic. She lived long enough to be kidnapped and taken to Flanders in an attempt to force her marriage, but she returned to marry Sir John Bale of Leicestershire. She died in 1652.

family well and could be relied upon to deliver a message that would not offend, and it was a message that was fully in tune with the puritan emphasis on personal faith, acceptance of one's sins, and redemption through piety. Rather, we should embrace the comfort that Cecily sought and found in God in her time of pain, and her parents' consolation that she died with inner peace, destined to a place in heaven. To a seventeenth-century puritan, these were indeed matters for rejoicing.

IV

Cecily's legacy was one of humility, her black marble ledger stone in the chancel of St. Mary's just as much a monument to sin as Greville's tomb. The same can hardly be said of her father's, which is an essay in self-aggrandisement from someone who had achieved but modestly.

Only four years old when his father died, Sir Thomas Puckering was brought up by his mother at the Priory. When his sister married Adam Newton, the tutor to Henry, prince of Wales, he forsook Warwick school to move to the royal household, to be educated alongside the prince and with a view to a career in his service. However, Henry died in 1612, and, after a tour abroad and marriage, Puckering returned to the Priory to lead the undemanding life of a landed gentleman living off his inheritance. Ambition does not seem to have been one of his stronger points, but with an estimated annual income of two thousand pounds it did not need to be.

Puckering became MP for Tamworth in 1621, and, three years later, he served as sheriff of Warwickshire. He was not popular in Warwick. He became embroiled in a dispute with the corporation over tithes due from the Priory, and lost. The town's minute book describes Puckering as 'a natural enemy to corporations', and the burgesses refused to adopt him as their nominee for Parliament in 1625, preferring Francis, the sixth surviving son of Sir Thomas Lucy of Charlecote. Despite living at the Priory, Puckering was, they said, 'but a stranger in the country', had 'a natural malignancy', and was 'not so commodious by sending corn to the market for the general good of the people, nor a man of such noble hospitality, as that worthy family … the Lucys.' Francis Lucy, it may be noted, lived in London.

Puckering's response was to accept a seat at Tamworth again, and to challenge the Warwick burgesses' right to control the nominations for the town's MP before a Parliamentary committee. It was not the way to repair his reputation with the locals. After an undistinguished political career, Puckering retired to the Priory on the dissolution of Parliament in 1629. His foundation of a hospital for eight poor women of Warwick in 1630 may have been an olive branch to the town, and in 1633 he gave land for the building of six houses for use by tradesmen, who were obliged to take apprentices nominated by him.

Puckering died in March 1637, less than a year after Cecily. Preposterously, his monument was erected against the south wall of the chancel, close to the sanctuary, ensuring that it would not go unnoticed, and ruining the concentration of drama on the tomb of Earl Thomas and Countess Katherine.

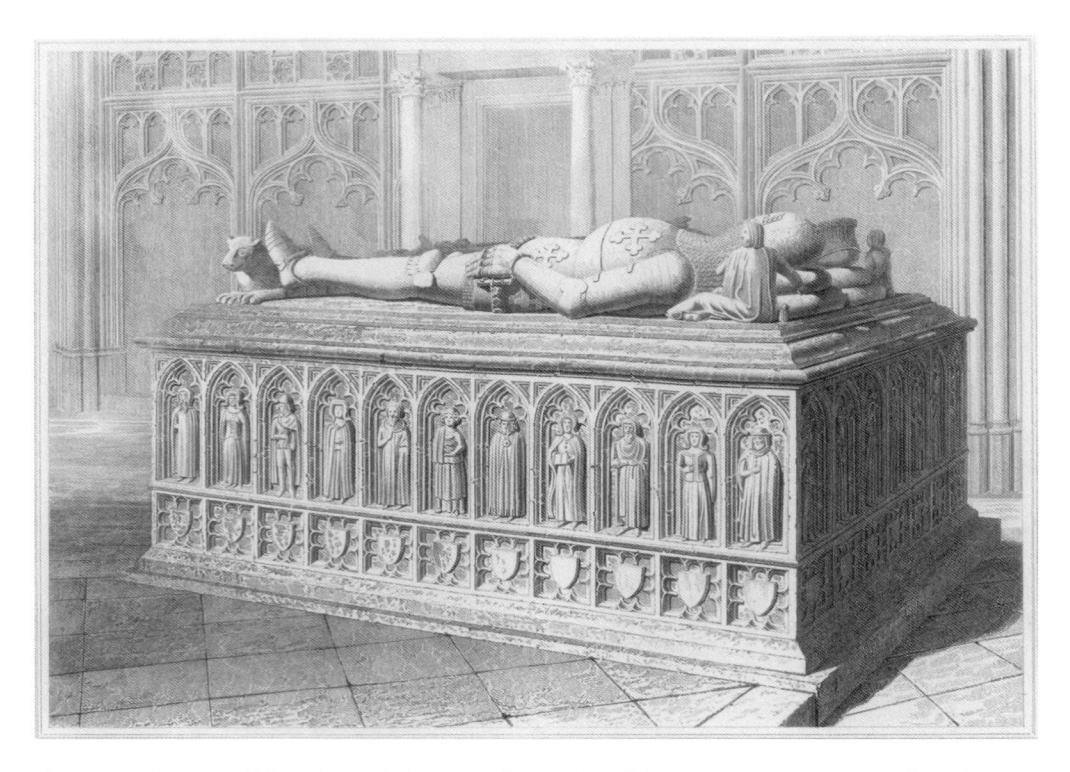

61. *A rare image of the chancel showing the tomb of Thomas Beauchamp and Katherine Mortimer with the memorial to Thomas Puckering behind it. It was drawn by Edward Blore for a book illustrating the tombs of 'noble and eminent persons' published in 1826. Blore had the good sense to show the Puckering tomb in minimal detail, so as not to distract from the subject matter or from the attractive blind tracery on the south wall.*

Admittedly it was by the graves of his daughter Cecily and his grandmother, Elizabeth Chowne, but that only underscores Puckering's appropriation of an intimate space. The Victorians sensibly moved it, though its cramped location in the outer vestry is less than ideal.

The memorial is the work of Nicholas Stone the elder, the leading mason-sculptor of his day and then at the pinnacle of his profession. Stone's portfolio of work is impressive. He undertook several commissions for James I, and he was the chief architect for Charles I's work at Windsor, becoming his master mason in 1632. Under the direction of Inigo Jones, he built both the Banqueting Hall in Whitehall and the renowned and novel Tulip staircase at the Queen's House, Greenwich. At the time of Puckering's death Stone was working on Goldsmiths' Hall in London, which he designed and built. Coincidentally, he also rebuilt Cornbury, the former house of Robert Dudley.

Puckering's memorial, which cost two hundred pounds, is made of black and white marble and rance (a dark reddish-brown limestone with white and red veins). It is surmounted by a segmental pediment broken by a coat of arms and supported by two columns and four pilasters. The tomb bears an inscription, in Latin, that tells of Puckering's life, with none of the poignancy and economy of Fulke Greville, nor the genuine achievement of Robert Dudley. The meagre and rueful epigraph, written by Puckering himself, cannot disguise the need to make the best of a bad job:

> … Who notwithstanding his education in the royal palace for the space of seven years, and having attained so high a degree of honour as to be the only person admitted fellow student to Prince Henry, eldest son to King James, and notwithstanding his having travelled through the greater and more polite [cultured] part of the Christian world for almost four years, yet upon his return to his country would not again re-embrace the life of a courtier … but being weary of the alluring charms which attend a Court and a city life he afterwards chose to live in the country as a method of life most proper for the serving of God and giving him an opportunity to be at leisure for himself …

It might have been better to have bowed to humbleness and said nothing. By his own admission, Puckering's one achievement of note was to be educated with Prince Henry, but he owed that to his brother-in-law, Adam Newton, and Puckering and Henry had different tutors anyway.

BEATAM PLACIDE EXPECTANS RESVRRECTIONEM

SVB ISTO TVMVLO REQVIESCIT THOMAS PVCKERING MILES
ET BARONETTVS, FILIVS IOHANNIS PVCKERING, DOMINI
CVSTODIS MAGNI SIGILLI ANGLIÆ, NATV MINNIMVS:
HÆRES TAMEN DVOBVS PRIORIBVS IN INFANTIA A MORTE
ABSORPTIS. QVI TAMETSI A PVERITIA IN AVLA REGIA PER
SEPTENNIVM INNVTRITVS, IN EOQ HONORIS ATQ FAVORIS
GRADV, VT SOLVS HENRICO PRINCIPI, IACOBI REGIS
FILIO PRIMOGENITO, STVDIORVM PARTICEPS ADMISSVS ESSET.
PERVAGATVS POSTEA MAIOREM CVLTIOREMQ. CHRISTIANI
ORBIS PER QVATVOR FERE ANNOS PARTEM, REVERSVS
TAMEN IN PATRIAM VITAM AVLICAM POST MORTEM
INCOMPARABILIS ILLIVS PRINCIPIS HERI SVI CLEMENTISSIMI
ATQ. AMANTISSIMI (QVEM DEVS OMNIPOTENS ERO SVMMA
IN IPSVM MISERICORDIA ET IVSTA IN POPVLVM INGRATVM
INDIGNATIONE SIBI IN CÆLVM ASSVMPSERAT) REAMPLECTI
NOLVIT: QVIN PERTÆSVS VTRIVSQ. VITÆ TAM AVLICÆ QVAM
VRBANÆ ILLECEBRAS, RVSTICAM (VTPOTE DEO INSERVIENDO
SIBIQ. VACANDO MAXIME IDONEAM) DEINCEPS DEGERE ELEGIT.
IN QVA CONSTANTER PERSEVERANS, SINGVLIS MVNERIBVS
FVNCTVS QVÆ SIVE REGIO FAVORE, SIVE POPVLARI
BENEVOLENTIA, IN EQVESTRIS DIGNITATIS VIROS
BENEMERITOS RVRI AGENTES CONFERRI SOLENT, CVRSVM
FELICITER PEREGIT, ANNVM AGENS ÆTATIS SVÆ
QVADRAGESIMVM QVINTVM

VXOREM HABVIT VNAM ELIZABETHAM NEMPE FILIAM
VNICAM IOHANIS MORLEY EQVITIS AVRATI, EX PROVINCIA
SVSSEXIANA: FILIAS EX EA SVSCEPIT TRES, QVARVM
MAXIMA NATV FRANCISCA INFANS OCCVBVIT, SECVNDA
CECILIA MERITO PATRI=CHARISSIMA SENEX (QVOD
VIX CREDI POTERIT) SINGVLARI PIETATE ÆTATE IVVENIS
DECIMO TERTIO ANNO ÆTATIS SVÆ MVNDO VALEDIXIT
TERTIA VLTIMA IANA 7.ᴹ AGENS ANNVM IAM SVPERSTES
SOLA MOX EST MORITVRA.

Puckering directed that his tomb be similar to Newton's, also made by Stone, in St. Luke's church, Charlton, as indeed it is. Newton was rather more successful than Puckering, and much closer to the Crown than a fellow student of a prince. Following his tutoring of Prince Henry, Newton became his secretary, and, after Henry's death, the treasurer of Prince Charles's household. He was dean of Durham from 1606 to 1620, due to royal influence, despite not being in holy orders. He acquired the manor of Charlton in 1606, and, in 1628, succeeded Fulke Greville as secretary to the marches of Wales, a position that swelled his wealth by a further two thousand pounds a year. On his death in 1630, he left money for St. Luke's to be totally rebuilt.

By mimicking Newton's memorial, Puckering is implying that he considers himself to be his equal, but their *curricula vitae* are very different. Surely, the allure of a monument appropriate to the rank that Puckering perceived to be rightfully his – its size, its location, its quality, its maker, its epigraph – got the better of him. As the proverb says, the bear wants a tail and cannot be a lion.

V

As tensions mounted nationally towards the end of the 1630s, a closing of the Protestant ranks in Warwick was in the air. Thomas Hall, very much a representative of the old guard, died in July 1639, having spent forty-three years as vicar of St. Mary's. His old friend Dugard had witnessed his will, and preached his funeral sermon. That November Hall's successor, Richard Venour, entertained Lord and Lady Brooke at dinner, along with Mr. and Mrs. Dugard, Mr. and Mrs. Bryan, and Peter Sterry. It was a remarkable gesture on the part of Brooke, echoing that of Richard Beauchamp towards Dean Younge. Perhaps it was intended to signify that the coldness between himself and St. Mary's was behind them.

In December 1640 Venour signed a petition of Warwickshire ministers against Archbishop Laud, who was impeached for high treason by the House of Commons that month; it had been organised by the moderate Dugard. The following August the town clerk of Warwick, Edward Rainsford, praised Brooke's contribution to 'the restitution of our religion, for our sky became

Left: 62. The memorial to Sir Thomas Puckering, by Nicholas Stone the elder (1639).

fearfully darkened, papal innovation coming on apace upon us' – despite Rainsford's resentment of Brooke's evasion of his responsibility to pay tithes due to the corporation, and his opposition to Brooke having nominated both MPs for the two 1640 Parliaments. Brooke had tried to have him dismissed as a result. But fear of popery, a term that was beginning to encompass anti-puritanism in general, was a unifying force. Three months after Brooke's attempt to remove Rainsford, Warwick was officially warned of an impending Catholic uprising, amid numerous rumours that quickly spread throughout the Midlands.

In March 1642 Parliament declared all county militia to be under its control, and Brooke was appointed the commanding officer of its forces in Warwickshire, Staffordshire, Leicestershire, and Derbyshire. Three months later it issued the Nineteen Propositions, which included the need for the king to obtain Parliament's approval for the appointment of privy councillors, ministers of state, new peers, and the commanders of forts and castles, as well as to the education and marriages of his children, to foreign policy, and to church government and liturgy. Charles's authority would have been eviscerated. Civil war became inevitable.

The fundamental problem was Charles I's unshakeable belief in the divine right of kings: that his authority to rule was derived from God alone, and that he was accountable only to God. This clashed with Parliament's political ambitions and with puritan emphasis on personal responsibility. Moreover, many believed that the country was under threat from state-sponsored papism. Politics and religion had become inextricably linked. John Doughtie, vicar of nearby Lapworth, wrote presciently of the link between the established church and the good order of society. Both, in his opinion, were dependent upon the authority of the monarch.

Many contemporaries thought religion responsible for the rift between Crown and Parliament. Thomas Dugard considered that the *Declaration of Sports*, which Samuel Clarke had refused to read at St. Mary's, 'was the cause of all the war and bloodshed in this nation', while Thomas Spencer at Budbrooke blamed a Jesuit plot, and drew no distinction between Catholics and royalists. In doing so, Spencer was echoing the views of his patron, Brooke. Brooke told his captains at Warwick that they were fighting the king to defend God's true religion against 'papistical malignants', a term that could well have encompassed the late vicar of St. Mary's, Thomas Hall, and he described his soldiers' opponents as either 'notorious papists or popishly affected persons'. Diametrically opposed to this was the antiquarian Sir William Dugdale, an implacable supporter of the Crown, who complained of seditious preachers who had 'poison[ed] the people with their antimonarchical principles'.

By June 1642 some one thousand seven hundred armed volunteers, plus hundreds more who were unarmed, were at Warwick castle, ready to fight for Parliament. They were supplied with two cartloads of ammunition, a wagon laden with gunpowder, bullets, and four cannons, for the castle's defence. The men were to receive a tempting 4s 8d a week, and were fortified with 'wine and strong drink'.

The following month, Brooke sent six pieces of ordnance to Banbury, a Parliament stronghold, with the intention of using it to supplement Warwick castle's armoury. It was seized by the royalist earl of Northampton, who brought it to Warwick with a somewhat different purpose, entering the town unopposed on 9 August. So began the extravagantly termed 'siege of Warwick'. Northampton's son, Lord Compton, bombarded the castle from the tower of St. Mary's. Return fire knocked off a pinnacle, but that seems to have been the only damage suffered by the church, despite one of the cannons on the tower misfiring and blowing up. The ordnance was promptly moved to West Street to continue the attack from there, but after two weeks, without any progress being made, Northampton sought to bring matters to a head. Five thousand of his troops faced seven thousand of Brooke's, two miles outside Warwick. Northampton, outmanned and with no prospect of further military support, withdrew his forces.

Warwick became a centre for a considerable number of soldiers who were prepared to fight for Parliament, and, by implication, for its more extreme religious doctrines. The parishioners of St. Mary's could not have been immune from their influence, for good or bad. The risk of opposing Parliament was evident when a force from Warwick castle paid a visit to Southam, the month after the 'siege'. One of the soldiers who took part described the minister, Francis Holyoake (he who thought Calvinists to be heretics), as 'very malignant' and 'of very evil and desolate conversation'. In other words, he was a royalist. His house was raided and a drum, ammunition, saddles, muskets and powder were confiscated. Five years later, by when the doughty Holyoake was approaching eighty, four-fifths of his estate were confiscated as a punishment for inciting his parishioners and keeping arms. Holyoake died in 1653 and was buried in the north transept of St. Mary's, though the memorial to him, erected by his grandson, is now in the southern one.

Brooke emphasised the need to teach royalist sympathisers like Holyoake a lesson in a speech he made in the House of Lords in December 1642. In it, he declared that their lordships should not 'out of any worldly respect for estate, wives, children, honour, good nature, compassion, care of trade, or laws, grow slack or lazy in our undertakings' but should 'proceed to shed the blood of the ungodly'. So violence, even murder, in the name of godliness trumped compassion: was this the message preached by Brooke's acolytes in the pulpit of St. Mary's?

Brooke was killed instantly at Lichfield in March 1643, shot through the eye by a sniper stationed on the central tower of the cathedral. A sympathetic chronicler thought that his memory ought to be 'deeply engraven in letters of gold on high-erected pillars of marble', but instead his body was laid in the family vault beneath the chapter house at St. Mary's, with no memorial. Thomas Spencer described the funeral as being 'honourable and warlike', which suggests a degree of pageantry, but, frustratingly, gave no other details.

You do not expect your MP to smash up your parish church, but that is just what William Purefoy did to St. Mary's in June 1643, three months

63. A miniature of Robert Greville, 2nd Lord Brooke, painted by Francis Smiadecki, a Polish artist working in England, ca. 1650.

after Brooke's death. Purefoy was from a well-established family from Caldecote, where Richard Vines (one of the lecturers who regularly appeared in Warwick) was the rector, and of whom Purefoy was a patron. Due to Brooke's support, Purefoy was nominated as Warwick's MP in both the Short and Long Parliaments of 1640. The uncompromising Purefoy became Parliament's political enforcer in Warwickshire, and commander of the garrison at Warwick castle. He would later be one of the commissioners who tried Charles I for 'traitorously and maliciously [levying] war against the present parliament and the people therein represented' – a role that many leading parliamentarians declined or evaded. If he had any compunction in signing Charles I's death warrant, he left no sign of it.

It is worth reproducing a lengthy extract from a royalist news sheet, *Mercurius Rusticus*, shortly after Purefoy's attack on St. Mary's. Written by the propagandist Bruno Ryves, it emphasises that it was directed not only at the church, but also towards the very structure of society, personified by the Beauchamps:

> In St. Mary's church in Warwick and the [Beauchamp chapel] are divers fair monuments of the Beauchamps, anciently earls of that place; which family long flourishing there had been great benefactors and beautifiers of that church, whereof Thomas Beauchamp (earl of Warwick, Earl Marshall of England, and one of the founders of the most noble order of the Garter …) built the choir now standing, in the midst whereof is his monument, and adorned the windows with pictures of himself, his wife, and children which were many; upon the surcoats of the men were their arms skilfully depicted, the women having the like, and mantles over which were the arms of their matches, their husbands being the prime nobility of those times: the like portraitures in glass, but much more rich and costly, were in the [Beauchamp chapel]. In this stood the monument of Earl Richard … in the opinion of judicious observant travellers, esteemed the rarest piece erected for any subject of the Christian world.
>
> But such is the barbarousness of the pretenders to reformation, that upon Wednesday 14 June [1643][17] the soldiers, by the appointment and encouragement of one whom (in these dangerous times wherein the dregs

---

17   This is an error, as 14 June was not a Wednesday in 1643.

of the people are made commanders for the advancement of rebellion) men call Colonel Purefoy (a man of mean desperate fortune but by the means of the late Lord Brooke chosen burgess of parliament for Warwick, and who had the greatest influence in seducing that unhappy lord to this desperate rebellion, in which he miserably perished), did beat down and deface those monuments of antiquity, and not content with this by the same command they break down the cross in the market place, not leaving one stone upon another, Purefoy all the while standing by, animating and encouraging them, until they had finished their so barbarous work.

Ryves concluded with a justifiable lament that the windows depicting the Beauchamp family contained 'nothing to offend the weakest Christian'.

The account does not tell us exactly what was attacked by Purefoy, but we can infer that it included the glass in the chancel. In the Beauchamp chapel the lowest tier of the east window, depicting Earl Richard, his two wives, and his children were smashed, as were the lower windows in the north and south walls. The reredos, a depiction of the Annunciation, was destroyed. The effigies of Ambrose and Robert Dudley were vandalised, but not irreparably.

Ryves laid the blame firmly at the hand of Purefoy personally, even to the extent of accusing him of having seduced Brooke to 'desperate rebellion'. That is a fabrication, necessary to defend Brooke as a member of the established order. Nonetheless, Ryves may have been right to imply that Purefoy was pursuing a personal agenda; official policy sanctioned only the removal of items of idolatry, not images of patrons, and destruction of market crosses, such as at Warwick, was not authorised by Parliament until the end of August 1643.

It may not be a coincidence that the desecration of St. Mary's came soon after Brooke's death. Purefoy may have been demonstrating his authority to Brooke's successor as commander of the parliamentary army in Warwickshire, the earl of Denbigh, who was no friend of Purefoy's. Whatever triggered Purefoy's actions, thankfully there does not appear to have been a repeat performance.

Purefoy died in 1659. The following year the anonymous *The Mystery of the Good Old Cause briefly unfolded* made no doubt as to which side it was on by declaring itself to have been published 'in the first year of England's liberty, after almost twenty years slavery'. It contained this account of Purefoy which was, the author assures us, 'fairly, and as far as possible, truly collected':

> [He] fought resolutely against the cross in the market place at Warwick and against the ancient monuments at the earl's chapel in St. Mary's church there, who took the mourners in brass there to be monks and friars, for which he had one thousand five hundred pounds given him, but when he should have fought with the enemy, hid himself in a barley field, for which a waterman who had been his soldier refused to carry him.

St. Mary's had been an obvious target for a man of Purefoy's zealotry, but it could have been much worse. Sir William Dugdale, never shy to draw attention to the depravity of Parliamentary troops, wrote of how, in 1642, they laid Lichfield cathedral to waste. Stained glass and monuments were smashed beyond repair; the nave was used for stabling and the chancel as a latrine; soldiers amused themselves by hunting cats with hounds throughout the church, and derided the sacrament of baptism by taking a calf to the font and sprinkling it with holy water. They were under the command of none other than Brooke.

Thankfully, the images of the four English saints in the east window of the Beauchamp chapel were unscathed, as were the statues surrounding it. Enough glass was left in the lower side windows to repair the east window, resulting in the hotch-potch that we have now, and from which we can still identify something of the original iconography. The heavenly choir and orchestra survived. The tombs were relatively unharmed, and it is a wonder that Richard Beauchamp was not melted down for gun metal or, as the *Mystery of the Good Old Cause* would have us believe, his tomb destroyed for a one thousand five hundred pound bounty.

The year after Purefoy's violation of St. Mary's, the earl of Denbigh sent papers to its minister, and to that of St. Nicholas's, with an instruction to read them to their congregations 'to better stir up the people to express their affections for the parliament'. One can only imagine how that was received by a church that had just seen a large part of its history vandalised and erased.

– 10 –

RESTORATION

I

WITH WARWICK being a garrison town, it was inevitable that the army's developing reputation for religious extremism spilled out from the castle. The religious community within St. Mary's parish was fragmenting beyond repair. Samuel Clarke complained that people from his parish at Alcester were driven to the protection of Warwick to seek safety from royalist soldiers, only to be exposed to the heresies of Anabaptism and sectarianism. The first Baptist chapel in Warwick was built as early as 1640, and became a strict sect that forbade both marriage to non-Baptists and attendance at 'Babylonish' Church of England services. By the 1650s a separate independent congregation met regularly in the town, led by the Greville family doctor who was also the surgeon to the garrison. A nascent Quaker community also emerged, and when their leader, George Fox, visited Warwick in 1655, the mayor did nothing to dissuade a re-enactment of Leviticus 24:16, 'anyone who blasphemes the name of the Lord is to be put to death. The entire assembly must stone them'. It was a common reaction at a time when Quakers were considered social disrupters, but thankfully it was not carried to its Levitical conclusion.

But there were clues that hard-line sentiments were softening or compromised. In 1655 St. Mary's sent three of its eight bells to Coventry for recasting. Christmas Day was supposed to be a normal working day, albeit one devoted to prayer and fasting, but in 1657 St. Mary's rang its bells in celebration. The following year saw the funeral at St. Mary's of Francis Greville, Lord Brooke, son of Robert, who died aged twenty-one. The ceremony was conducted with all the honours appropriate to his rank. The procession was led by Garter King of Arms – it is hard to imagine a finer representative of royal chivalry – followed by peers and members of the Warwickshire gentry, who attended irrespective of their stance in the Civil Wars, and finally the mayor with his mace, the burgesses of Warwick, and gentlemen of the shire. Admittedly the sermon was preached by a committed presbyterian, Thomas Manton, a lecturer at Westminster abbey who the previous year had prayed with Oliver Cromwell when he was considering an offer to anoint him as king. Yet even Manton was to waver. Three years later, when the army deposed Oliver's son, Richard, he swiftly called for the restoration of Charles II and was part of a parliamentary delegation to negotiate with him in the Dutch city of Breda before his return from exile. Though Manton could not accept the Book of Common Prayer, he became more moderate and willing to compromise. Like many of his fellow believers, he was horrified by the disintegration of the national church, and much preferred the chance of unification, even on imperfect terms.

The stance of St. Mary's vicar, Richard Venour, was also shifting. In 1648 he had endorsed the *Warwickshire ministers' testimony to the trueth of Jesus Christ and to the Solemn League and Covenant*. The Solemn League and Covenant was an alliance between Parliament and the Scots made in 1643 to defend both countries against papism, and to commit to a common presbyterian church. Organised by John Bryan, the man who had delivered Cecily Puckering's funeral oration and was later preacher and chaplain to the Warwick garrison and then vicar of Holy Trinity, Coventry, the *Warwickshire testimony* rejected tolerance of Protestant schismatics: there could only be one true 'godly' church. It was signed by forty-three ministers, about a fifth of all ministers in Warwickshire, so Venour was part of a sizeable minority. Other signatories included Dugard, who had succeeded Bryan at Barford; Henry Butler at St. Nicholas; and Thomas Spencer, still at Budbrooke.

Those subscribing to the *Warwickshire testimony* swore to honour it to the death. However, the restoration of the monarchy saw the Solemn League and Covenant repudiated, and the Book of Common Prayer again made compulsory. Ministers who refused to accept it were ejected from their livings, John Bryan and Samuel Clarke among them. But Dugard and Venour conformed, and on 2 September 1660 Venour delivered an oration in St. Mary's to explain his change of heart.

No doubt coloured by the increasing diversity of religious sects in Warwick, with its attendant threat to order, Venour lamented the loss of authority brought about by the abolition of bishops in 1646. The absence of church government led, he said, to 'a great distraction and confusion'. In his view set forms of liturgy were commanded by Christ, citing Matthew 6:9 and Luke 11:2, though that was straining it as both verses refer only to the Lord's Prayer. He argued that the Book of Common Prayer was the product of 'wise, judicious, and very learned men' since 1552, who 'sealed the truth of the reformed religion' and those who rejected it were like 'an evil physician, who to cure a mole, a freckle, a wart, or small wen [boil] in a fair face doth kill the person to effect it'. Abolishing bishops was the work of those who did 'eagerly desire and greedily gape after [their] authority and estates', and, with an unhappy mix of similes, were 'greedy cormorants who, ostrich-like, could devour anything'. It was a total rejection of what he had put his name to in the *Warwickshire testimony*.

Venour continued:

> So the expulsion of the liturgy opened a wide gap to all the whimsical fancies, fanatic opinions, errors, heresies, and blasphemies that have so abounded, and so much infested the Church of God ever since: while every man was left to his own abilities, inventions and expressions; and every man that could but talk a little, and make use of any good language, was presently cried up for a gifted brother, and completely fitted for the ministry, without any more ado.
>
> And hence, no doubt, hath been abundance of nonsense (if not worse) uttered by men of weak abilities, parts and gifts, in celebrating the mysteries of God. And hence have sprung those swarms of sectaries that have so long annoyed us.[18]

Venour was clearly getting something off his chest, disillusioned with the events of the past twenty years that had enabled men like Abiezer Coppe to peddle their heresies in his own parish. Venour would surely have added George Fox and the Baptists to his list of swarming sectaries. However, he did not reject the importance of the Word of God:

---

18   Richard Venner (or Venour), '*Panoplia, or the whole armour of God explained etc*' (London, 1662). 'Panoplia' means 'spiritual protection'.

> Those [who] set [the Book of Common Prayer] too high, that make it equal in authority with the holy Scriptures, as if it were ... sent by immediate inspiration from God, as the oracles of God were ... [do as] the Children of Israel did by the brazen serpent, (reserved and kept as a monument of God's mercy to their ancestors) was so doted upon, as that they gave divine honour to it: Then did that good King Hezekiah ... break it in pieces, that God might no longer be dishonoured thereby.

That was a nod to puritan values, but now they were to be subservient to conformity within the established church. Venour was rejecting not only presbyterianism, but also the type of intense personal relationship with God that had sustained Cecily Puckering in her suffering. But Venour's plea for conformity was in vain, as the split was permanent. A survey of 1676 recorded that over seven per cent of the population of Warwick were Nonconformist, and therefore worshipping outside the Church of England.

II

In a ceremony at the Banqueting House in Whitehall in November 1660, the Dutch states of Holland and West Friesland presented the newly restored Charles II with twenty-eight paintings and twelve sculptures, in recognition of their alliance with England. The gift included Titian's *Madonna and Child in a landscape with Tobias and the Angel,* and Paolo Veronese's *The mystic marriage of St. Catherine of Alexandria,* a depiction of a symbolic betrothal to God. The titles of these pictures alone would have been an anathema to the hotter puritans, but the extremists were now either in retreat or sidelined. Moreover, attitudes towards art were changing. Charles I had woven fine art into the majesty of kingship, and his son's swift acquisition of a collection to replace that lost to the monarchy after 1648 was clear recognition that to display fine art was to display power. Oliver Cromwell had also grasped the point, surrounding himself with the trappings of a head of state and being content to leave hanging at his principal residence, Hampton Court (built by a cardinal), paintings such as *Madonna and Child with St. Elizabeth* and the *Assumption of the Virgin Mary.* It was only fitting for a man who came to be addressed as 'your Highness', and who was buried with full heraldic pageantry among royalty at Westminster abbey.

In truth, puritans had always had an uneasy relationship with religious art. Robert Dudley owned thirteen paintings with religious subject matters at the time of his death, including a triptych showing Christ being taken down from the cross, many of which he acquired after 1580. The justification was that displaying such paintings was acceptable if they were not used for idolatrous purposes, a distinction accepted by the Church of England in 1562. Therefore there was no problem in using them (for example) to decorate a long gallery, so Cromwell was merely following an established practice.

Religious imagery was now starting to spread beyond a domestic context, and reappear in churches. A window at Bristol cathedral, made during the 1660s, shows biblical scenes. But St. Mary's went much, much further than that, for in 1678 a new painting of the day of judgment was executed above the western door of the Beauchamp chapel, replacing the 'decayed' original. The subject matter is intimately associated with purgatory, the antithesis of the fundamental tenet of the Church of England, predestination. It is, therefore, surprising, to say the least, to see this image appear within thirty years of the execution of a king accused of being a papist; painted in a town that had been exposed to some of the most vociferous puritan preachers in England; and unveiled at a time when anti-Catholic sentiment was reaching a crescendo. In 1673, just five years beforehand, parliament had passed the Test Act, which prohibited Catholics (and Nonconformists) from holding public office, and in 1678 itself the accusations of Titus Oates that prominent Catholics were plotting against the king whipped up an anti-Catholic frenzy, with over twenty innocent men executed.

It was against this background that the Beauchamp chapel's painting of the day of judgment was made, but, to cap it all, its central grouping is a deliberate imitation of that in the 'Antichrist' bishop of Rome's Sistine chapel, complete with the godly horror of full-frontal nudity, male and female. It was blatant plagiarism, but the reputation of Michelangelo Buonarroti of Florence had nothing to fear from Richard Bird of Warwick.

The painting had been commissioned on the initiative of Sir William Dugdale, a prolific scholar whose *Antiquities of Warwickshire* set new standards for local history. It is thanks to him that the wording of contracts for the Beauchamp chapel have been preserved, and that we know something of the medieval stained glass and monuments at St. Mary's that were destroyed by puritan iconoclasm. His respect for the past led him to persuade Lady

Above: 64. The painting of the day of judgment in Beauchamp chapel.
Below: 65. The painting of the day of judgment in the Sistine chapel.

The similarity of the central grouping, around Christ, is obvious, but Bird departed from the original further out, beyond the need to adapt the painting to the smaller and differently shaped space.

Katherine Leveson, Robert Dudley's granddaughter through his illegitimate son Robert, to establish a trust for the restoration of the Beauchamp chapel and of her ancestors' monuments in it. Its trustees were Dugdale and his heirs and the mayor of Warwick from time to time, and the fund was endowed with fifty pounds for the initial works, and thereafter forty pounds a year, charged on Lady Katherine's manor of Foxley in Northamptonshire. A tablet of white marble was made to commemorate her generosity, and erected behind the altar of the Beauchamp chapel to hide the damage caused when Purefoy smashed the reredos. Now on the north wall, it is by Joshua Marshall, the royal master mason.

There were a few in the parish who would have positively welcomed the return of an illustration of the day of judgment to St. Mary's. Catholics in Warwick had kept a low profile after the early years of Elizabeth's reign, a wise policy at times such as 1595, when the papist priest William Freeman was hanged at Warwick, and in 1604 when another priest, John Sugar, was hung drawn and quartered, and his remains displayed at the town's gates. A lay Catholic, Robert Grissold of Rowington, was treated more leniently, being merely hanged on the same day as Sugar, whom he had assisted.

It is difficult to know how many Catholics there were in Warwick in the wake of the Restoration, but the 1676 survey suggests that there were as few as nine in St. Mary's parish, and only two in St. Nicholas's, out of an adult population of 1,246 and 596 respectively. This is almost certainly an under-estimate, but even so the numbers were small compared with the Warwickshire Catholic hotbeds of Coughton, Baddesley Clinton, and the Wixford and Bidford-on-Avon area. Others in Warwick were, if not Catholic, at least sympathisers. One was Roger Edes, twice mayor, while another was Sir Henry Puckering, who had inherited the Priory. Sir Henry was the son of Adam Newton, the man whose tomb Sir Thomas Puckering had copied, and he added Puckering to his name when he inherited the Priory in 1654.

In 1685 the openly Catholic James Stuart succeeded his brother Charles to become King James II, and two years later a Catholic chapel was built in Saltisford, suggesting that there was sufficient adherence to the old faith in Warwick to justify it – and to pay for it. This would be of passing interest were it not for the fact that accusations were made that the new vicar of St. Mary's, Roger Edes' son William, had laid the keystone over the doorway, asked that the initial of his first name be carved upon it, and gave sixpence to the workmen so they could buy themselves a drink.

William Edes was also said to have entertained papish priests, and even a bishop, at the vicarage; attended the Catholic chapel's consecration; and tried to have the bells of St. Mary's rung for the occasion. When the ringers failed to respond to the summons, the parish clerk, James Fish, supposedly fetched some who had retired, and offered to pay them ten or twenty shillings. Edes denied the charges, supported by other witnesses, some of whom thought that they were 'raised much with a design to prejudice [him]'. Fish's testament does not survive.

It is difficult to know what to make of this. Edes, born and bred in Warwick, would have been well-known, so it is strange that his public actions surrounding the building of the Catholic chapel were a matter of dispute, and if the accusers were right Fish too was a papist sympathiser. The charges coincided with a bitter dispute between Edes and the corporation over his pay, and with tension between the Crown and the corporation – indeed, James II was to suspend the corporation's charter in 1688. James II's unpopularity among the town's burgesses had been heightened by his *Declaration of Indulgence*, which offered toleration to both Catholics and Nonconformists, and was issued a month before Edes' appointment. Perhaps Edes had become a lightning conductor for anti-papist and anti-Jacobean sentiment in Warwick. Despite Edes' father and brother probably being Catholics, there is no firm evidence that William was, and in the 1715 parliamentary election he supported the Whigs, not something one would expect of a high churchman. How and why Fish got dragged into the allegations is a mystery.

Edes attracted controversy beyond his supposed Catholicism and the row over his pay. He sacked his corporation-appointed assistant at St. Mary's, violently threatening to 'pistol [whip] him or any man who shall dare to preach in his pulpit without his leave'. That makes Thomas Hall's treatment of Samuel Clarke in 1633 seem quite tame. He was accused of inciting his 'wild and debauched' brother to wield his sword before the mayor and threaten to kill him, twice on the same day. And Edes had, in the words of the corporation minutes, become 'so out of charity with [the corporation] that he left them out of his prayers', clearly seen as a neglect of a spiritual duty and a calculated affront. It was quite a start to his ministry at St. Mary's.

The burgesses soon had enough, and in 1689 they resolved to take steps to remove Edes from both St. Mary's and his position as master of the school. However, the following year a compromise was reached over his pay, and as part of the deal he gave up the mastership. The other allegations seem to have been dropped.

Clearly William Edes was a disruptive figure in the town, and inciting his brother to intimidate the mayor, or threatening bodily harm to a priest of St. Mary's, were not the acts of a reconciler – not to mention conduct inappropriate for a vicar. As it was, Edes remained at St. Mary's until 1706, when he resigned to become rector of Kinwarton. The chapel in Saltisford that may or may not have borne his initial over the door did not last long, as it had been demolished by 1737.

III

On Wednesday 5 September 1694, at about two o'clock in the afternoon, a fire broke out near the corner of Leycester Place and High Street. It is said that sparks from a torch being used to light an oven at the premises of Joshua Perks set the thatched roof of his bakehouse alight, but that was never verified. A strong south-westerly wind quickly fanned the fire towards the north-east, burning much of High Street, Swan Street, New Street, Church Street, and Northgate Street, as well as part of the north side of Jury Street and the east side of Market Square. Prisoners had to be let out of the gaol in Northgate Street for their own safety, and, unsurprisingly, some did not return. By the time the fire had been extinguished some six hours later, about one hundred and fifty houses had been damaged or destroyed, but thankfully there were no fatalities. The disaster became known as the Great Fire of Warwick.

One can only imagine the panic and confusion as desperate townspeople tried to save their houses, their possessions, and their public buildings. We have no eye-witness accounts of the fire itself, but there is one from Northampton, which suffered a similar fate in 1675. Its author, who described himself as 'a country minister', wrote:

> …a lively image I cannot draw, because my bosom cannot hold their passions, nor my pen weep out their tears. No words can report the cries, fears, dangers, distractions, carefulness, and amazedness of young and old

66. A late seventeenth-century fire engine, as shown on the manufacturer's business card, dated 1678. The engines were of little use, as they were heavy to manoeuvre, they got stuck on poor surfaces, and the throw of water was so poor that they had to be taken close to the fire, putting both men and machine at peril. At least the firefighters were remarkably well-dressed. Warwick's engine was kept in St. Mary's but was badly damaged in the Great Fire. It was repaired by Nicholas Paris, the blacksmith who did much work at St. Mary's, at a cost of five pounds.

> ... Oh! The roaring of fire and wind, what a thunder in the air! What clouds of smoke! What tearing cracks of timber! ... What could the helpless [elderly, children, and infirm] do? Whither could they creep or run?[19]

Taking their cue from measures learned in London, people started removing thatched roofs, and even demolishing houses, to try to prevent the spread of the fire. Dr. William Johnson, a physician living at the west end of Smith Street in what is now known as Landor House, took it upon himself to raze Edward Heath's house on the corner of Jury Street and the Butts,

---

19 Anon. (Edward Pearse), *The state of Northampton from the beginning of the fire, Sept. 20th 1675 to Nov. 5th* (London, 1675), p.11.

without his consent and without the authority of the mayor. The fire stopped before it reached the site, and Johnson was required to pay compensation.

Some moved their goods into St. Mary's, in the hope that its stone walls would afford protection. According to the author William Field, the townspeople unwittingly took smouldering items into the church which created a fire within and set the roof alight, but there is no contemporary evidence of this. It seems implausible that people did not know that their goods were burning, and the absence of any mention of it in official reports in the days after the fire casts further doubt on its truth. The flames probably leapt across Church Street, which was narrower than it is now, and took hold on the wooden roofs of the nave and transepts. The tower collapsed. Ironically, the town's fire bell, bought in 1670 at a cost of £1 8s, survived, and is on display in the crypt.

All the memorials in the nave and transepts were lost. The most important casualty was the tomb of Earl Thomas Beauchamp II and his Countess Margaret. The brass is the only part of the tomb that survived, and it is now on the wall of the south transept. Others included a tomb of someone we cannot identify, that was recessed into the south wall, but its grandeur shows that he was someone of importance and the dress indicates that he was a knight. A chest tomb in the north transept commemorated Thomas Fisher, who died in 1577, and his first wife Winifred. In the cross aisle, in front of the pulpitum, was the tomb chest and effigy of William Peyto (died 1407), a family usually associated with Chesterton, about seven miles south-east of Warwick. However, they were also lords of the manor of Wolfhampcote, out of which John Peyto, William's father, had surrendered the church and its advowson to Earl Thomas I before they were given to St. Mary's in 1392. A Thomas Peyto also had a tomb chest with an effigy, in the nave, but it is not clear what relation he was to William.

Several ledger stones were also destroyed, including those of William Berkeswell and John Rous. John Alestre, who was dean from 1510 to 1516, is said to have been buried in the grave in the south transept vacated by Earl Richard Beauchamp, but no visible trace of it remains. The brass of Thomas Huggeford, one of Earl Richard Beauchamp's executors, and his wife Margaret was lost, as was that of his parents, Robert and Margaret. Both are notable for being two of the only twenty or so known late-medieval brasses that showed a couple holding hands, a clear connection with the

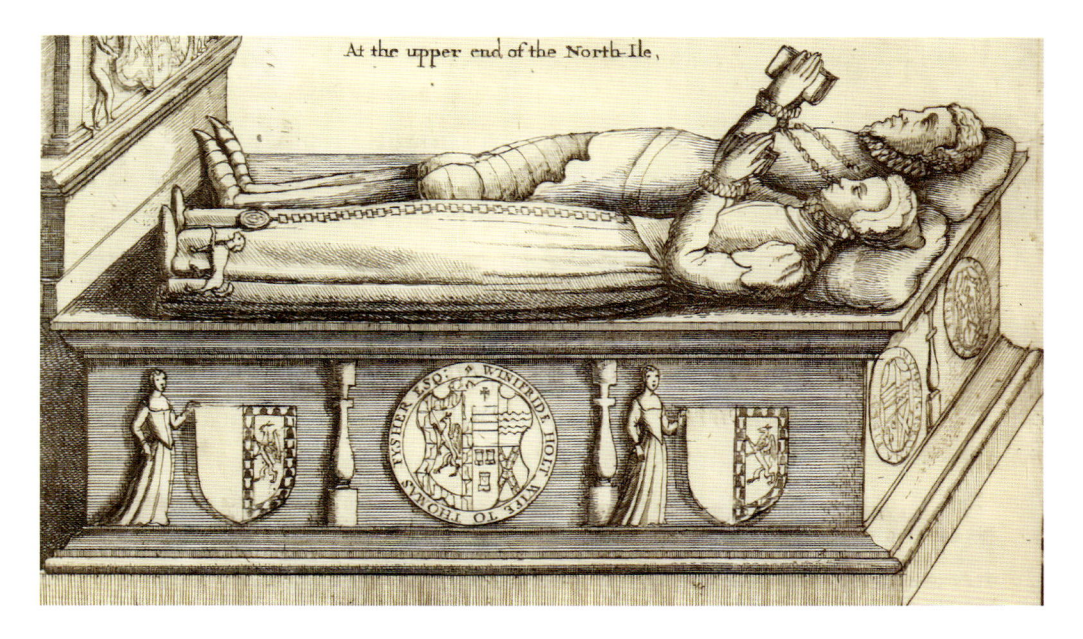

67. The tomb of Thomas Fisher in the north transept, lost in the 1694 fire.

family's service to the Beauchamps. Thomas Oken's brass was saved from his memorial, and can be seen at the entrance to the north transept.

Other parts of the church were damaged, particularly the chancel, which suffered a partial collapse of the roof, but the stone vault gave it some protection. It seems likely that much of the damage to the tomb of Earl Thomas Beauchamp I and Katherine Mortimer that is evident now was caused at this time; certainly some of the weepers were repaired with plaster in the years after the fire. The pulpitum also survived, but it fell foul of Georgian aesthetics, and it was removed in 1795.

The Beauchamp chapel was saved by the efforts of James Fish, the churchwarden, parish clerk, and alleged Catholic sympathiser, who organised four unknown men to contain the fire, presumably with nothing more than buckets and water, with the risk of collapse about them. Their bravery was rewarded with a shilling each. At that time the opening above the portal of the Beauchamp chapel was unglazed, admitting flames that burned the wooden gallery and screen, and scorched the image of the day of judgment around it. The stalls along the west wall also caught, and the two westernmost windows were badly damaged. It must have been close.

IV

The day after the fire, a meeting of local worthies took place to discuss what was to be done. The attendees included Fulke, the fifth Lord Brooke and the third son of the radical Robert Greville, and Sir Henry Newton Puckering. They became closely involved in organising and controlling the rebuilding of the town through a Committee formed for that purpose.

The initial estimate of the cost of the damage to the town was one hundred thousand pounds, though this was soon revised to nearer ninety, and the final total was just over sixty. Of that, the losses at St. Mary's accounted for twenty-five thousand pounds, though there is no breakdown of that figure. There was no insurance.

It would be inappropriate to tell the story of St. Mary's in the aftermath of the fire without first conveying an impression of the deprivation faced by its parishioners. The most urgent task was to provide for those who had suffered, their plight exacerbated by a serious food shortage. They were supplied with food, bedding, and tools to enable them to earn a living. The corporation adapted two barns to accommodate twenty-eight of the poor, though how quickly it did so is uncertain. Inevitably, there were allegations of looting from the outset, and it was reported that people were seeking alms from parishes in other counties, falsely claiming to be from Warwick and to have been impoverished by the fire. Later, legitimate sufferers would be given the right to ask for alms from anywhere in the country, in relaxation of the usual rule that caring for the poor was solely the responsibility of their own parish.

Letters were sent to every town in Warwickshire on the day after the fire, pleading for donations to aid the dispossessed. The initial funds were raised from the gentry, including Brooke and Puckering. Within five days £528 was distributed among 143 people, and further payments were made the following week after the receipt of £279 from the bishop of Worcester and the Worcester parishes. A brief issued by King William III and Queen Mary II required every parish in England to undertake a door-to-door appeal for funds, not only from householders but also from 'servants, strangers, and others'. Money was sent from as far afield as Chichester and Suffolk. Perhaps not surprisingly, given their own recent plight, numerous London parishes contributed. However, according to an author writing in 1730, the appeal raised only eleven thousand pounds, leaving a substantial shortfall.

There are numerous examples of hardship, but three must suffice here. Abraham de Commun was a gunsmith who had recently set up his trade in the High Street. His was one of the first houses to be destroyed, and he lost everything. Worse, he had bought some of his tools on credit, and his suppliers were pressing for payment. He was anxious to pay them, not only because they were entitled to their money, but also to protect his creditworthiness and reputation for his future business dealings. John King rented rooms in a house on the north-east side of Market Square. The property was partly burned by the fire, partly torn down as a fire break, and part remained standing. King and his family had nowhere else to go, so they continued to live there, even though it had no roof. One day the chimney collapsed, nearly killing them. King complained that his landlady continued to charge him rent, but she refused to abate it. Presumably she needed the income.

The fire also saw the demise of one of Warwick's largest inns, the Bear in High Street, run by a widow, Sarah Bunter. This impressive building had a frontage of twelve bays, and the site went through to Brook Street. It was valued at £400, and a further £410 was claimed for its contents, including £250 for the loss of bedding and furnishings, £30 for wood and coal, £30 for wine, and £75 worth of hops. It was never replaced.

Besides providing for sufferers, the Committee had to consider how to rebuild the town. By the end of September it had resolved to seek an Act of Parliament to regulate the work, and on 11 February 1695 the *Act for the rebuilding of the town of Warwick, and for determining the differences touching houses burnt or diminished, by reason of the dreadful fire there* received royal assent, based on the precedents of the Acts passed for rebuilding London. It was steered through the House of Commons by William, Lord Digby, one of Warwick's two MPs.

The purposes of the Act were to regenerate the town quickly and attractively and to create a town centre in which gentlemen would wish to reside. Provision was made for the widening of Church and Northgate streets, the straightening of Swan Street, new building lines, and for rationalising plot boundaries to facilitate the construction of party walls and to allow for a uniform appearance. The work was to be supervised by Commissioners and a Court of Record, essentially offshoots of the Committee.

The only significant alteration to the street pattern that would be made was the stopping up of Pebble Lane. This ran north-east from New Street to join Northgate Street, and it was replaced by an extension of Old Square, which then went only as far as New Street, through to St. Mary's. A square was created at the end of the new stretch of road for 'the greater grace and ornament of the Church', enhancing the prominence of St. Mary's which was now clearly visible from Market Square. One casualty of the new layout was the site of the vicar's house, that had been on the corner of Pebble Lane but had burned down. It was used in part to widen Northgate Street.

The Act was surprisingly prescriptive in setting out regulations for new buildings. All rebuilt houses fronting High, Castle, Church, Northgate, and Swan streets, as well as Old Square and the eastern side of the Market Square, were to have two storeys, each with a floor-to-ceiling height of ten feet. The ground floor had to be fourteen inches above street level, with steps only as approved. There could also be a cellar, and a garret if permitted by the Court. To reinforce the appeal of these streets, the Act gave the Court power to banish 'noisome trades' from them, even though they may have been carried on there before the fire. Under this power, butchers and candle makers were banned from High, Jury, Castle, Church and Northgate streets.

Rebuilding brought its own difficulties for the population of St. Mary's, particularly cashflow. Nicholas Paris was a successful blacksmith, clockmaker, and gunsmith, who carried out much work at St. Mary's. He lost his premises in Jury Street, along with his tools and stock, but he seems to have rebuilt promptly, presumably a necessity to enable him to profit from Warwick's rebuilding. However this left him short of funds, and in December 1696 he successfully applied for a payment of fifteen pounds on account of the work he was then doing in regilding Richard Beauchamp's tomb.

V

The immediate priority for St. Mary's was to repair the chancel sufficiently to enable it to function as the parish church. Within days after the fire, Roger Hurlbutt and Thomas Masters were instructed to 'cover the chancel with a roof of boards and poles of oak', clearly a temporary fix, and seating was added by way of benches placed around Thomas and Katherine's tomb. They were not removed until 1851.

Hurlbutt was a carpenter by trade and, along with William (presumably his brother), had been responsible for panelling the state rooms at the castle.

They were also builders, between them constructing Warwick's Market Hall, the stables at Packwood House, and, most notably, Ragley Hall at Alcester. The Hurlbutts' reputation is such that they have been called two of the 'more important provincial builder-architects of late seventeenth century England',[20] so it is perhaps surprising that they do not appear to have had any greater role in rebuilding St. Mary's. However, William probably died in 1698, and, other than the refronting of Landor House in 1692, no major work has been attributed to either of them after 1683, so perhaps Roger came out of retirement to carry out emergency works to St. Mary's.

Work on the chancel took longer than anticipated. Responsibility for its repair fell on the corporation, a consequence of arrangements made at the time of the dissolution of the college in 1544. However, it was short of funds due to its own losses in the fire, and, in May 1695, the Court allocated one hundred pounds 'for the more speedy repairing of [the chancel] and making it ready for public service', and a loan of three hundred and fifty pounds was made by the Commissioners.

We do not know what arrangements were made for worship in the meantime, but some alternatives seem to have been considered. A letter, undated but clearly written in the aftermath of the fire, seeks the assistance of the prospective recipient in 'grant[ing] us liberty to make a place for public worship' presumably in property owned by them, assuring them that it would be taken care of, and no damage done. Unfortunately we do not know who wrote it, who it was written to, or, indeed, if the letter was ever sent. In any event, the chancel was being used for services by the summer of 1697.

There were at least three candidates for the role of architect (or, more accurately, surveyor, as the term 'architect' was not then in common use) for the rebuilding of St. Mary's. A design was submitted by William Weale, of whom little is known but presumably he was a local man, given that Weale was an established name around Warwick. Rather more famous was Sir Christopher Wren, but as he had largely retired from detailed work, the drawings were made by his senior draughtsman, Nicholas Hawksmoor, and submitted under Wren's name.

---

20   By Howard Colvin in *A Biographical Dictionary of British Architects, 1600-1840* (New Haven, CT, 2008), p.208.

Neither Weale nor Wren was appointed; rather, the Commissioners chose Sir William Wilson of Sutton Coldfield. Wilson's reputation was more as a sculptor than as a surveyor, though one of undistinguished ability and, it transpired, one not afraid of taking short cuts. His equestrian statue commissioned for Nottingham castle was to be made from one piece of stone, but it was discovered that one of the legs was wooden. His knighthood, incidentally, was not through birth, but by courtesy of his wife's family. They were so horrified that she had married the poor son of a baker (Wilson had an income three pounds a year, she had eight hundred) that they procured the honour for him.

68. What St. Mary's might have looked like: the south elevation of a design drawn by Nicholas Hawksmoor, while working for Sir Christopher Wren. The restrained cupola above a lantern at the crossing adds interest and a note of modernity into what is otherwise a traditional Gothic style. The tower is a triumph, a happy marriage between Gothic and baroque. The lower height of the second tier compared with the first creates dramatic tension, unlike Wilson's where they are the same depth, and the spire stretches the entire structure towards heaven.

What Wilson lacked in experience – he had never built a church before – he made up for in self-belief. Asked to act as surveyor in the building of a free school in Leicestershire designed by Wren, Wilson drastically altered the plans. A meeting was arranged between Wilson, his client, and Wren, at which Wren declared a preference for Wilson's design over his own. At least, that is Wilson's version of the conversation. He was a brave choice.

The new foundations of St. Mary's were laid in November 1697 by William Smith and Samuel Dunckley. The former, from Tettenhall in Staffordshire, was the elder brother of Francis, who also worked at St. Mary's. The Smiths were the sons of a respected and successful bricklayer, and were probably recommended by Andrew Archer, a member of the Committee, for whom they were building Umberslade Hall (Tanworth-in-Arden) and who also had a house in Jury Street. They came to be considered the leading master builders in the Midlands. Francis is known in Warwick for both the Court House and the house now known as Abbotsford, in Market Square, but the brothers' grandest work is the mighty west range at Stoneleigh abbey (1720-26).

69. Francis Smith, drawn from a portrait attributed to Hamlet Winstanley. There is nothing subtle about this rather stodgy work. Smith holds a pair of compasses, an established symbol of intellect and so distinguishing him from the jobbing mason he started off as. Beneath the compasses is a drawing of the domed building in the background, the Radcliffe Camera in Oxford, of which Smith was the master builder. Smith died in 1738 and is buried at St. Mary's, but there is no memorial to him, and the location of his grave is unknown.

The subsequent fame and success of Francis Smith overshadows the work of Dunckley, who does not receive the credit he deserves for his role in rebuilding Warwick. A mason by trade, Dunckley lived in what is now Barrack Street, then a poor part of town, and was for a time a minister at the Baptist chapel on Castle Hill. He became an invaluable servant of the Court of Record. Dunckley was one of those appointed to conduct a survey of the damage immediately after the fire, and to advise on the appropriate amount of compensation. He also drew up the plans for the adjustment of site boundaries and for the widening of the streets, staking out the new lines. And, as we shall shortly discover, he has left us with a fine legacy of his remarkable talent.

VI

Work on St. Mary's started above ground in early 1698, when the Smith brothers and Dunckley were appointed to build the nave, transepts, and tower for a fee of £2,300, plus another fifty pounds if it was decided that they had done a good job. The stone for the exterior was taken partly from the grounds of the Priory, partly from a site at Coten End, and partly from within the churchyard itself. A quarry had been excavated along the northern boundary of the churchyard in January 1696, to assess the suitability of the stone. It was used despite the stone cutters complaining about its poor quality; they were paid by the usable piece, so they bore the loss of substandard material.

The churchyard quarry was the cause of a petition for compensation from the vicar, still the troublesome William Edes, on the grounds that it prejudiced his income from allowing sheep to graze in the churchyard. The outcome of the claim is not known, but the initial decision clearly did not satisfy Edes, as he complained again some fifteen months later. The quarry was later filled with debris from the burnt houses, much of which had been collected in the Butts. Bones disturbed by quarrying were taken into the crypt, which was already being used as a charnel house, possibly since Elizabethan times. The bones were returned to the churchyard in 1704, and the crypt became a mausoleum for the great and the good.

Timber for the new church was supplied by Thomas Masters who, together with John Phillips of Broadway, made the roof, with the lead provided by Richard Lane, the then mayor. The newly created square at the west end of the church was used as the carpenters' workshop. Nicholas Paris and William

Marshall of Henley-in-Arden undertook the ironwork, including the window frames and bracings for the tower. They were appointed only after they had objected to the use of Birmingham suppliers, on the grounds that preference should be given to those who had suffered from the fire.

Paris also made the clock for the tower, part of the mechanism of which is now displayed in the crypt, though it is probably more accurate to say that he made (at most) only the clock hands and faces, buying in the other components. Marshall's work included a set of gates for the pulpitum arch, for which he was paid one hundred and ten pounds, and another five pounds if Lord Digby thought he deserved it. There is no mention in the accounts of Marshall having received his bonus, but that is not to say he did not. These gates were removed with the pulpitum in 1795, and one is now at the west door to the Beauchamp chapel, the other at its north entrance.

Constructing the new church was proving to be a drain on available funds, and in May 1698 the Court gave one month's notice to recall eight loans that had been made to assist in rebuilding houses, worth in total nine hundred pounds. By November, work had progressed sufficiently to enable a contract to be entered into with Francis Badson of Binton, near Stratford-upon-Avon, for paving the floor with Wilmcote stone, later supplemented with stone from Bearley. Glazing was entrusted to two Warwick glaziers, William Hyron and Richard Hancox, and one from Coventry, Hugh Canter, using glass 'of the best sort' from Stourbridge. Installation commenced in August or September 1700.

A serious problem had emerged in January of that year. The tower had reached just over half of its intended height when cracks began to appear in its supports. Advice was taken from Edward Strong, one of Sir Christopher Wren's master masons, who concluded that the Warwick stone being used to build the pillars could not bear the required weight. As a result, the tower was replaced by that which we see today, standing proud of the west door, with piers made of stronger Shrewley stone. One blessing that resulted from the move is that the church was spared its intended portico: All Saints' Northampton, rebuilt after the 1675 fire there, was not so fortunate, as it had a portico added in 1701.

The three master masons, the Smith brothers and Dunckley, had to bear the cost of the error, and were out of pocket to the tune of £230. It also imperilled their fifty-pound bonus, and the Committee sought consent to pay it from those who had suffered loss from the fire, fearing they would begrudge it. In

70. All Saints' church, Northampton, 1680-86, with a portico added in 1701. Had it not been for the failing tower, the west front of St. Mary's could have looked more like this.

fact, one hundred and twenty-two townspeople signed a resolution to confirm their agreement, including some who had been badly affected, suggesting that they sympathised with the masons. The Committee seems to have wanted to make a point though, and reduced the bonus by ten pounds.

In November 1702, with the tower substantially complete, twenty-four lights and two barrels of pitch for illumination were taken to the top of it, to celebrate the defeat of the French navy off Vigo. It must have been a nervy occasion, but marking the visit of King William III by lighting bonfires in the Market Place, a mere fourteen months after the Great Fire, does not seem to have been a good idea either.

VII

The total cost of rebuilding St. Mary's cannot be quantified because the accounts are incomplete, but it has been estimated at about eight thousand pounds, or even a few hundred pounds above that. Either way, it left in the shade the cost of rebuilding All Saints' Northampton, at less than five thousand pounds. The Smith brothers and Dunckley were paid about four thousand five hundred pounds between them, which includes the cost of their workmen and materials, which they had to meet. A benefactors' board in the church records that Queen Anne contributed one thousand pounds, but this was supposedly for the town generally, and for relief of its sufferers. It was paid in four instalments, and, with the first tranche received in October 1704 (at least six months after the work at St. Mary's had been completed) and the last in July 1706, it was hardly a display of spontaneous royal munificence, and came only after lobbying by the Committee. Whatever the stated purpose of the gift, most of it was applied towards the cost of rebuilding St. Mary's.

There are signs that the Commissioners were prepared to spend money to produce a church that was worthy of the rejuvenated town that they were creating. This goes some way to explaining why the cost was so much higher than at All Saints' Northampton. The new tower, with a height of 128 feet to the battlements, soars thirty feet higher than the failed tower would have done. The balustrade and urns newly installed around the nave roofline were extended around the chancel, an incongruous baroque (and pagan) decorative feature, thankfully removed by 1885.

The bells, increased to a ring of ten, were made by Abraham Rudhall of Gloucester, described by one contemporary as 'the greatest bell-founder of this age', at a cost of £218. The intention had been to salvage metal from the old bells, which was duly melted down for the purpose. However, the metal was stolen, allegedly by one Pickford, and efforts to retrieve it were unsuccessful, despite hunting for it in Birmingham, Towcester, Kings Norton, and Stratford. The new bells were installed between the latter part of 1702 and early 1703, and conveyed from Gloucester to Stratford by boat and then by road. Three of them are still in use.

The font was commissioned from John Nost, a Dutchman living in London, whose work included fine sculptures for Hampton Court. Costing thirty pounds, it is made of marble and was decorated with gilt. Like the

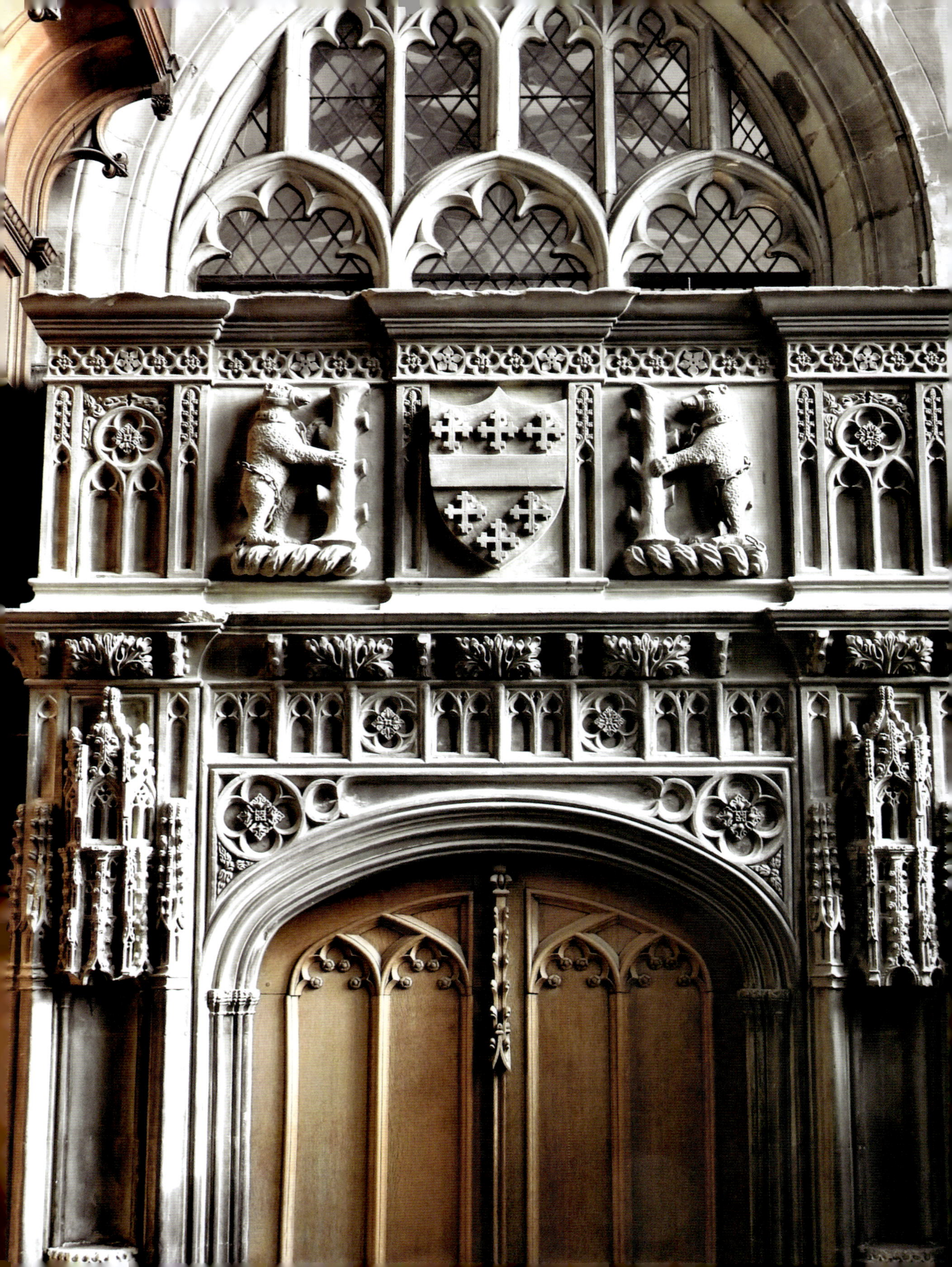

Left: 71. Samuel Dunckley's portal to the Beauchamp chapel, completed by 1708.

Smith brothers, Nost had worked at Umberslade Hall for Andrew Archer, which may explain his choice for St. Mary's. The first person to be baptised at the new font, on 10 February 1705, was John, the son of Thomas and Ann Rippingall, who had married at St. Mary's in 1702.

Perhaps the finest example of quality inside the church is Dunckley's portal to the Beauchamp chapel. It was completed by 1708, and Dunckley was paid forty pounds for it out of the Leveson trust. One may quibble with Nikolaus Pevsner's verdict that it is a Gothic pastiche 'which will today deceive all but the connoisseurs'[21] – the prominent shields flanked by large bear and ragged staff devices are clearly not a reproduction of the medieval design – but not his appreciation of it. Dunckley died in 1714, and was buried at St. Mary's. Though his memorial is lost, he leaves us with this splendid testimony to his abilities. It is a powerful reminder that the animosity between conformists and Baptists that had erupted fifty years earlier was not all-pervasive.

VIII

To say that the rebuilt St. Mary's has provoked a mixed reaction is an understatement. The initial response was positive. According to Daniel Defoe, who visited Warwick in 1716, the new church was 'a fine building', and four years later Samuel Gale considered it to be 'very elegant'.[22] In 1755 John Sabin wrote that the church and tower were 'uncommonly beautiful', 'charming', and 'serv[ed] as monuments to proclaim the refined judgment of Sir William Wilson,'[23] but as Sabin was the parish clerk, promoting St. Mary's as a visitor attraction, he may not have been wholly objective.

Others have been rather less complimentary, with the turn of the nineteenth century seeing particularly strident condemnation. Samuel Ireland, writing in 1795, was under the misapprehension that Wren had been

---

21   Chris Pickford and Nikolaus Pevsner, *The buildings of England: Warwickshire* (New Haven, CT, 2016) p.655.

22   S. Gale, 'An account of a journey made at Easter 1720', in *Bibliotecha Topographia Britannica* Vol. 3 (London, 1790), pp.53-65, p.56.

23   John Sabin, *A brief description of the collegiate-church and choir of St. Mary, in the Borough of Warwick* (Warwick, 1757) p.1.

the architect, which caused him much vexation. Ireland lamented that he was 'sorry to say that [the design] is in many parts very inferior to the general excellence of that great architect'. He continued:

> To censure any work of so distinguished an artist may appear arrogant … he has most absurdly, and I doubt not but that public opinion will accord with mine, blended together the inferior and discarded monuments of [Grecian and Roman style] without either sense or meaning. The jumble is nowhere more palpable than in the forms of the windows, where a double row of cumbrous circular, or Saxon, arches are terminated above by such grotesque and barbarous forms as to baffle all conjecture as to what order or country they could belong.[24]

William Field echoed – or, to be more accurate, copied – this twenty years later. He also believed Wren to have been responsible, albeit admitting to serious doubts as to whether it was indeed the work of 'that consummate master'. Field too wrote of the 'cumbrous Saxon arches' of the window, and denigrated the nave as an 'absurd mixture of different modes', and a 'strange violation of all architectural rule … terminated by such grotesque and barbarous forms as were never before seen'.[25] He criticised an unidentified commentator who had praised the new church by declaring that either he had never seen it, or, if he had, he must have totally forgotten what he saw. In 1834 John Gough Nichols called the nave 'tasteless, incongruous, and deformed',[26] and shortly afterwards Sir Stephen Glynne, an assiduous recorder of medieval church architecture, followed Ireland and Field in using the b- word: barbaric. The renowned ecclesiastical architect of the late Victorian era, William Butterfield, thought the nave windows so barbarous (that word again), that he wanted to block them up as far as the transoms, which he would have straightened out.

Recent opinion has been more sympathetic. A guide to English churches published in 1958, edited by no less a figure than John Betjeman, considered the exterior to be 'noble', and the vaults and arcades of the nave 'a *tour de*

---

24 Samuel Ireland, *Picturesque views on the upper, or Warwickshire, Avon* (London, 1795), p.144.
25 Field, p.105; see *Further reading*.
26 John Gough Nichols, *Description of the Beauchamp Chapel* (London, 1838), p.1.

72. The interior of the nave. Its distinctive architecture must have provoked mixed reactions among the parishioners.

force'.²⁷ In 1995, one architectural historian exercised more restraint than his predecessors of two hundred years beforehand, judging the design to be 'a curious and rather awkward mixture of Gothic and classical motifs'.²⁸ But perhaps the most perceptive comment was made by Marcus Whiffen in 1947, when he wrote of the nave's 'splendid swagger'.²⁹

The problem was how to connect the new with the old. Wren's proposals departed little from tradition, retaining clerestory windows and Gothic tracery, with only the cupolas, dome, and tower introducing more fashionable notes. Wilson was much more radical. He designed a structure that is Gothic at heart, but he abandoned the clerestory, opting instead to make the aisle vaulting the same height as that of the nave. This is a feature popularised by the baroque style that can be seen in churches such as St. Philip's cathedral in

---

27   *Collins guide to English parish churches*, (London, 1958), p.380.
28   Howard Colvin, *A Biographical Dictionary of British Architects, 1600-1840* (New Haven, CT, 1995), pp.1063-1064.
29   Marcus Whiffen, *Stuart and Georgian churches outside London, 1603 to 1837* (London, 1947), p.19.

Birmingham (1710-15), but it is rarely employed in a Gothic-style aisled nave such as at St. Mary's. Combined with the treatment of the ribs, the overall effect resembles hall churches in Germany, especially those of Westphalia and Saxony.

Having a single-height nave enabled Wilson to insert exceptionally large windows in it, the shape and treatment of which have their roots in Gothic but forego the medieval intricacies of trefoils and cusps. Rather, the plain lines of the mullions and tracery combine to form an outline that resembles candles, three in each window. If this was a deliberate referencing of the light of God and the Holy Trinity – and there is no evidence that it is – it was lost on Matthew Bloxam, the author of *The Principles of Gothic Ecclesiastical Architecture* (1829). He unflatteringly compared the shape of the tracery to a horse collar.

The overall effect of the nave may be Gothic, but there are distinct baroque elements. Capitals are decorated with foliage, found in medieval English Decorated architecture, but perhaps too idiosyncratic alongside the aggressively plain Perpendicular chancel. There is more baroque in the angels at the rib springs, looking down somewhat wistfully on the congregation. In the vaulting, cartouches imitate the panels in the chancel, though without their presence, and somewhat inconsequential and lost in comparison.

The tower is even more of a conflation of styles. 'Less is more', the lesson taught by the Perpendicular builders, and taken to extremes by the skeletal ribs of the chancel, is uncompromisingly defied by the fussy tower. Harmonious and elegant it is not, its disparate styles jarring. Field called it a 'jumbling mixture of round and pointed arches' with little 'taste and judgment'. Blind Gothic windows, decorated with foliated shaft rings that are anachronistic to the chancel, jostle for attention with baroque angels and cartouches, and classical balustrades and niches. It would have been even worse had the niches been filled with statues, which was Wilson's intention before Henry Puckering refused to sanction the cost.

Twelve heraldic shields beneath the baroque battlements take us back to the traditions of the Middle Ages and to the legends of yore; they include the ragged staff and an emblem representing Rohund, father of the fair Felice. Atop, clumsy medieval-style pinnacles, that should crown the tower and soar towards heaven, instead make it look top-heavy, almost squashing it down. This effect is exacerbated by even-depth tiering and narrow bands (known as 'strings') that surround the tower and break up the vertical. As a result, and

73. *A detail of the tower, showing blind windows, foliated shaft rings, niches, and a baroque angel above the clock face. The clock was made by Nicholas Paris of Jury Street.*

despite its height, the tower lacks the emotional impact of those of the great Cotswold or Lincolnshire wool churches, and of the designs for St. Mary's proposed by Wren.

There is, though, a complication. Wren's son, also Christopher, listed among his father's papers a perspective drawing of the tower which, he said, was erected 'after an unsuccessful attempt in execution of a defective prior design by other hands'.[30] Frustratingly, the drawing is now lost, but some have

---

30 Christopher Wren, *Parentalia or Memoirs of the family of the Wrens, etc* (London, 1750), p.342.

74. The shields on the north face on the tower reflect the traditional ancestry of the earls. From left to right: a ragged staff; a shield with eight crosslets, a fictive device thought to represent Rohund, the father of Felice; and Newburgh, later quartered with Beauchamp to form the arms of the earls of Warwick.

concluded from this entry that the tower we see now was designed by Wren. One of his biographers accepted that the attribution of the tower to Wren was 'basically correct', and explained the problem that it does not look like a Wren tower by suggesting that the colonnettes (thin decorative columns), strings, and niches may have been added by Wilson to, as he sniffily put it, 'adapt Wren's bolder conception to meet provincial taste and to match the church'.

This will not do. For one thing, when the tower was being built there is no record of Wren being paid for anything other than Edward Strong's advice on its positioning and choice of stone. Secondly, all the surviving drawings show spires, including one on which Hawksmoor lightly sketched a spire on to a relatively squat tower. This seems to give a clear indication of the evolution of the architects' thoughts, rejecting a spire-less tower. Surely, if Wren had designed the tower, it would not have resembled the current one without the niches.

The more plausible explanation is that Wren's son is referring to a concept drawing prepared by his father's office, showing how the new

75. One of Hawksmoor's drawings, showing the possible treatment of the tower. The faint addition of a spire suggests that this was how his thoughts were evolving. There is nothing that resembles the present tower in Wren's papers.

tower could be positioned proud of the west end of the nave following Strong's recommendation. This would also explain why the drawing was in perspective, and why there are no elevations of the tower listed among Wren's papers.

Despite the criticisms of both nave and tower, it all works. Even William Field begrudgingly admitted that, overall, the church was 'handsome and stately', and Matthew Bloxam, so cutting with his comments on the nave windows, surprisingly thought the tower to be above criticism. Arguably, what Wilson has incorporated into the tower is a homage to the church's architectural past and present. We shall never know whether he did so consciously, but contradicting the established precepts of architecture did not seem to bother him. After all, the construction of a Germanic hall church nave in a quasi-Gothic style, with classical and baroque overtones, shows that he was not shy of flouting convention. Wilson could do orthodox – his chapel in Hall Green, Birmingham (subsequently extended and now known as the Church of the Ascension), built by William and Francis Smith, is charming and inoffensive – but one cannot accuse him of producing a standardised solution at St. Mary's.

One may carp about a contamination of architectural purity, but Wilson was not solely responsible: his design was approved by the Committee, and he was answerable to it. There seems to have been a conscious decision to select a design that was bold, while at the same time respecting the medieval context demanded by the chancel. Perhaps Wilson's critics have not given him enough credit for seeking an imaginative solution. He produced a building that is no dull recreation of the past, but one that is light and assured, modern yet not drastically at odds with its forebear. The awe-inspiring nave, like the chancel, is free of distraction, the eye being drawn immediately to its length and height. Visible from several villages around Warwick, the tower's soaring appearance on the skyline must have conveyed, both to the local population and to approaching visitors, a message not just of restoration, but of confidence, of a church and town emerging stronger from adversity.

The tower and nave reflect the purpose of those who commissioned them, proclaiming the optimistic message of the town's rebirth that they were keen to emphasise. It is a sentiment reflected in a letter written in 1707 by the mayor of Warwick, in which he said that all those he had consulted preferred a design for the floor of the Beauchamp chapel that ''twill be uncommon and rich'. Perhaps it was Wilson's willingness to embrace this positive attitude that explains his appointment, despite his lack of experience. Wren's clerestory nave may have been too backward-looking, not rescued by baroque cupolas and spires. And, with its narrative of authority and its defiance of convention, the new church follows the principles behind the design of both the chancel and the Beauchamp chapel, and so is, indeed, faithful to the old.

Contemporaries considered St. Mary's to be worthy of the portrayal of Warwick as a reinvigorated town, fit for gentlemen. The St. Mary's of 1708 was just as much a product of status and promotion as it had been in the times of Earls Roger, Thomas Beauchamp II, and Anne Beauchamp. William Wilson, the Smith brothers, Samuel Dunckley, and the Committee that supported them, can truly be said to have embraced and enhanced St. Mary's fine heritage, faire and goodly.

GLOSSARY

achievements items of military equipment belonging to a deceased knight, such as his sword, shield, gauntlet, helm, and crest. They were customarily hung above the grave.
advowson the right to appoint a priest to a benefice.
anchorite a devout recluse who lived simply, often being given accommodation in a cell adjacent to or even inside a church.
antiphon a sentence or verse that is sung, for example before or after the singing of a psalm.
archdeacon a priest who acted as an official of the bishop, responsible for administration within the diocese.
canon a priest who is a member of a *college*.
cartouche an ornate frame, typical of the baroque style.
chancel that part of a church that contains the principal, or high, altar. It is almost always at the church's east end, the direction of Jerusalem. From the Latin *cancellus*, meaning the screen that separated the space from the nave and so, by extension, the space itself.
chantry a foundation of at least one priest, whose principal role was to say prayers for the souls of persons nominated by the founder. It could be attached to an altar, or be a dedicated chapel.
chapter often used as a synonym for *college*, though technically *chapter* does not include the *dean*. Can also mean a formal meeting of the *canons*.
chapter house a room built to house meetings of the *college*.
clerestory a row of windows above the height of the aisles of the nave.
college a group of *canons* attached to a collegiate institution, such as St. Mary's.
corbel a stone block, usually on top of a *pilaster* or column, where the vault or ribs join on to them. Ribs are said to *spring* from them.
cusp an element of *tracery*, being a projection formed by two inter-locking arcs, often with a decorated end (*see image 76*).
dean the head of the *college*.
escutcheon a shield shape that usually bears heraldic arms.

GLOSSARY

hearse (a) a portable frame placed over a coffin or grave and draped with cloth, and used for holding candles (b) a frame built on to a wagon used to transport a body, which was draped with cloth.

high altar the altar situated in the chancel, used to celebrate high mass, the most elaborate form of mass.

honour the land and other property assets held by an earldom.

hoodmould the moulding around an arch-shape, such as on the top of a window or doorway.

Host consecrated bread, considered by Catholics to have become the body of Christ.

latten a copper and zinc alloy, similar to brass, but also containing tin and lead

ledger stone an inscribed stone, set into the floor, that memorialises the deceased.

lierne a *rib* that is decorative rather than weight-bearing.

mark a unit of currency equal to two-thirds of one pound.

mortmain licence a licence issued by the Crown that authorised the applicant to give property to the church.

mouchette curved, sometimes S shaped, stonework that forms a pattern within a more regular frame. It is a feature usually associated with windows, but at St. Mary's it is used for the bracing of the flying ribs in the chancel.

mullion stonework that divides a window vertically.

nave the main body of the church.

obit a re-enactment of the funeral service on an anniversary of death.

ogee a design of *tracery* in the shape of a double curve, upwards to a central point and downwards from it, like a { rotated ninety degrees clockwise (*see image 76*).

pall a cloth draped over the *hearse* or coffin.

pilaster a pillar carved in low- or high-relief, so not fully formed in circumference. Also known as a vaulting shaft if it is used to receive *ribs*.

piscina a receptacle for the disposal of holy water.

76. Blind tracery, an ogee curve above a trefoil pattern, and cusps with decorated ends, on the north wall of the chancel.

251

prebend the entitlement to income of a *prebendary,* usually a mixture of property interests that may have been scattered across several parishes.

prebendary someone in receipt of a *prebend*; in practice, synonymous with *canon.*

preferred appointed to a *prebend.*

pulpitum a high screen made of wood or stone that separated the *chancel* from the *nave*; also known as a *rood screen*, from the crucifixion cross, or rood, that was always placed on top of it.

pyx a small container that held consecrated bread for use after mass, perhaps to take the sacrament to the sick.

quire often treated as synonymous with *chancel* (as Earl Thomas Beauchamp did in his will), but strictly speaking it excludes the *sanctuary.*

reredos a woven or carved screen behind an altar, depicting a biblical scene.

rib a structure that helps transfer the weight of the *vault* to the side walls.

rood, rood screen see *pulpitum.*

rood loft a gallery or platform on top of the pulpitum.

sacristy a room used principally for the storage of plate, other items used for worship, and treasures.

sanctuary an area surrounding an altar, bounded by rails, wall, or screen to exclude the public from it and to emphasise the sanctity of the altar.

sedila built-in seating near the high altar for use by priests during mass. The one at St. Mary's unusually has four seats; two or three is more normal.

spandrel (or *spandril*) the space between the outer curve of an arch and the wall, roof, or frame. The term is used in this book to refer to the space between a flying rib and the wall or vault.

spring see *corbel.*

tracery a pattern formed by stonework, most obviously in windows but also as mouldings on walls and above doors, when it is said to be 'blind' (*see image 76*).

transept a projection north or south from the junction of the *chancel* and the *nave.* If both are present, the footprint of the church becomes cruciform.

transom stonework that separates a window horizontally.

trefoil an element of *tracery* in the shape of three leaves (*see image 76*).

Use of Sarum a form of liturgy originating at Sarum (Salisbury) cathedral, and used widely in England by the late Middle Ages.

vault (a) a curved roof (b) a burial chamber.

vestry a room used principally for the storage of vestments.

FURTHER READING

I HAVE shunned a full bibliography in favour of listing the sources that I have found particularly useful or interesting, and so providing a clearer signpost to those who would like to explore topics further.

I express my gratitude to all the authors whom I have consulted. It goes without saying that the use I have made of their texts is entirely my responsibility, and any errors are mine and mine alone.

Generally

Philip Chatwin: numerous articles published in the volumes of *Birmingham Archaeological Society Transactions*
William Field, *An historical and descriptive account of the town and castle of Warwick etc.* (Warwick, 1815)
History of Parliament online at historyofparliamentonline.org
A History of the County of Warwick ('Victoria County History'), volumes 2 and 8
Thomas Kemp, *A history of Warwick and its people* (Warwick, 1905)
Oxford Dictionary of National Biography online at doi.org
Sir William Dugdale, *Antiquities of Warwickshire* (London, 1656)

Chapters 1 to 5

Andrew Budge, 'Change in architectural style: the adoption of the macro- and micro- architectural motifs in 14th century collegiate churches in England and Wales', unpublished PhD thesis, Birkbeck College London, 2017
Fred. Crossley, *English church monuments AD 1150-1550* (London, 1921)
David Crouch (ed.), *The Newburgh earldom of Warwick and its charters 1088-1253* (Stratford-upon-Avon, 2015)
Charles Fonge (ed.), *The cartulary of St. Mary's Collegiate Church, Warwick* (Woodbridge, 2004)

Timothy Guard, *Chivalry, kingship, and crusade* (Woodbridge, 2013)

John Harvey, *The master builders: architecture in the Middle Ages* (London, 1971)

John Hunt, 'Rethinking Berkswell; the 12th century church of St. John the Baptist, Berkswell', *Birmingham and Warwickshire Archaeological Society Transactions* Vol 122 (2020), pp.39-70

Arthur Leach, *History of Warwick School* (London, 1906)

Richard Morris, 'The architecture of the earls of Warwick in the fourteenth centuries' in W. M. Ormrod, *England in the fourteenth century* (Woodbridge, 1986), pp.161-174

Nicholas Orme, *Going to church in medieval England* (New Haven, CT, 2021)

Velma Richmond, *The legend of Guy of Warwick* (New York, 1996)

Nigel Saul, *English church monuments in the Middle Ages* (Oxford, 2009)

Nigel Saul, *For honor and fame: chivalry in England 1066-1500* (London, 2012)

Dorothy Styles, *Ministers' accounts of the collegiate church of St. Mary Warwick 1432-1485* (Stratford-upon-Avon, 1969)

Chapter 6

Alexandra Buckle, 'Entumbid Right Princely: The re-internment of Richard Beauchamp, Earl of Warwick, and a lost rite' in H. Kleineke and C. Steer (eds.), *The Yorkist Age: Proceedings of the 2011 Harlaxton Symposium* (Donington, 2013)

Alexandra Buckle, 'Fit for a King': Music and Iconography in Richard Beauchamp's chantry chapel', *Early Music*, 38/1, 2010, pp.3-19

Alexandra Buckle, 'Of the finest colours: music in stained glass at Warwick and elsewhere' *Vidimus* 46 (2010)

Richard Marks, 'Entumbid right princly: the Beauchamp chapel at Warwick and the politics of interment', in C. Barron and C. Burgess (eds.), *Memory and commemoration in Medieval England*, Harlaxton Medieval Studies 20, (Donington, 2010), pp.163-184

Richard Marks and Paul Williamson (eds.), *Gothic: Art for England 1400–1547* (London, 2003)

Linda Monckton, 'Fit for a King? The Architecture of the Beauchamp chapel', *Architectural History*, 47, 2004, 2, pp.5-50

Alexandra Sinclair (ed.), *The Beauchamp Pageant* (Donington, 2003)

Chapters 7 to 10

Benjamin Brook, *Memoir of the life and writings of Thomas Cartwright* (London, 1845)

John Bryan, *The virtuous daughter: a sermon preached at St. Mary's in Warwick etc.* (London, 1640)

Patrick Collinson, *The Elizabethan puritan movement* (London, 1967)

Fred. Colville, *The worthies of Warwickshire who lived between 1500 and 1800* (Warwick, 1870)

Michael Farr (ed.), *The Great Fire of Warwick, 1694* (Stratford-upon-Avon, 1992)

Anthony Geraghty, *The architectural drawings of Sir Christopher Wren* (Aldershot, 2007)

Andor Gomme, *Smith of Warwick* (Stamford, 2000)

Andrew Hopton (ed.), *Abiezer Coppe: selected writings* (London, 1987)

Ann Hughes, *Politics, society and civil war in Warwickshire, 1620-1660* (Cambridge, 1987)

Ann Hughes, 'Thomas Dugard and his circle in the 1630s – a 'Parliamentary Puritan' connexion', *The Historical Journal*, vol. 29 no. 4 (1986), pp.771-793

Thomas Kemp (ed.), *The Black Book of Warwick* (Warwick, 1898)

Peter Marshall, *Heretics and believers* (New Haven, CT, 2017)

Darren Oldridge, 'Conflicts within the established church in Warwickshire ca. 1603-1642' unpublished PhD thesis, University of Warwick, 1992

Richard Venner (or Venour), '*Panoplia, or the whole armour of God explained etc*' (London, 1662)

INDEX

References in bold are to image numbers

A

d'Abetot, Urse 61, 62, 63, 149
Aethelflaed, Lady of the Mercians 32
Agincourt, battle of 118, 132
Alcester 76, 87, 180, 192, 200, 201, 218, 233
altars 18, 20, 21, 24, 25, 26, 85, 157, 163, 164, 170, 201
    at St. Mary's 18, 43, 53, 84, 87, 95, 96, 97, 101, 144, 145, 153, 161, 163, 164, 167, 168, 173, 190, 191, 224
angels 64, 99, 104, 244, **4**, **73**
    in Beauchamp chapel 120, 128, 137, 138, 140, **40**, **41**, **42**
    in nave 244
appropriation of churches to St. Mary's 37, 69, 85, 89, 154, **14**
archbishop of Canterbury 41, 47, 53, 55, 58, 130, 156, 184, **5** *and see* saints, Thomas Becket; Laud, William
archbishop of Sens 72
archbishop of York 122, **31**
Archer, Andrew 235, 241

B

Baginton 141, 154
Baptists 218, 220, 236, 241
Barford 39, 197, 204, 219
Barnet, battle of 143
bear, Beauchamp emblem 65, 102, 116, 128, 146, 149, 187, 190, 211, 241, **13**
Beauchamp chapel, St. Mary's **30**, **71**
    appearance of, pre-Reformation 145, 146
    building of 124, 125
    consecration of 144
    day of judgment, painting of, in 136, 222, 224, **64**
    desecration of (1643) 214-6
    Dudley tombs in 185-7, 190, **52**, **53**, **54**
    Great Fire and 229
    Lancastrian imagery in 142
    narrative of 128-41, 146
    purposes of 119-20, 123, 157, 163
    reputation of 116, 117
    statuary in 137, 138, 146, 164, 217, **40**
    tomb of Richard Beauchamp in 127, 128, 148, 164, 217, **44**
        craftsmen of 127, 137, 148
        influences on 128, 129, 135-6, **33**, **37**, **38**
        narrative of 128-33, **35**, **36**, **39**
        significance of 148
    windows in, glass of 127
    cost of 125, 146
    heavenly choir and orchestra 138, 140, 141, 146, 217, **41**, **42**
    maker of 125
    saints in east window 130, 132, 157, 164, 217, **32**, **34**
bailiffs of Warwick *see* Warwick, mayors of
Beauchamp, Eleanor, duchess of Somerset 136 n10, 141, 142

INDEX

Beauchamp Pageant 121, 122, **31**
Beauchamp, Sir John, brother of Earl Thomas I 78, 107
Beauchamp, Walter de 61
Beauchamp, William, Lord Bergavenny, brother of Earl Thomas II 85, 86, 89, 97
Beaudesert 42, 43, 179
Beausale 154
bells of St. Mary's 93, 159, 177, 218, 225, 239
Berkswell 42, 43
Beverley 84, 91
Bidford-on-Avon 54, 224
Bird, Richard 222
bishop of Coventry and Lichfield 123, 144, **31**
bishop of Hereford 55-56
bishop of Le Mans 72
bishop of London 56, 163
bishop of Salisbury 185
bishop of Worcester 37, 39, 40, 46, 51, 57-63, 77, 84, 123, 144, 152, 164, 168, 169, 175, 230, **31**
Black Death 85, 99, 101
Black Prince, the *see* Edward of Woodstock
Bordesley abbey 54, 67, 68, 89, 90
boy bishops 26, 27, 158
Brailes 34, 39, 54
Bridlington *see* Saint John of Bridlington
Bristol 58
    cathedral 111, 222
Bryan, John 197, 204-6, 211, 219
Budbrooke 37, 63, 77, 80, 84, 87, 162, 176, 197, 212, 219
Burgundy 22, 72, 135, 136, **4**, **37**
Butler, John 174
Butterfield, William 242

C
Calais 71, 79, 111, 118, 119, 142, **17**
Calvin, Jean 23, 169

Cambridge, King's college 123, 127
Candlemas 26, 27, 157, 163
canons 16, 17, 18
    of St. Mary's 34, 37, 39, 40, 41, 42, 45, 53-63 *passim*, 68, 69, 76-85 *passim*, 88, 96, 112, 124, 150, 151,153, 155, 157, 161, **1**
        rules of behaviour 82
        and see college of St. Mary, absence from
    Alestre, John 153, 228
    Berkeswell, William 124, 161, 164, 228
    Blake, John 77, 79, 97, 111
    Buckingham, John de 78, 79, 80, 124, 161, **17**
    del Fen, Albanus 77, 97
    Hengham, Ralph de 59, 60, 62, **12**
    Leicester, Robert de 68, 83
    Leycester, Peter de 63, 80
    Mile, Robert 77, 78, 161
    Morton, William 97, 100
    Pirton, Richard 77, 97, 124, 161
    Plesset, John de 57
    Plesset, Robert de 57, 58, 63
    Southam, Nicholas de 77, 153
    Vaughan, David 158, 179
    Watwood, John 159, 160
    Younge, Thomas 125, 161, 211
Canterbury cathedral 66, 123, 127, 130, 157
Catholics, post Reformation 156, 158, 162, 166, 167, 169, 172, 175, 180, 196, 204, 212, 222, 224, 225, 229
Cartwright, Thomas 180-5, 191, 193, 200, 204, **51**
Chaddesley Corbett 85, 154
chantries 40, 66, 67, 87, 119, 120, 121, 124, 125, 132, 138, 141, 151, 153
chaplains at St. Mary's 34, 41, 57, 60, 87, 153, 162
Charlecote 39, 207
Chichester cathedral 106

257

chivalry 103, 109, 112, 119, 121, 123, 128, 129, 130, 133, 143, 172, 174, 187, 194, 219
Clarence, George, duke of 143, 144, 150
Clarke, Samuel 182, 198-201, 202, 212, 218, 219, 225, **59**
Claverdon 39, 48, 52, 54, 62
Clerks of the Blessed Mary 96, 97
Clinton, Geoffrey de 40
college of St. Mary
    absence from 18, 57, 59, 68, 69, 80, 88, 151, 161
    bishops of Worcester and 37, 39, 40, 46, 53, 55, 57, 58, 59, 62, 63, 77, 80, 82, 84, 151, 152, 157, 159-60, 161
    dissolution of 150, 161, 162, 233
    earls of Warwick, relationship with 15, 16, 46, 47, 49, 59, 62, 63, 67, 70, 77, 88, 150
    finances of 50, 55-6, 60, 68, 84-5, 86, 151, 152-4
    foundation of 16, 34, 36-9, 45, **8, 10**
        reasons for 39-42
    management of 53-5, 68-9, 76, 77-81, 84, 151, 154, 161
    popes and 16, 41, 42, 55, 56, 58, 68, 76, 85, 90, 91
    refoundation (1367) 76, 77, 79-81
    schools of 82, 83, 85, 93, 109, 176, **18**
collegiate church of St. Mary
    altars *see* altars at St. Mary's
    building of (*ca.* 1150) 42-3
    chancel of 20, 21, 26, 45, 70, 86, 93, 96, 114, 144, 146, 164, 173, 175, 198, 207, 208, 216, 239, 244, 248, 249, **21, 26, 29**
        architectural features and influences 15, 95, 98, 98-100, 109-12, **6, 22**
        construction 91-2
        and Great Fire 229, 232, 233
        tomb of Thomas Beauchamp and Katherine Mortimer 15, 101-9, 173, 208, 229, 232, **2, 23, 24, 25, 61**
    chapter house of 15, 45, 92, 93, 96, 162, 194, 214, **20, 57**
    crypt of 15, 42-5, 91, 92, 96, 194, 228, **11**
    Dean's chapel in 125, 146, **43**
    endowments and gifts to 18, 37, 39, 52-3, 69, 70, 85, 86-7, 88, 89, 112, 113, 141, 154, 161
    Great Fire of Warwick and 228-9, 230, 236, 237
        criticism of Wilson's design 241-3
        rebuilding after 232-49
    Lady chapel in 83, 96 *and see* Beauchamp chapel
    nave of 15, 69, 81, 91, 92, 162, 164, 228, 236, 239, 242-4, 248, **72**
    pre-Reformation appearance 20, 21, 24, 95, 100, 112, **19** *and see* altars at St. Mary's
    pulpitum of 21, 24, 95, 96, 97, 100, 228, 229, 237
    rebuilding of (*ca.* 1369-94) 90-93 *and see* chancel of, architectural features and influences (*supra*)
    tower of
        pre-Great Fire 69, 92, 93, 162, 213, 228, **19**
        post-Great Fire 15, 236-9 *passim*, 241, 244-8, **73, 74**
    transepts of 29, 92, 95, 96, 103, 109, 112, 113, 119, 178, 214, 228, 229, 236, **28, 50, 67**
    vestry of 18, 19, 45, 92, 93, 209, **3, 62**
    and see Beauchamp chapel; college of St. Mary
communion 24, 83, 86, 163, 170, 173, 175, 184, 199, 201

Compton Mordak (Verney) 34, 59, 77, 78, 154, **8**
Coombe abbey 51, 54
Coten End, Warwick 33, 34, 69, 236
Coppe, Abiezer 202-4, 220
Coughton 87, 124, 168, 224
countesses of Warwick
    Beauchamp, Anne, 15th countess 115, 120, 141
    Beauchamp, Anne, 16th countess 115, 120, 121, 123, 124, 136, 136 n10, 141, 142, 143, 148, 249, **44**
    Despenser, Isabel 115, 120, 144
    Ela 48, 49, 52, 62
    Ferrers, Margaret 87, 99, 112, 115, 152, 164, **27**, **28**, **29**
    Gundreda 46, 49, 101
    Mortimer, Katherine 71, 77, 85, 99, 100-1, 102, 107, 109, 115
        tomb of 15, 101-9, 173, 208, 229, 232, **Frontis**, **23**, **24**, **25**, **61**
Coventry 20, 33, 50, 51, 52, 54, 92, 130, 152, 180, 198, 199, 203, 204, 218, 219, 237
    archdeacon of 41, 42, 53
    bishop of, and Lichfield 123, 144, **31**
    diocese of, and Lichfield 69
Crécy, battle of 71, 72, 74
creeping to the Cross 26, 27, 157, 163
Cromwell, Oliver 197, 219, 221, 222
Cromwell, Thomas 16, 156, 160, **47**
curates of St. Mary's 155
Cure workshop 186, 187

D
day of judgment, paintings of 20, 136, 222, 224, 229, **64**, **65**
Digby, Lord William 231, 237
Dean's chapel, St. Mary's 125, 146, **43**
deans of St. Mary's *see* canons of St. Mary's
Declaration of Sports 199, 201, 202, 212
Dod, John 185
Domesday Book 31, 32, 33, 61

Dominican friars in Warwick 59, 152, 153
doom paintings *see* day of judgment, paintings of
Dubricius, supposed 1st bishop of Warwick 32, 96
Dudley, Ambrose *see* earls of Warwick, Dudley, Ambrose
Dudley, John, earl of Warwick, later duke of Northumberland 164-7, 174, 175, **48**
Dudley, Robert, earl of Leicester 15, 167, 168, 169, 183, 184, 190, 193, 195, 209, 224, **49**
    funeral of 185-6
    Order of St. Michel and 172-4, 176, 187, **49**
    puritanism and 171, 181, 182, 191, 222
    relationship with town of Warwick 174, 176-7, 179, 180
    tomb of 186, 187, 194, 216, **54**, **56**
    and see Beauchamp chapel
Dudley, Robert, Lord Denbigh *see* Noble Impe, the
Dugard, Thomas 197, 198, 200, 202, 211, 212, 219
Dugdale, Sir William 213, 217, 222, 224
Dunckley, Samuel 235, 236, 237, 239, 241, 249, **71**

E
earls of Warwick
    Beauchamp, Guy 63, 67-8, 69, 70, 71, 115, 129
    Beauchamp, Henry (later duke of Warwick) 115, 120, 121, 123, 132, 136, 136 n10
    Beauchamp, Richard
        life of 118, 119, 130, 132, **31**
        patronage of music 141
        reburial of 144-6
        reputation of 121, 123, 130
        tomb of 127-30, 133-4, 136-7, 148, 164, 217, **35**, **38**, **39**, **44**

will and executors of 15, 28, 116, 123, 124, 125, 127, 128, 136, 137, 228
and see Beauchamp chapel
Beauchamp, Thomas (died 1369) **15**
   canons and 77-79
   life of 70-74, 101, 109, 111, 112
   rebuilding of St. Mary's and 89-91
   refounds college 79-81, 84
   tomb of 15, 101-9, 173, 208, 229, 232, **Frontis**, **23**, **24**, **25**, **61**
   Warwick castle and 74
   will and executors of 77, 92, 97, 111
   and see collegiate church of St. Mary, chancel
Beauchamp, Thomas (died 1401) 75, 77, 79, 87, 92, 97, 99, 104, 111, 114, 115, 123, 124, 151, 152, 167, 249, **29**
   endowments and gifts to St. Mary's 26, 85, 113
   tomb of 112, 228, **27**, **28**
   Warwick guilds and 153
   will of 112-3, 130
Beauchamp, William 62-3, 70, 102
Beaumont, Henry de *see* Newburgh, Henry de
Dudley, Ambrose 15, 167, 168, 171, 173, 176, 179, 180, 181, 183, 184, 190, 191, 192, 193
   tomb of 186, 187, 194, 216, **53**
   and see Beauchamp chapel
Mauduit, William 48, 49, 61, 62
Neville, Richard ('Warwick the Kingmaker') 115, 120, 136, 141, 142, 143
Newburgh I, Henry de 33, 34, 36, 41, 49
Newburgh II, Henry de 47, 49, 63
Newburgh, Roger de 36, 37, 39-43, 46, 50, 52, 53, 54, 55, 59, 84, 101
Newburgh, Thomas de 47-8, 49, 52, 62, 64
Newburgh, Waleran de 41, 47, 48, 49, 81
Newburgh, William de 47, 81
Plessis, John de 48, 49, 51, 58, 61
Easter, services and ceremonies 24, 25, 26, 157, 163, **6**
Edward of Woodstock (the 'Black Prince') 74, 95, 108, 127 n9, 130
Elfael 71
Elmley castle 63, 67, 77, 113
Eton college 123, 125, 127
Eucharist *see* mass

F
Fish, James 225, 229
Fisher, John 169, 176, 177, 179, 180
Fisher, Thomas 163, 168, 228, **67**
Flanders 111, 141
font at St. Mary's 239, 241
Fulbrook (Warwickshire) 154

G
Garter, Order of the 72, 89, 102, 109, 118, 119, 128, 130, 133, 148, 168, 172, 173, 175, 187, 215, **15**, **33**
Gloucester 58, 239
   cathedral 66, 92
Gower 33, 47, 72
grammar school, attached to St. Mary's 82, 83, 85, 176, **18**
Greetham (Rutland) 37, 68, 84
Greville, Francis, 3rd Lord Brooke 218
Greville, Sir Fulke 180, 192
Greville, Fulke, 1st Lord Brooke 192-6, 201, 207, 209, 211, **57**
Greville, Fulke, 5th Lord Brooke 230
Greville, Robert, 2nd Lord Brooke 196-200, 211-7, 230, **63**
Grey, Henry, marquis of Dorset 155, 166
Grey, Lady Jane 166, 167, 174

INDEX

Griffin, Rafe 176, 177, 179, 180, 182
guilds 85, 95, 152-4, 162, 163, 174, 177
Guy of Warwick 63-7, 89, 90, 109, 121, 146, 149, 174, **13**
Guy's Cliffe 66, 74, 120, 121, 124

H
Haselor 85, 154
Hawksmoor, Nicholas 93, 233, 234, 246, 247, **19**, **68**, **75**
Heathcote 86, 87
Hereford cathedral 60
Holyoake, Francis 201, 213, 214
Huggeford, John 20, 50, 143
Huggeford, Thomas 20, 124, 228
Hurlbutt, Roger 232, 233

I
images of reverence 19, 20, 23, 27, 84, 96, 97, 130, 137, 142, 156-9 *passim*, 161-4 *passim*, 167, 170, 191, 217, 222, **48**
indulgences 90, 91, 156, 157, 159, **46**

J
Jeanne d'Arc 118
Jewish community in Warwick 53

K
Kenilworth 46
    abbey 54
    castle 40, 48, 92, 95, 168, 174, 180, 185, 186, 187
Kingmaker, the, *see* earls of Warwick, Neville, Richard
kings of England
    Charles I 196, 199, 209, 211, 212, 215, 221
        at St. Mary's 198
    Charles II 219, 221, 224
    Edward I 62
    Edward II 67, 71
    Edward III 71, 72, 78, 89, 95, 100, 108, 109, 127 n9, 134
    Edward IV 142, 143
        at St. Mary's 142
    Edward VI 165, 166, 174
    Henry IV 28, 87, 101, 118, 119, 123, 130, 132, 146
    Henry V 118, 120, 123, 127, 132, 142
    Henry VI 118, 123, 127, 132, 142, 143
        at St. Mary's 142
    Henry VII 127 n9, 150, 154
    Henry VIII 143, 155, 156, 158, 159, 161, 162, 165, 166, 167, 187, 197
    James I 170, 180, 192, 194, 197, 199, 209
    James II 224, 225
    Richard II 72, 87, 106, 123, 127 n9, 130, 132, 134, 148, 153, **31**, **36**
    Richard III 121, 124, 143, 150
    William III 230, 238
Knollys, Lettice 187, **53**

L
Lady chapel, at St. Mary's 83, 96, 119, 140
Latimer, Hugh, bishop of Worcester 156, 157, 158, 159, 160
Laud, William, archbishop of Canterbury 196, 197, 200, 201, 211
Leamington Priors 32
lecturers in Warwick *see* preaching
Leek Wootton 32
Leveson, Lady Katherine 224
    Leveson Trust 241
Lichfield cathedral 60, 78, 108, 214, 217
Lincoln cathedral 37, 45, 78, 79, 111, 180
Lord Leycester hospital 85, 154, 174, 177, 181, 185, **55**

M
Magdeburg cathedral 111, 112
mass, celebration of 18, 19, 21, 22, 24, 26, 83, 91, 93, 96, 97, 153, 156, 158, 163, 176, 191
    and see communion

Massingham, John 148
Mercurius Rusticus 215-6
Marshall, William 237
Michelangelo 222
Milan, Missaglia workshop 128, 130
Mortimer, Roger 68, 71, 102
Mortmain, Statutes of 69, 85, 86, 151
music at St. Mary's 18, 83, 97, 119, 140, 141, 144, 170
Myton 31, 124

N
Nonconformists 221, 222 *and see* Baptists, Quakers, Ranters
Northampton 226, 237, 238, 239, **70**
Noble Impe, the 186, 187, 188, 190, **52**
Nost, John 239, 241

O
Oken, Thomas 177, 179, 229, **50**
Oxford, Divinity School 125

P
Paris, Nicholas 227, 232, 236, 237, 245
Parr, William, marquis of Northampton 165, 174-6, 177
pews, seating in church 20, 21
Peyto, William 228
Pillerton Hersey 69, 76, 85, 89, 91, **14**
Pinley priory 54
Poitiers, battle of 71, 72, 74, 75, 90
Power, Walter 20, 86, 87, 97, 161, 173
preachers, preaching 21, 59, 171, 177, 182, 183, 184, 191, 193, 197, 199, 201, 202, 203, 204, 213, 222, 225
prebends, prebendaries *see* canons and deans
predestination 170, 196, 201, 222
presbyterianism 171, 180, 182, 184, 193, 196, 197, 198, 203, 219, 221
Preston Capes 141
Preussenreisen 111, 132
'Princes in the Tower', at St. Mary's 144

Priory, the 168, 173, 174, 176, 183, 204, 207, 208, 224, 236 *and see* St. Sepulchre's Priory
Prudde, John 125, 127, **32**
Puckering, Cecily 204-7, 208, 209, 219, 221, **60**
Puckering, Sir Henry Newton 224, 230, 244
Puckering, Sir John 183, 185, 204
Puckering, Sir Thomas 204, 207-11, 224, **61**, **62**
Purefoy, Sir William 214-7, 224
purgatory 21, 22, 23, 27, 64, 90, 91, 112, 156, 158, 162, 163, 164, 170, 222, **4**
    Beauchamp chapel and 120, 136, 137
puritans, puritanism 170, 171, 176, 177, 179, 180, 184, 193, 196, 197, 199, 200, 201, 202-7, 212, 221, 222

Q
Quakers 218
queens of England
    Anne 239
    Elizabeth I 15, 29, 167, 168, 169, 171, 172, 175, 176, 177, 180, 181, 182, 185, 186, 187, 192, 193, 194
        religious changes under 170
    Jane Grey 166, 167, 174
    Mary I 162, 166, 167, 168, 175
        St. Mary's during reign of 167
    Mary II 230

R
ragged staff 65, 96, 113, 128, 145, 146, 149, 187, 190, 241, 244, 246, **13**, **45**, **55**, **56**, **74**
Ranters 203
Reformation, the 16, 155-9, 162-4, 169, 170, 190, **48**
relics 23, 27, 43, 45, 67, 132, 156, 157, 161, 162, **5**
    at St. Mary's 23, 159
Rody, Nicholas 124

INDEX

Roe, Richard 193, 197, 199, 200
rood screen *see* pulpitum
Rouen 36, 41, 64, 118, 119
Rous, John 32, 34, 48, 93, 120, 143, 149, 164, 228
    Rous Roll 121, 123
Rudhall, Abraham 239

S
St. Albans 130, 142
St. Mary's Warwick *see* college of St. Mary; collegiate church of St. Mary
St. Paul's cathedral, London 37, 45, 60, 78, 106, 107, 152, 186, 193, 194
St. Sepulchre's priory, Warwick 32, 34, 36, 43, 48, 52, 54, 55, 56, 59, 68, 84, 101, 152, 168, **2**
saints
    Alban 127, 130, 132, **32**
    Barbara 138, **40**
    Christopher 19
    John of Bridlington 130, 132, 142, **34**
    Katherine of Alexandria 116, 138, 221, **40**
    Margaret of Antioch 138
    Mary Magdalene 23, 138
    Thomas Becket 23, 130, 155, 157, 164, **5**
    Winifred of Shrewsbury 130, 132, 142
Sarum 37, 42, 45, 58, 80
    Use of 17, 140
serfs, serfdom 31
Sherbourne 32, 39
Shrewley 237
Shrewsbury 118, 132, 133, 193
Sidney, Sir Philip 193, 194, 196
Skyllington, Robert 91, 92, 95
Smith, Francis 235, 236, 237, 239, 241, 248, 249, **69**
Smith, William 235, 236, 237, 239, 241, 248, 249

Snitterfield 39, 68
song school, attached to St. Mary's 83, 93, 109
Southam 171, 201, 213
Southwell minster 111
Spelsbury 85, 86, 89, 154
Spencer, Thomas 192, 197, 200, 212, 214, 219
Spyne, Guy 87, 124
Stratford-upon-Avon 33, 50, 51, 52, 237, 239
Stone, Nicholas 205, 209, **60**, **62**
Strong, Edward 237, 246
Surrey, duke of 87
Sutton Coldfield 78, 234
swan, de Bohun emblem 128, 129, 130, 142, 149, **33**, **45**
Swansea 34

T
Tanworth-in-Arden 62, 235
Tattershall, collegiate church of Holy Trinity 28, **7**
Tewkesbury 143
    abbey 120
Throckmorton, Job 180, 183, 192
Throckmorton, Thomas 168
Throgmorton, John 124
transubstantiation 18, 21, 27, 158, 170
treasurer of St. Mary's 81, 88, 96, 150, 151, 160
Turchil of Arden 31, 32, 33, 45, 121

U
Umberslade Hall 235, 241

V
vicars of St. Mary's 18, 27, 53, 57, 69, 81, 82, 83, 88, 96, 144, 151, 152, 153, 155, 160, 161, 162, 177, 179
    Bordman, Andrew 184, 185
    Delene, Martin 179, 183, 184, 191
    Edes, William 224, 225, 226, 236

Hall, Thomas 197, 198, 200, 202, 211, 212
Venour, Richard 211, 219, 220, 221
Wall, William 161, 162, 168
Virgin Mary 18, 20, 21, 23, 26, 90, 156, 157, 170, 221
    St. Mary's and 23, 32, 95, 97, 109, 119, 128, 136, 137, 140, 145, 148, 160

W
Walden, Robert 87, 153
Warwick 33, 53, 59, 81, 84, 180
    castle 32, 33, 34, 46, 48, 50, 61, 64, 67, 68, 74, 77, 87, 89, 90, 101, 110, 124, 143, 159, 165, 168, 176, 192, 193, 194, 196, 197, 218, 232, **16**
    in the Civil Wars 213, 215-6
    churches in
        All Saints' 32, 33, 34, 36, 37, 39, 40, 45
        St. Helen's 32, 37, 55, 56, 84
        St. James's 37, 55, 77, 84, 85, 153, 154, 174
        St. John's 37, 37 n1, 84, 85
        St. Laurence's 32, 37, 55, 84, 85, 124
        St. Mary's *see* college of St. Mary; collegiate church of St. Mary
        St. Michael's 32, 37, 52, 54, 77, 84, 85, 124, 161
        St. Nicholas's 32, 37, 84, 162, 163, 167, 182, 197, 199, 200, 202, 217, 219, 224
        St. Peter's 37, 37 n1, 84, 159
    corporation of 162, 169, 174, 176, 177, 179, 193, 198, 199, 207, 212, 225, 230, 233
    economy of 32, 33, 46, 50-1, 101, 154
    Great Fire of 226-31
        losses suffered by people 231
        rebuilding of town after 231-2
    and see collegiate church of St. Mary, rebuilding after Great Fire
    mayors of 16, 169, 174, 177, 199, 218, 219, 224, 225, 226, 228, 236, 248
    'siege' of 213
Warwick, Guy of, *see* Guy of Warwick
'Warwick the Kingmaker' *see* earls of Warwick, Neville, Richard
weepers **37**
    on tomb of Thomas Beauchamp I 107, 108, 109, 229, **25**
    on tomb of Richard Beauchamp 134, 135, 136, 136 n10, 143, 146, 148, **35, 38, 44**
Wellesbourne 39, 54
Wells cathedral 66
Westminster abbey 106, 118, 123, 125, 127, 186, 194, 195, 219, 221
Westminster, St Stephen's college 78, 80, 89, 109
Whittlesford 85, 154
Wilson, Sir William 234, 235, 241, 243, 244, 246, 248, 249
Winchcombe, Richard 125
Windsor
    castle 74, 89, 209
    St. George's chapel 89, 109, 130, 159
Wolfhampcote 85, 154, 228
Wolverton (Warwickshire) 141
Worcester, bishops of 51, 53, 230 *and see* college of St. Mary and bishops of Worcester; Latimer, Hugh
Wren, Sir Christopher 233, 234, 235, 237, 241, 242, 243, 245, 246, 248, 249, **19, 68, 75**

Y
Yevele, Henry 106, 107
York minster 37, 45, 78